P9-CBJ-849

# SUPER CROOKS

## BOOK ONE: THE HEIST

WRITER: **MARK MILLAR**

ARTIST: **LEINIL YU**

CO-PLOTTER: **NACHO VIGALONDO**

INKER: **GERRY ALANGUILAN**

COLORIST: **SUNNY GHO**

VARIANT COVER ARTISTS: **DAVE GIBBONS & BRYAN HITCH**

INKING & COLORING ASSISTANCE: **MICHAEL JASON PAZ & JAVIER TARTAGLIA**

LETTERER: **VC'S CLAYTON COWLES**

EDITOR: **NICOLE BOOSE**

COLLECTION DESIGNER: **SPRING HOTELING**

SPECIAL THANKS: **JENNIFER GRÜNWALD, BILLY KIRKWOOD, ROBERT FLORENCE & GREG HEMPHILL**

SENIOR VICE PRESIDENT OF SALES: **DAVID GABRIEL**

SVP OF BUSINESS AFFAIRS AND TALENT MANAGEMENT: **DAVID BOGART**

SVP OF BRAND PLANNING & COMMUNICATIONS: **MICHAEL PASCIULLO**

SUPERCROOKS CREATED BY MARK MILLAR AND LEINIL YU

SUPERCROOKS. Contains material originally published in magazine form as SUPERCROOKS #1-4. First printing 2012. ISBN# 978-0-7851-6610-8. Published by MARVEL WORLDWIDE, INC., a subsidiary of MARVEL ENTERTAINMENT, LLC. OFFICE OF PUBLICATION: 135 West 50th Street, New York, NY 10020. Copyright © 2012 Millarworld Limited and Leinil Francis Yu. All rights reserved. $19.99 per copy in the U.S. and $21.99 in Canada (GST #R127032852); Canadian Agreement #40668537. "Supercrooks," the Supercrooks logo, and all characters featured in or on this issue and the distinctive names and likenesses thereof, and all related indicia are trademarks of Millarworld Limited and Leinil Francis Yu. "Icon" and the Icon logos are trademarks of Marvel Characters, Inc. No similarity between any of the names, characters, persons, and/or institutions in this magazine and those of any person or institution is intended, and any such similarity that may seem to exist is purely coincidental. This work may not be reproduced by any means without written consent from the authors, except in small amounts for review purposes. ALAN FINE, EVP - Office of the President, Marvel Worldwide, Inc. and EVP & CMO Marvel Characters B.V.; DAN BUCKLEY, Publisher & President - Print, Animation & Digital Divisions; JOE QUESADA, Chief Creative Officer; TOM BREVOORT, SVP of Publishing; DAVID BOGART, SVP of Operations & Procurement, Publishing; RUWAN JAYATILLEKE, SVP & Associate Publisher, Publishing; C.B. CEBULSKI, SVP of Creator & Content Development; DAVID GABRIEL, SVP of Publishing Sales & Circulation; MICHAEL PASCIULLO, SVP of Brand Planning & Communications; JIM O'KEEFE, VP of Operations & Logistics; DAN CARR, Executive Director of Publishing Technology; SUSAN CRESPI, Editorial Operations Manager; ALEX MORALES, Publishing Operations Manager; STAN LEE, Chairman Emeritus. For information regarding advertising in Marvel Comics or on Marvel.com, please contact Niza Disla, Director of Marvel Partnerships, at ndisla@marvel.com. For Marvel subscription inquiries, please call 800-217-9158. Manufactured between 8/27/2012 and 10/8/2012 by R.R. DONNELLEY, INC., SALEM, VA, USA.

10 9 8 7 6 5 4 3 2 1

**THIS IS A REALLY WELL WRITTEN AND A REALLY WELL DRAWN BOOK. TRUST ME. YOU'LL BLOODY LOVE IT. IF ANY OF YOU BUYING THIS BOOK ARE DUMB ENOUGH TO READ THIS BEFORE YOU ACTUALLY READ THE STORY THAT FOLLOWS IT THEN, APART FROM NEEDING THERAPY WITH YOUR OCD, JUST TRUST ME. IT'S GREAT.**

There. That's what you needed, right? That's all an introduction should be. Nice and concise, straight to the point. Now, assuming by this point you went off, got a drink and immersed yourself in the adventure that comes right after these pages and, in the interests of squeezing just a few more minutes or reading out this book, have remembered there was some guy waffling on at the front, let me tell you some shit.

I first got to know Mark through his writing. When I was drawing *The Authority* (written by Warren Ellis, which you should also own and, if you don't, go and buy it now before I burn your *X-Men* collection), Mark was writing *Superman Adventures* for DC Comics. Although it was based on the Warner Bros. animated Superman shows, which meant it had to look a very particular way, just like the animation style, I was enjoying it as my favourite *Superman* comic DC produced and the reason was simple. It was very well written.

You could see Mark learning. He's always been an ideas machine but in *Superman Adventures* he was learning to craft a real story around each idea and, issue by issue, each self-contained story was a joy to read.

Warren and I were sure he was the guy to write *Authority* after we left and we were right. He could think big, he could think crazy and he wasn't afraid to start where others, including us, would draw the line.

I found myself sitting on the toilet reading his first issue and saying "You can't do THAT!" I was both shocked and overjoyed because he gave me something new with something that was so familiar to me and that's a pattern I've seen repeated with everything he writes.

It wasn't long before he and I hooked up. Joe Quesada, then newly minted as Marvel Editor in Chief, called me and said, "Dood, the lunatics are running the asylum up here, come and par-TAY." Millar had been asked to retool the *Avengers* for their new Ultimate Line and Mark had asked for me. We spent all day on the phone and knew we'd found a good creative partner in the other. *The Ultimates*, our take on the *Avengers* comic and the root of the *Avengers* movie you've all seen three times now, was born. It was a huge break for both of us and established our creative credentials in such a way as to give us the freedom to leave Marvel and DC to create our own projects. Look at what Mark went and did with that.

That pattern of surprising you with a take on something familiar continued with every issue of the book I drew. You think you know super heroes but Mark can take that, change it, warp it and throw you a curve you just aren't expecting. It happened on *The Authority* and it happened on *The Ultimates*. It happened on *Kick-Ass*, *Wanted*, *Superior* and *Nemesis* and it's happened again here.

It isn't complicated, actually. In fact, it's face-palmingly simple. He comes up with the ideas everybody else can't believe they haven't thought of first, writes a terrific story around them and then gets the best artists the industry has to draw them.

He's had some great partners on these projects but in *Superior* and again here, Mark worked with the mad Filipino genius, Leinil Francis Yu. I've known Leinil's work for years and years and he's always shown an incredible confidence I can only envy. With *Superior* and especially here, his work has taken a real leap and I don't mean just in his drawing ability. In *Supercrooks* he's managed to fully pull you into the visual world of the story Mark's written and then beat you over the head until your nose bleeds. Each moment, each outrageous idea and scene Mark's demented Pictish brain has thought of, Leinil has managed to draw in a way that carries you to the next spluttering outrage of a scene. His environments, his characters, action, everything the work of a true industry master. Obviously I hate him. Passionately.

As storytellers go, Mark and Leinil grab you, take you into the back room and beat the shit out of you with your own legs and then have you asking for more. And you know there's more coming, there has to be.

This wild mix of *X-Men* and *Ocean's Eleven*, like *Wanted*, *Nemesis*, *Superior* and *Kick-Ass* really pisses me off. It pisses me off because I didn't draw it and it pisses me off because Leinil did it better than I could have.

You know what, Fuck off. Don't read it, read my books instead. You don't need another Millar and Yu book, especially one this much ridiculous, delicious and demented fun.

Fuck it, I'm going to burn your *X-Mens* anyway. And your *Archies*.

———

Bryan Hitch has drawn comics for over a quarter of a century and having drawn nearly everything, also co-created two of the most influential comics ever, *The Authority* and *The Ultimates*. He's English, quite handsome in his own way, lives near London with his enormous family but is willing to travel to tear up your comics if you haven't been reading his latest book, *AMERICA'S GOT POWERS*, co-created with British TV superstar and comic nutcase, Jonathan Ross.

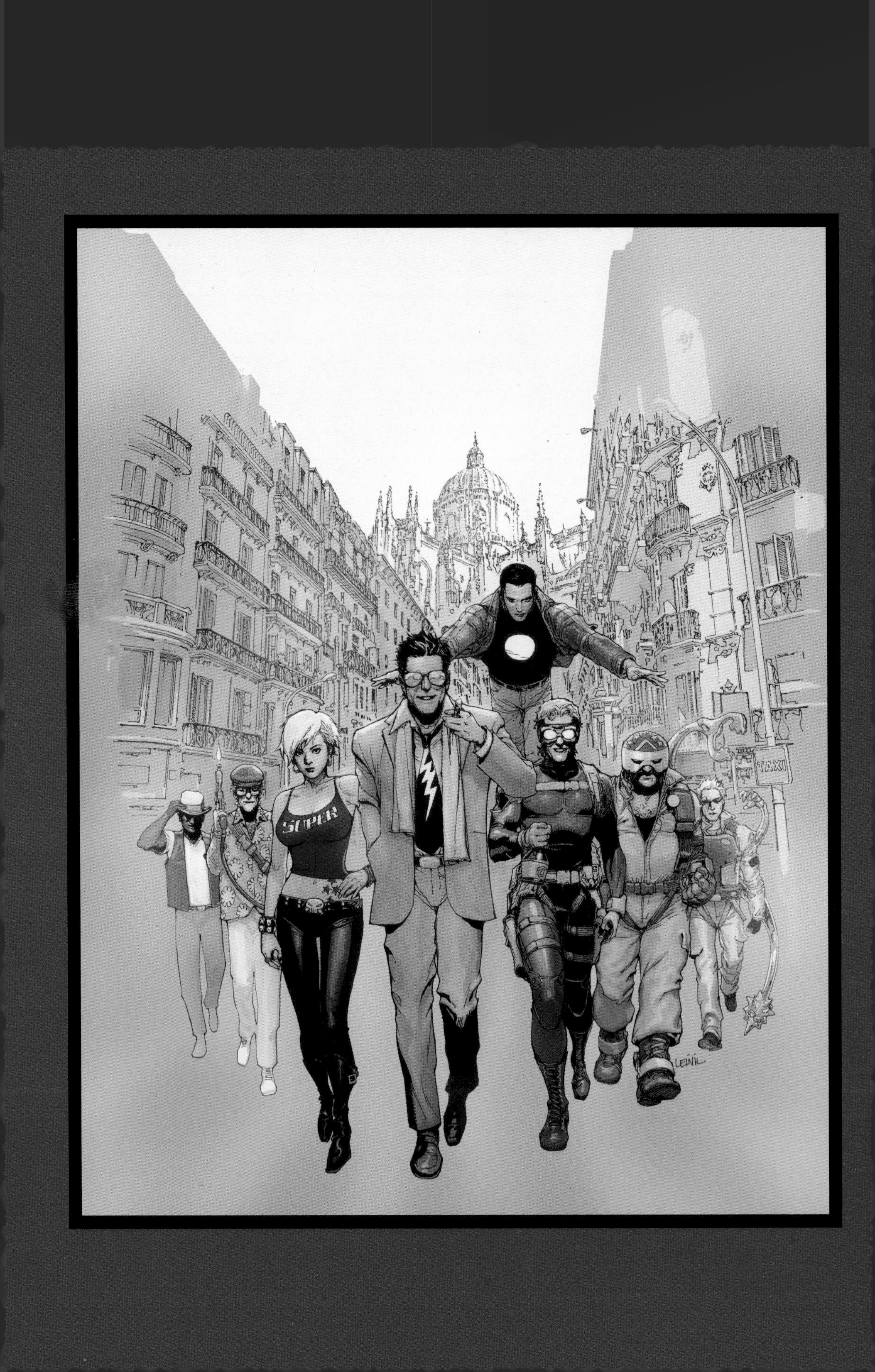
SUPER
TAXI
LEINIL

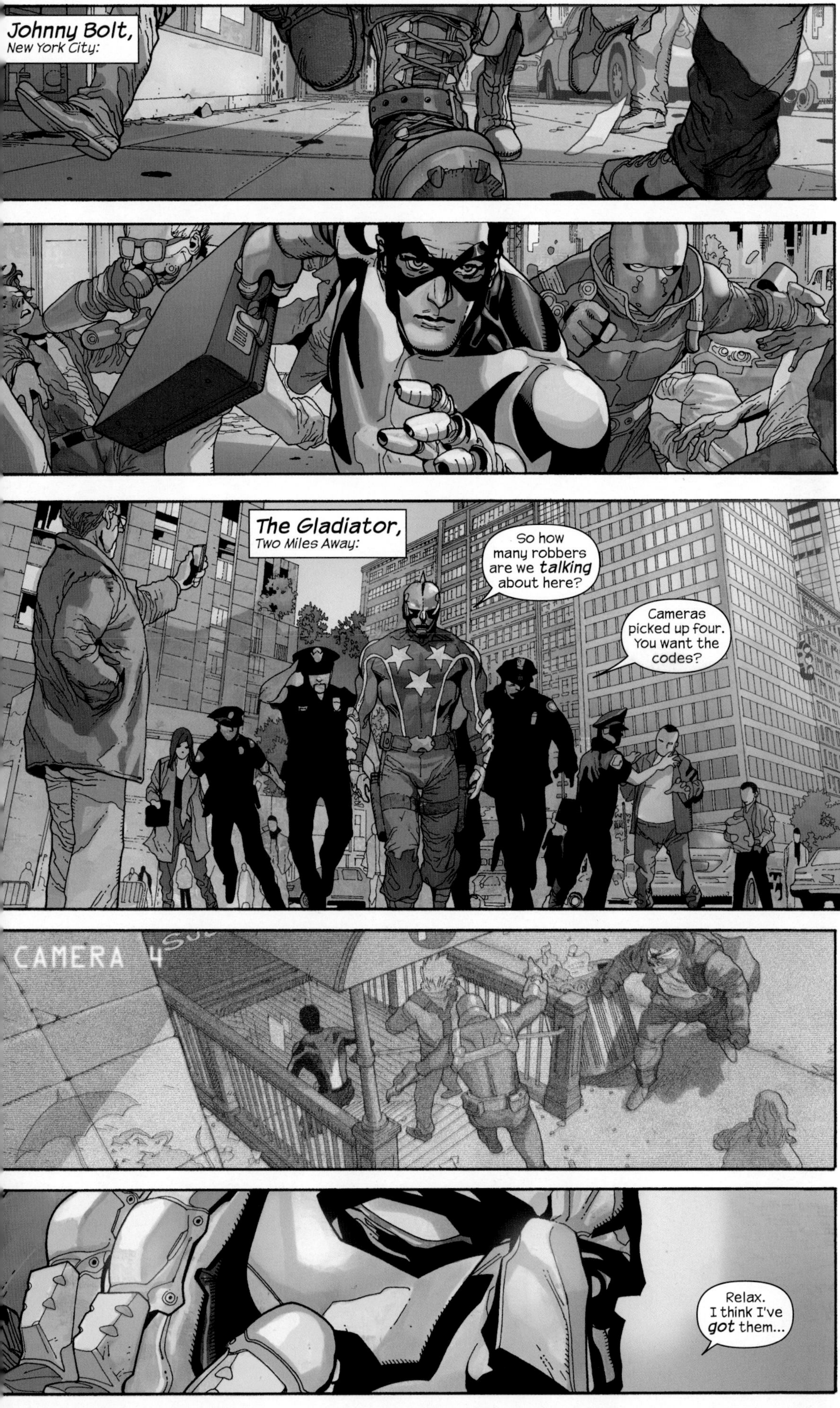
Johnny Bolt,
New York City:
The Gladiator,
Two Miles Away:
So how many robbers are we talking about here?
Cameras picked up four. You want the codes?
CAMERA 4
Relax. I think I've got them...

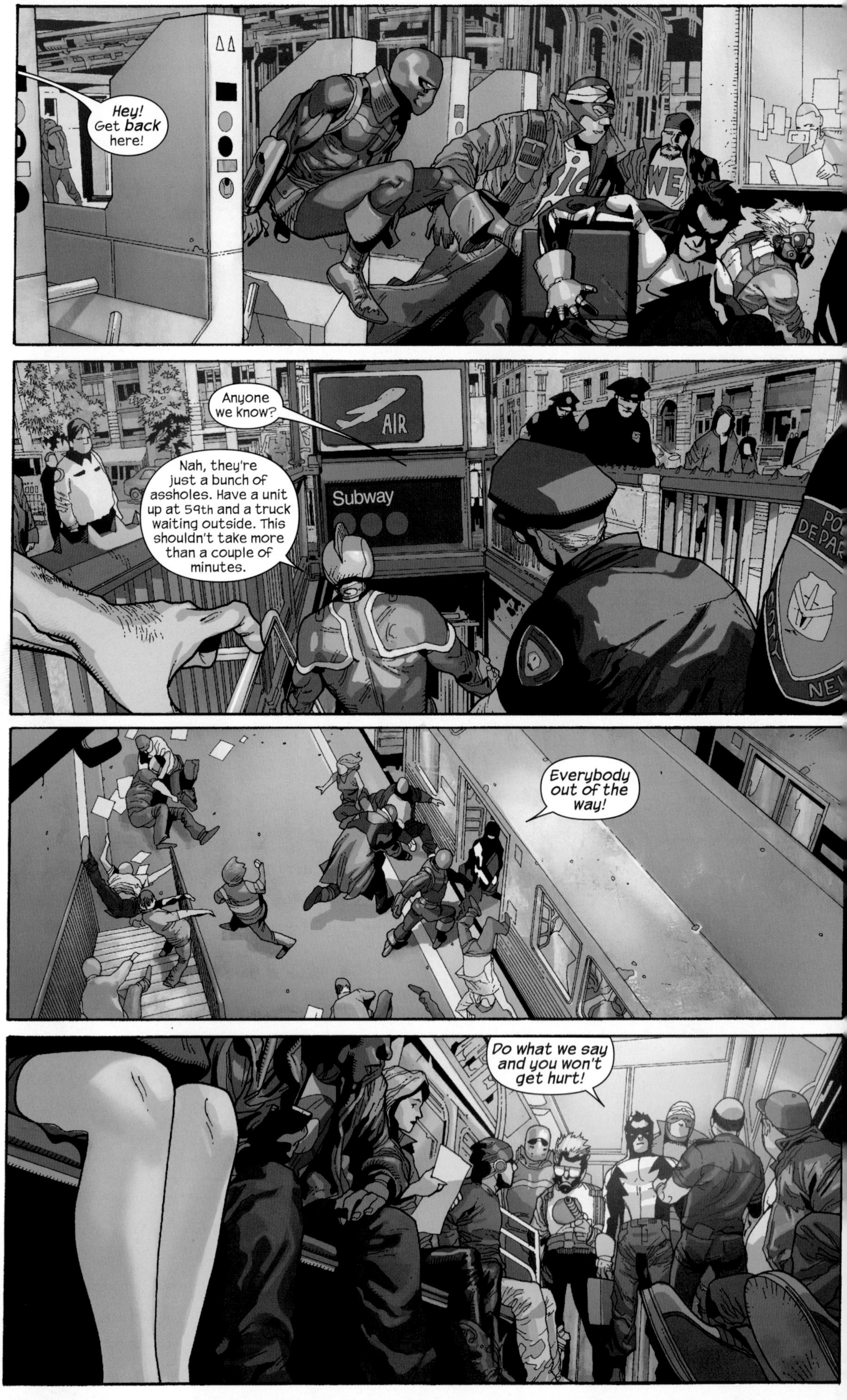
Hey! Get back here!
Anyone we know?
Nah, they're just a bunch of assholes. Have a unit up at 59th and a truck waiting outside. This shouldn't take more than a couple of minutes.
AIR
Subway
Everybody out of the way!
Do what we say and you won't get hurt!

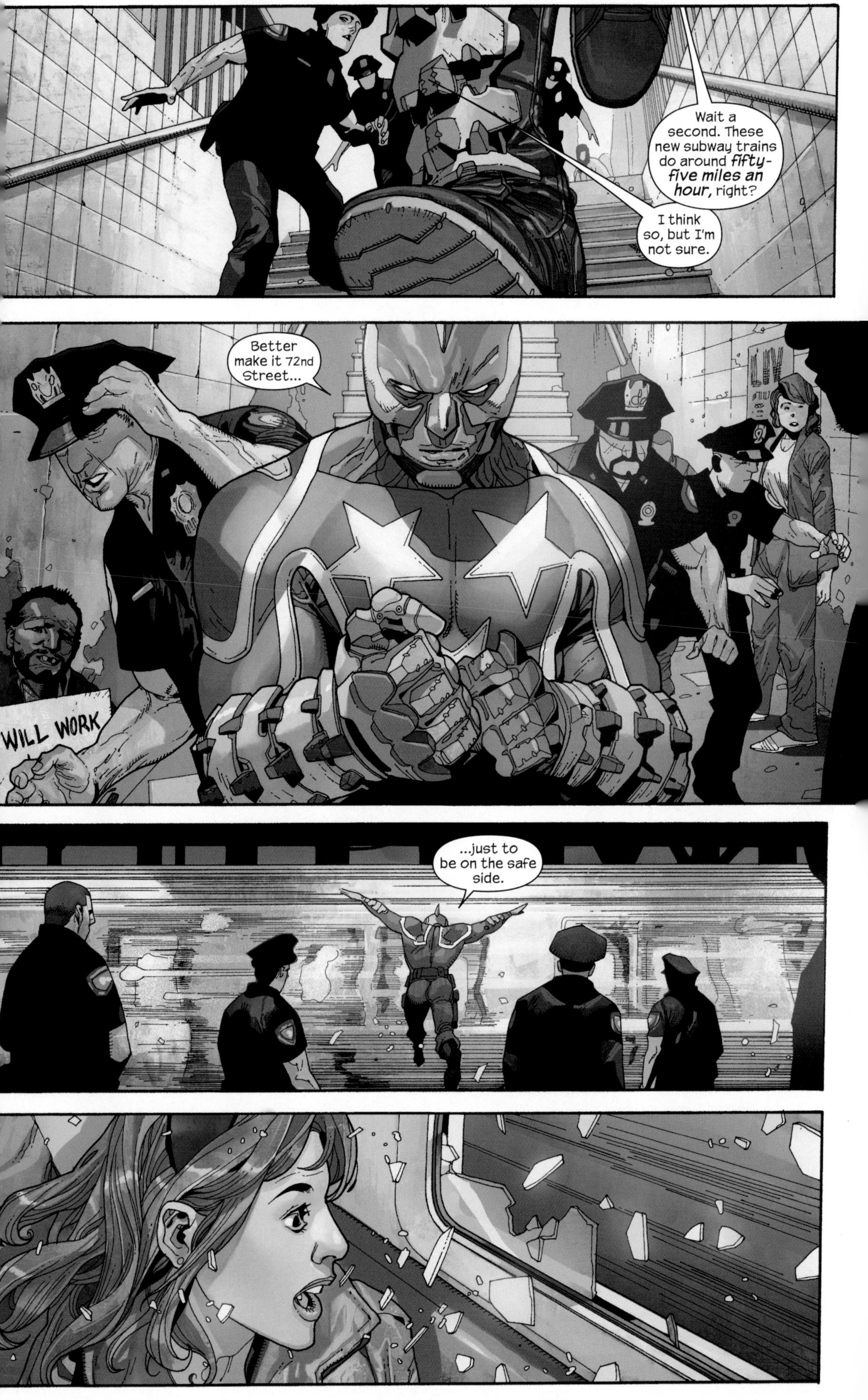

Wait a second. These new subway trains do around *fifty-five miles an hour,* right?
I think so, but I'm not sure.
Better make it 72nd Street...
WILL WORK
...just to be on the safe side.

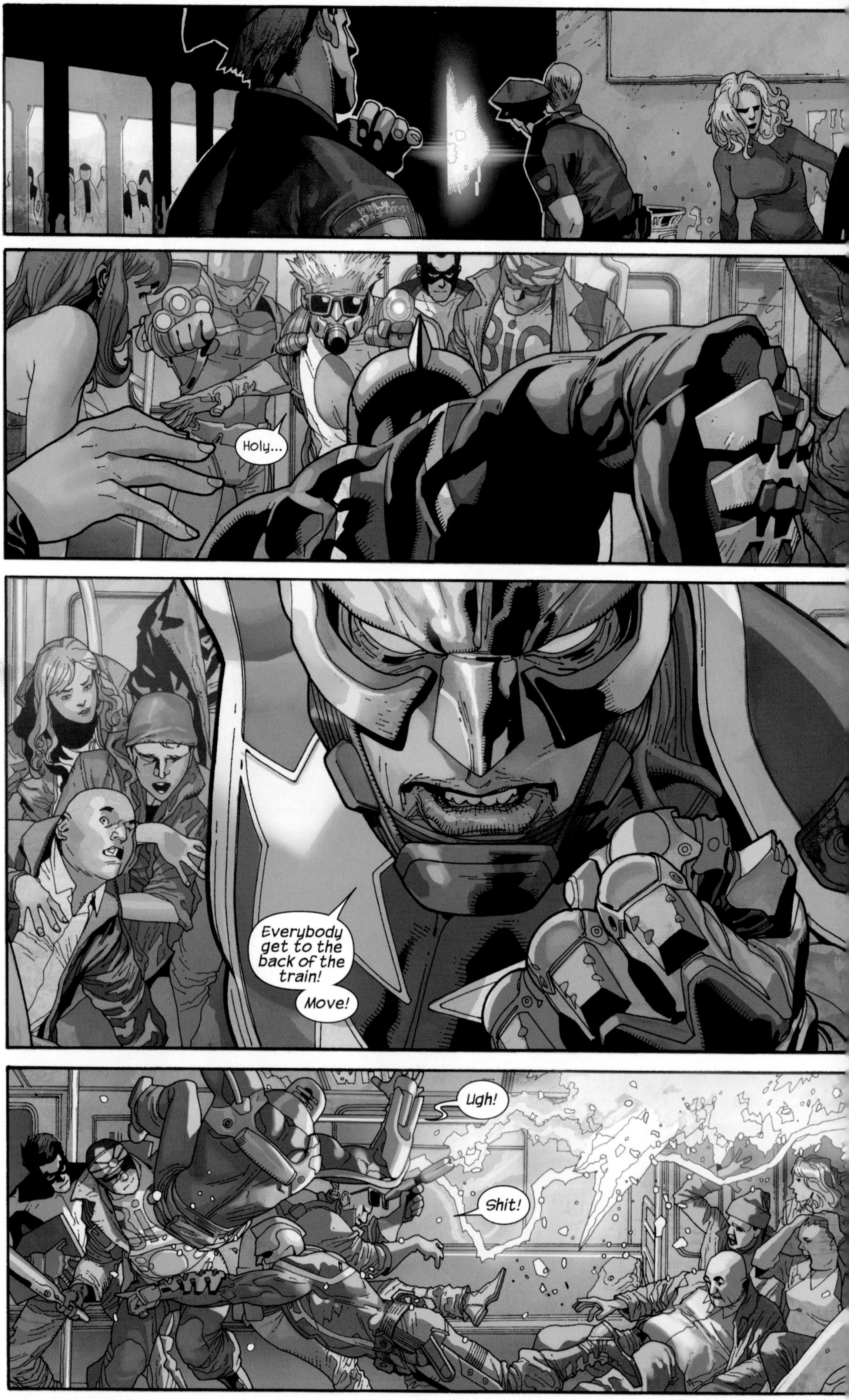
Holy...
Everybody get to the back of the train!
Move!
Ugh!
Shit!

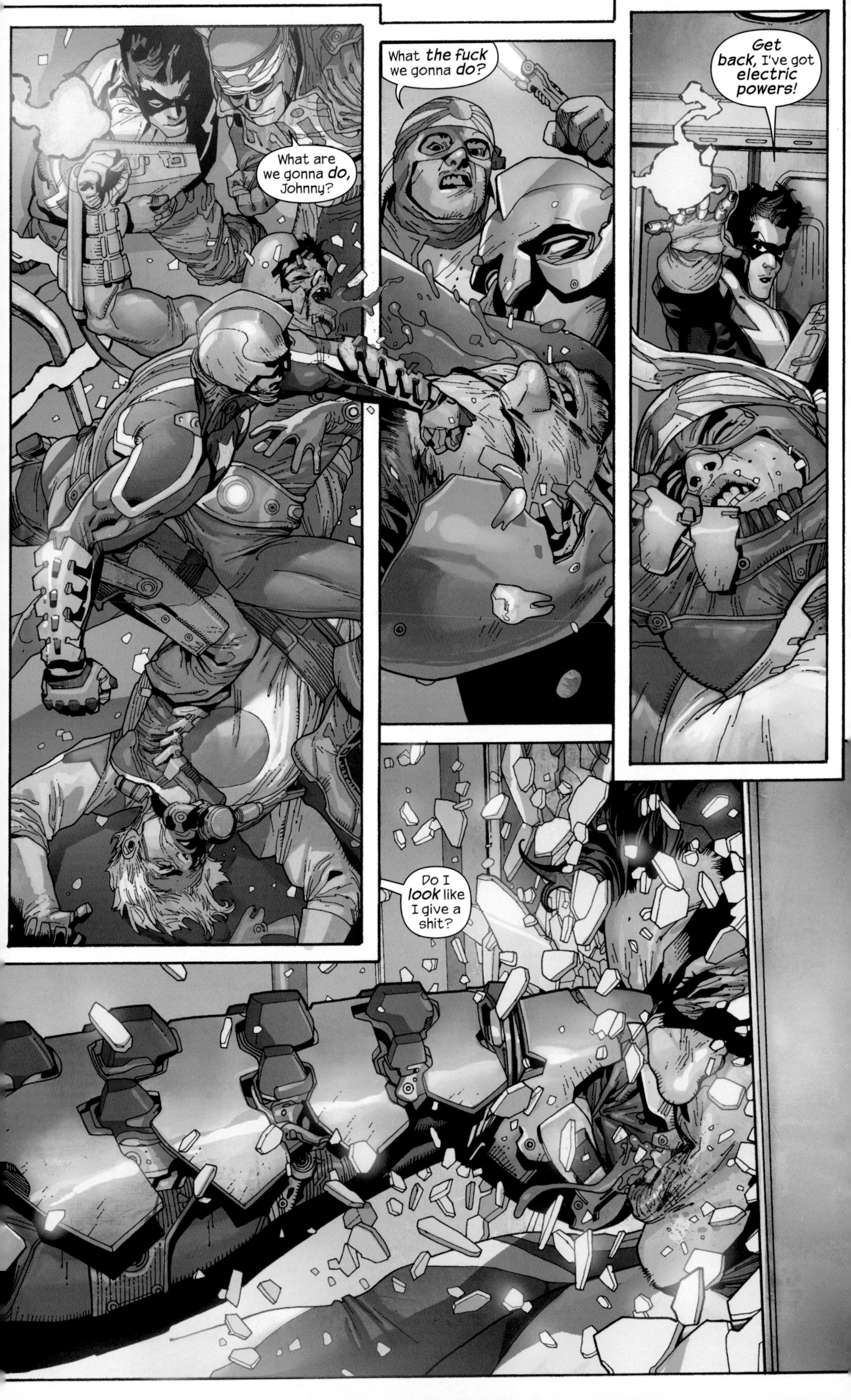
What are we gonna *do,* Johnny?
What **the fuck** we gonna *do?*
Get *back,* I've got *electric powers!*
Do I *look* like I give a shit?

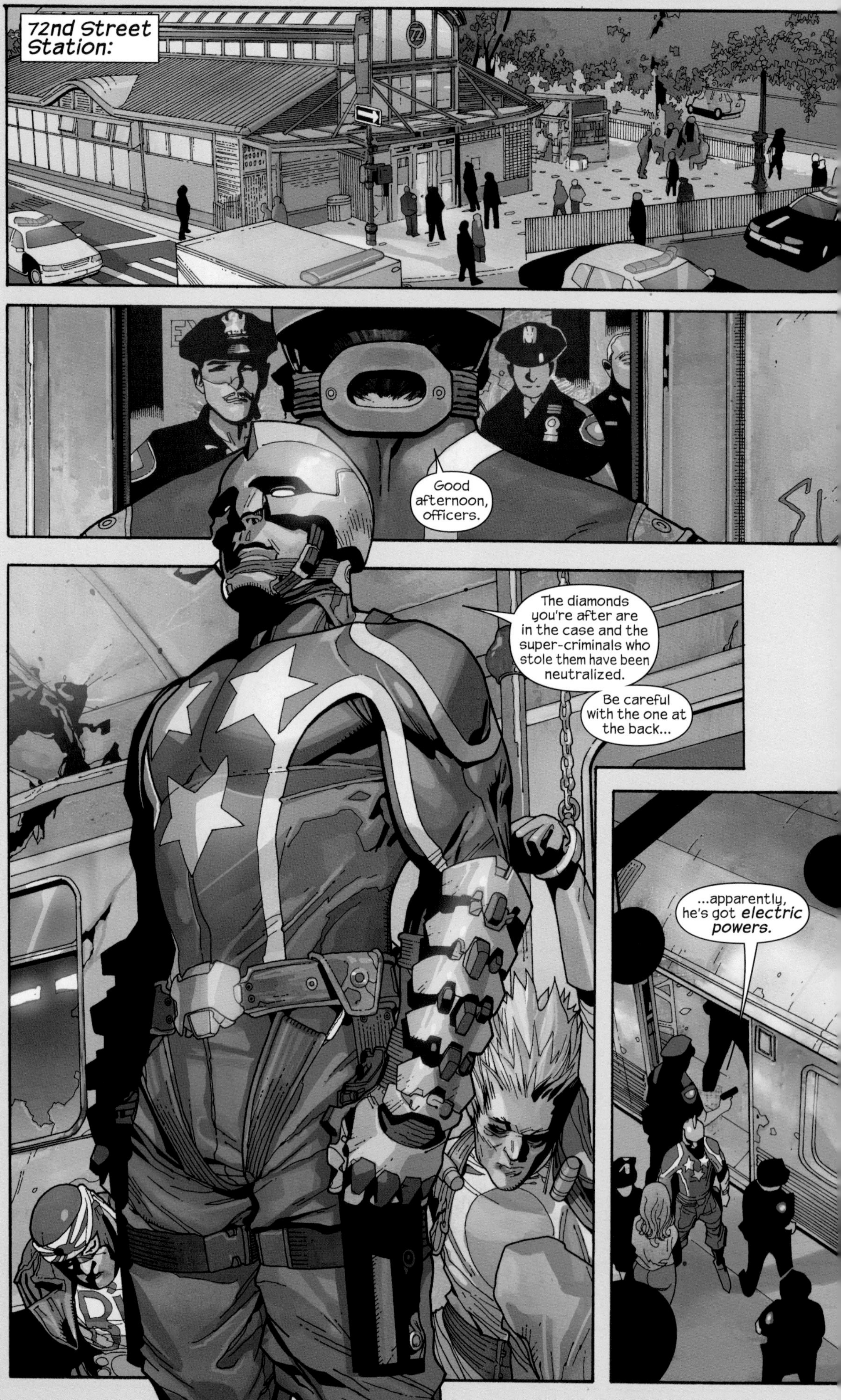
72nd Street Station:
Good afternoon, officers.
The diamonds you're after are in the case and the super-criminals who stole them have been neutralized.
Be careful with the one at the back...
...apparently, he's got *electric powers.*

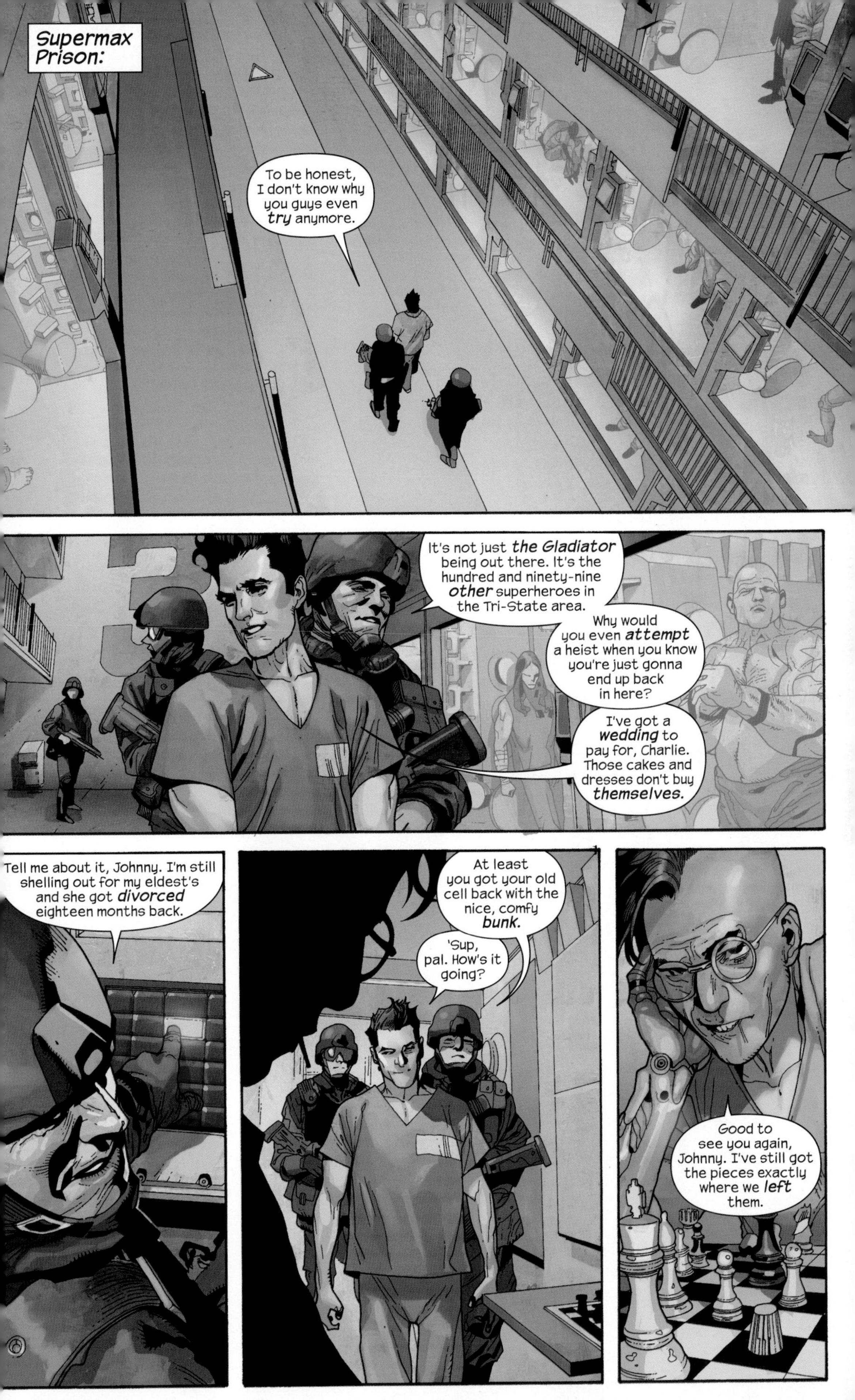
Supermax Prison:
To be honest, I don't know why you guys even *try* anymore.
It's not just *the Gladiator* being out there. It's the hundred and ninety-nine *other* superheroes in the Tri-State area.
Why would you even *attempt* a heist when you know you're just gonna end up back in here?
I've got a *wedding* to pay for, Charlie. Those cakes and dresses don't buy *themselves.*
Tell me about it, Johnny. I'm still shelling out for my eldest's and she got *divorced* eighteen months back.
At least you got your old cell back with the nice, comfy *bunk.*
'Sup, pal. How's it going?
Good to see you again, Johnny. I've still got the pieces exactly where we *left* them.

SUI
CRO

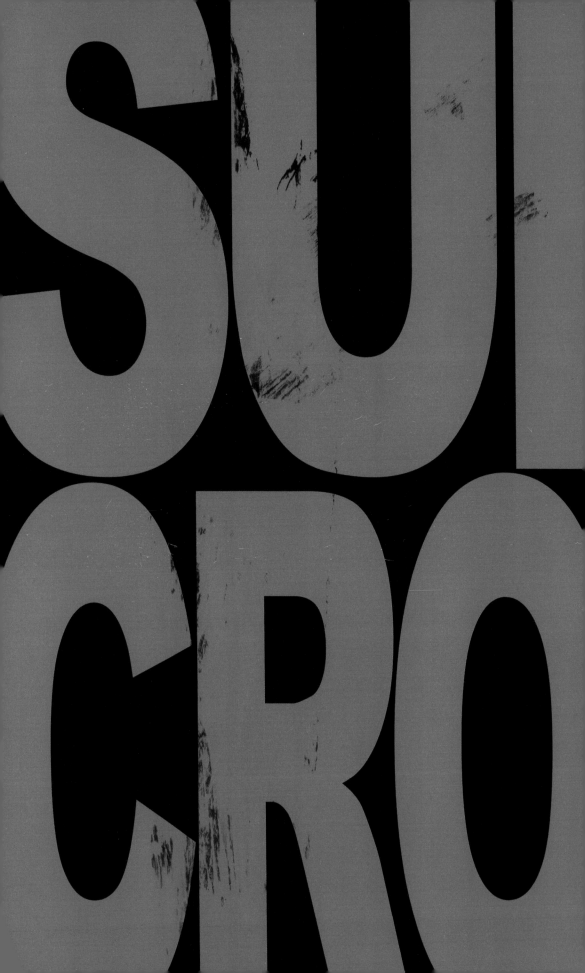

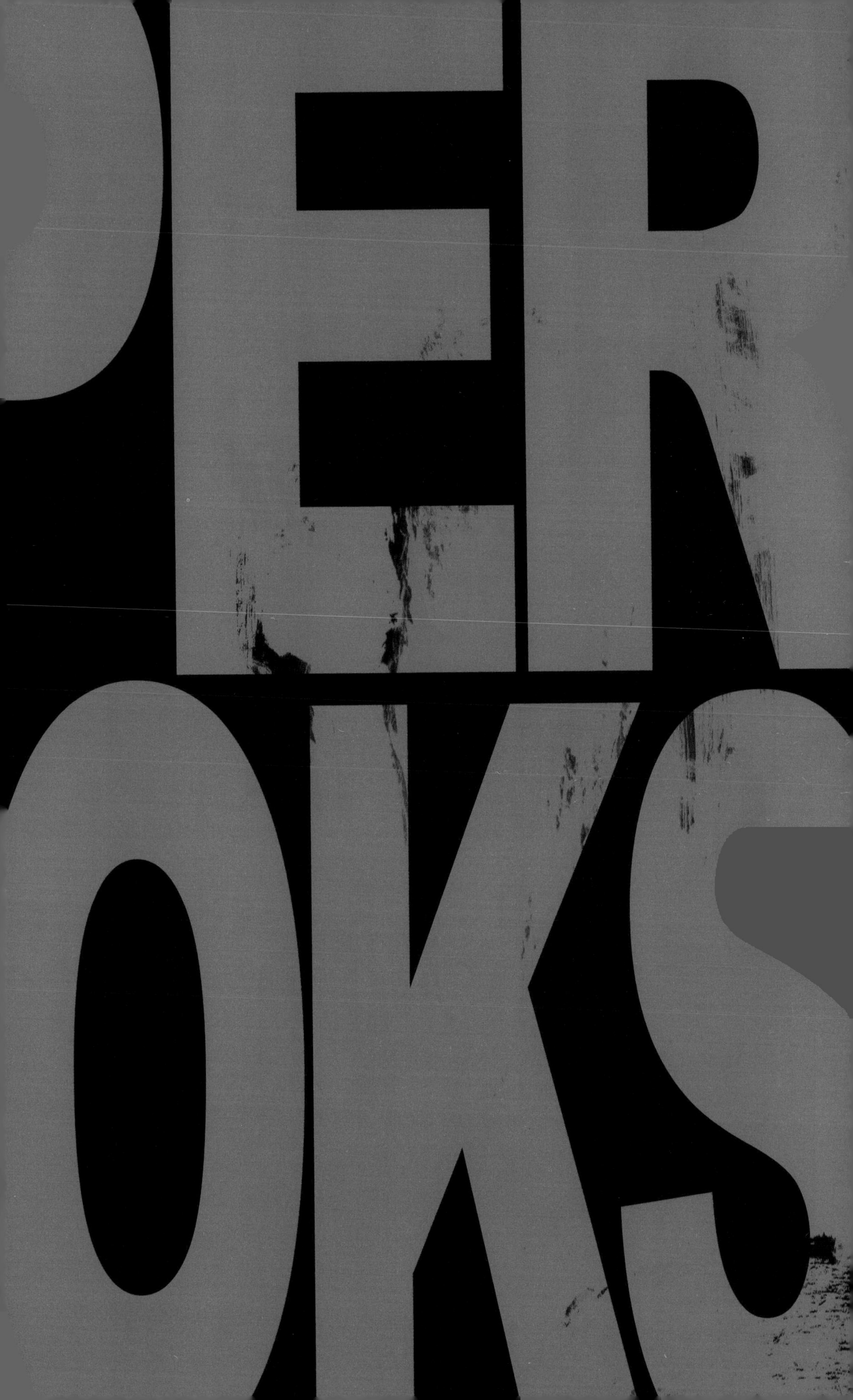

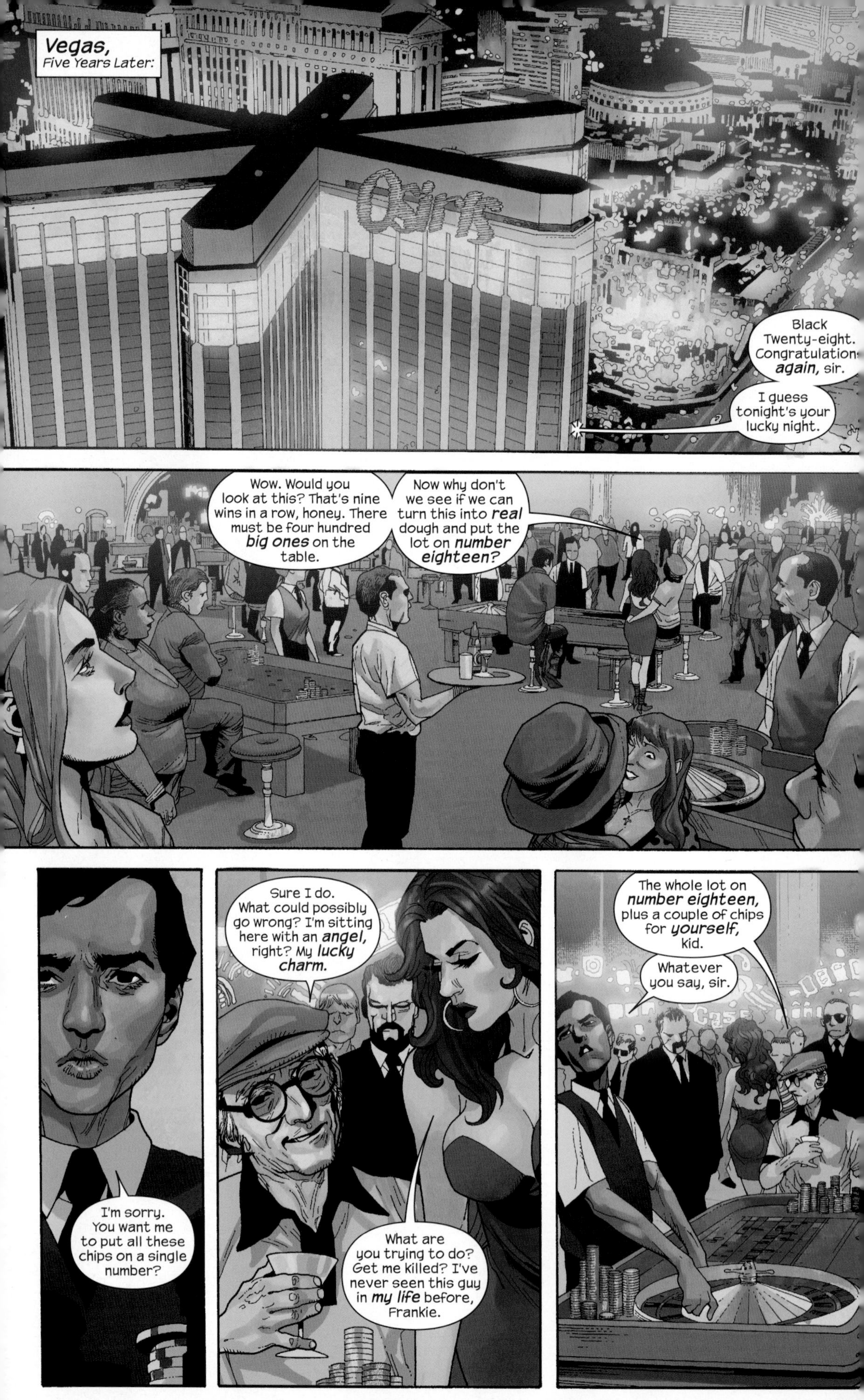
Vegas,
Five Years Later:
Black Twenty-eight. Congratulations *again,* sir.
I guess tonight's your lucky night.
Wow. Would you look at this? That's nine wins in a row, honey. There must be four hundred *big ones* on the table.
Now why don't we see if we can turn this into *real* dough and put the lot on *number eighteen?*
I'm sorry. You want me to put all these chips on a single number?
Sure I do. What could possibly go wrong? I'm sitting here with an *angel,* right? My *lucky charm.*
What are you trying to do? Get me killed? I've never seen this guy in *my life* before, Frankie.
The whole lot on *number eighteen,* plus a couple of chips for *yourself,* kid.
Whatever you say, sir.

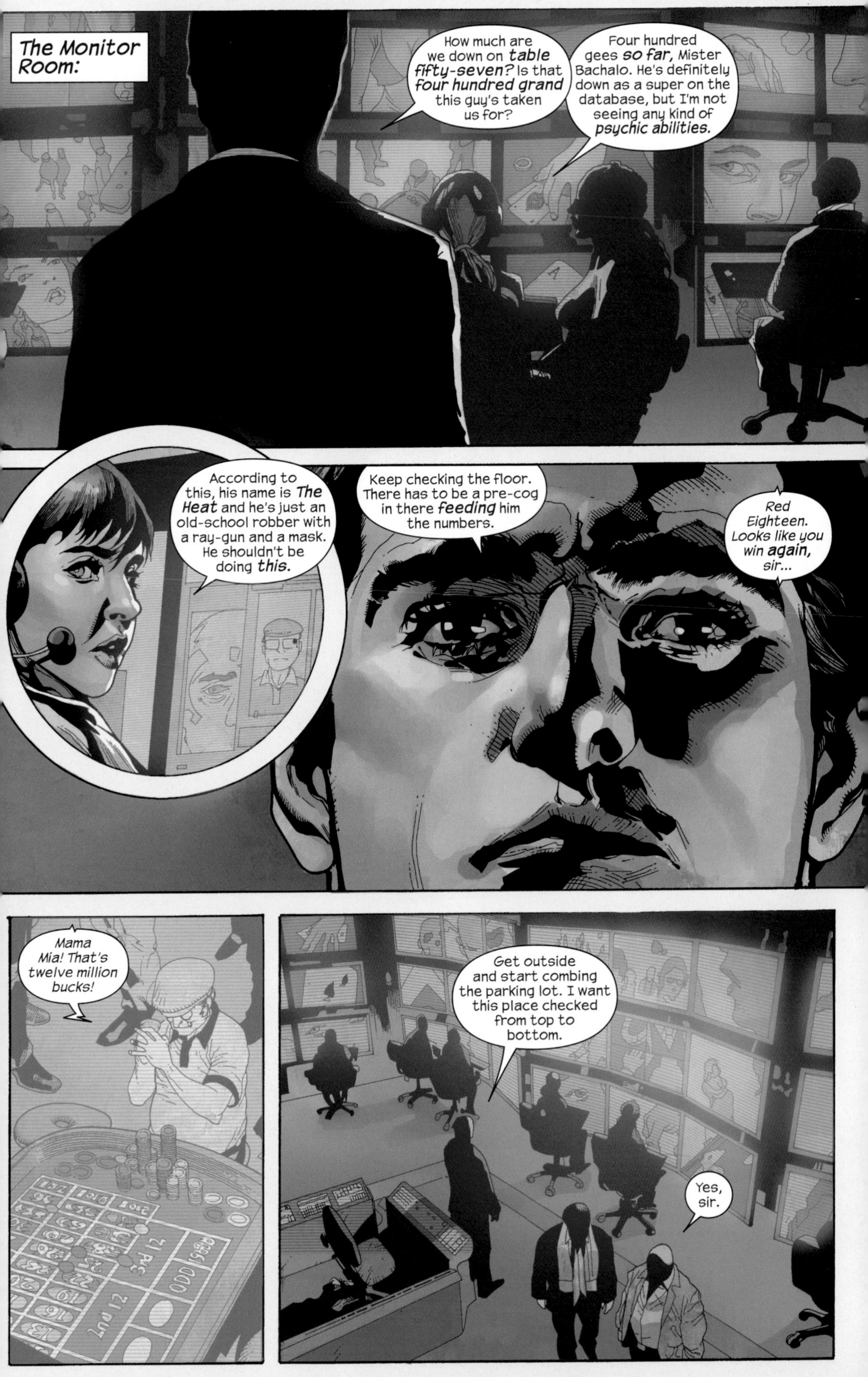
The Monitor Room:
How much are we down on table fifty-seven? Is that four hundred grand this guy's taken us for?
Four hundred gees so far, Mister Bachalo. He's definitely down as a super on the database, but I'm not seeing any kind of psychic abilities.
According to this, his name is The Heat and he's just an old-school robber with a ray-gun and a mask. He shouldn't be doing this.
Keep checking the floor. There has to be a pre-cog in there feeding him the numbers.
Red Eighteen. Looks like you win again, sir...
Mama Mia! That's twelve million bucks!
Get outside and start combing the parking lot. I want this place checked from top to bottom.
Yes, sir.

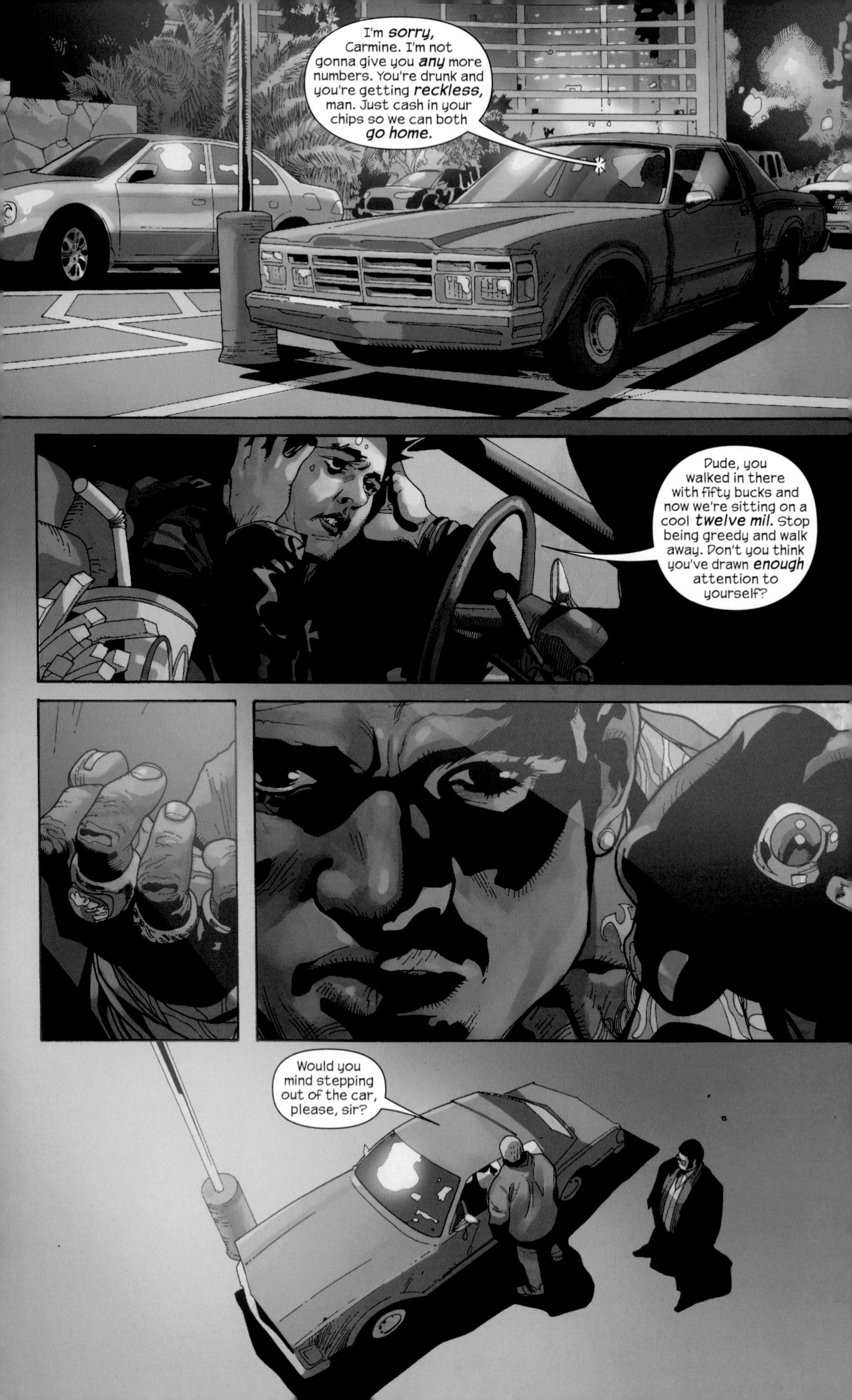
I'm sorry, Carmine. I'm not gonna give you any more numbers. You're drunk and you're getting reckless, man. Just cash in your chips so we can both go home.
Dude, you walked in there with fifty bucks and now we're sitting on a cool twelve mil. Stop being greedy and walk away. Don't you think you've drawn enough attention to yourself?
Would you mind stepping out of the car, please, sir?

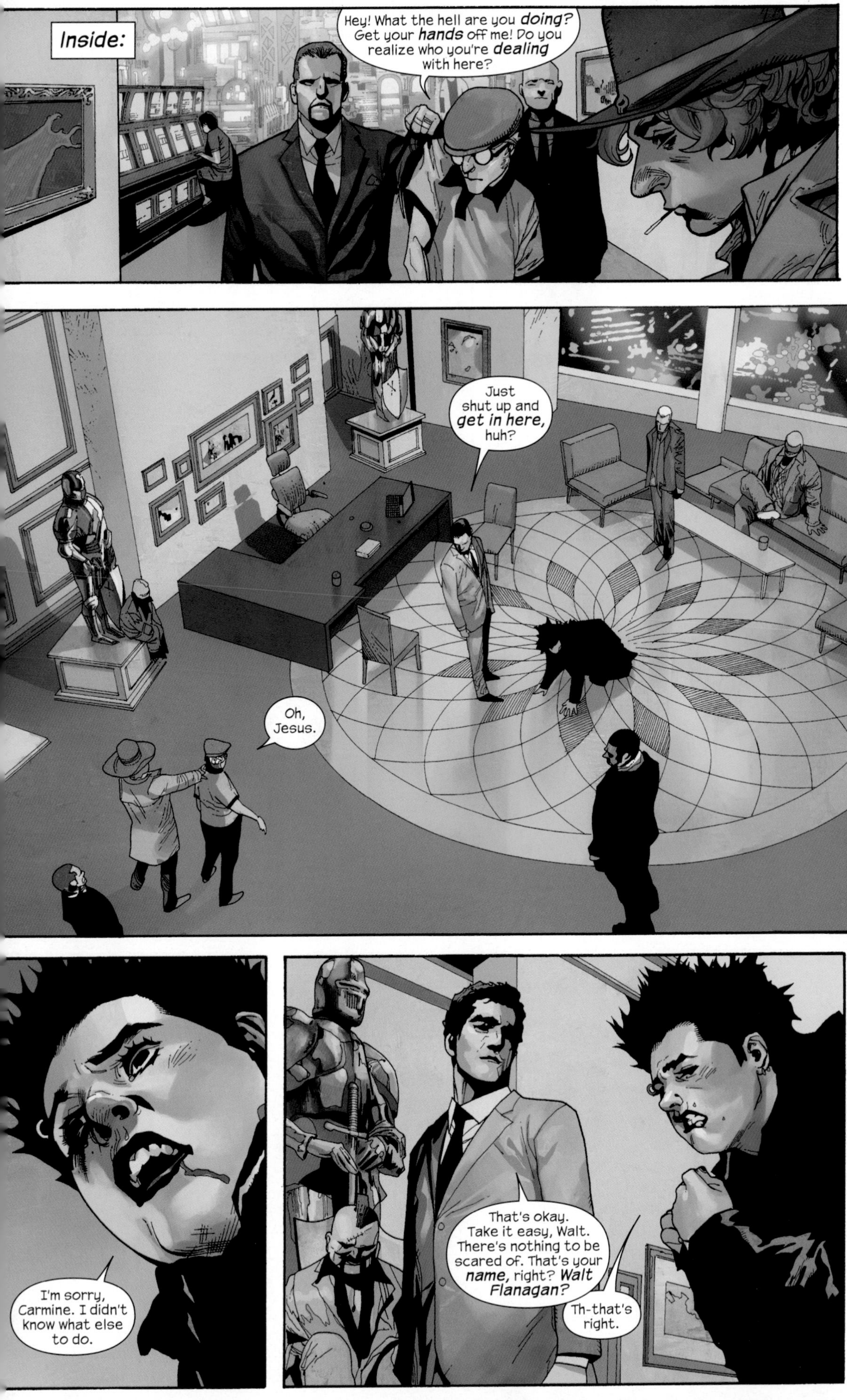

Inside:
Hey! What the hell are you doing? Get your hands off me! Do you realize who you're dealing with here?
Just shut up and get in here, huh?
Oh, Jesus.
I'm sorry, Carmine. I didn't know what else to do.
That's okay. Take it easy, Walt. There's nothing to be scared of. That's your name, right? Walt Flanagan?
Th-that's right.

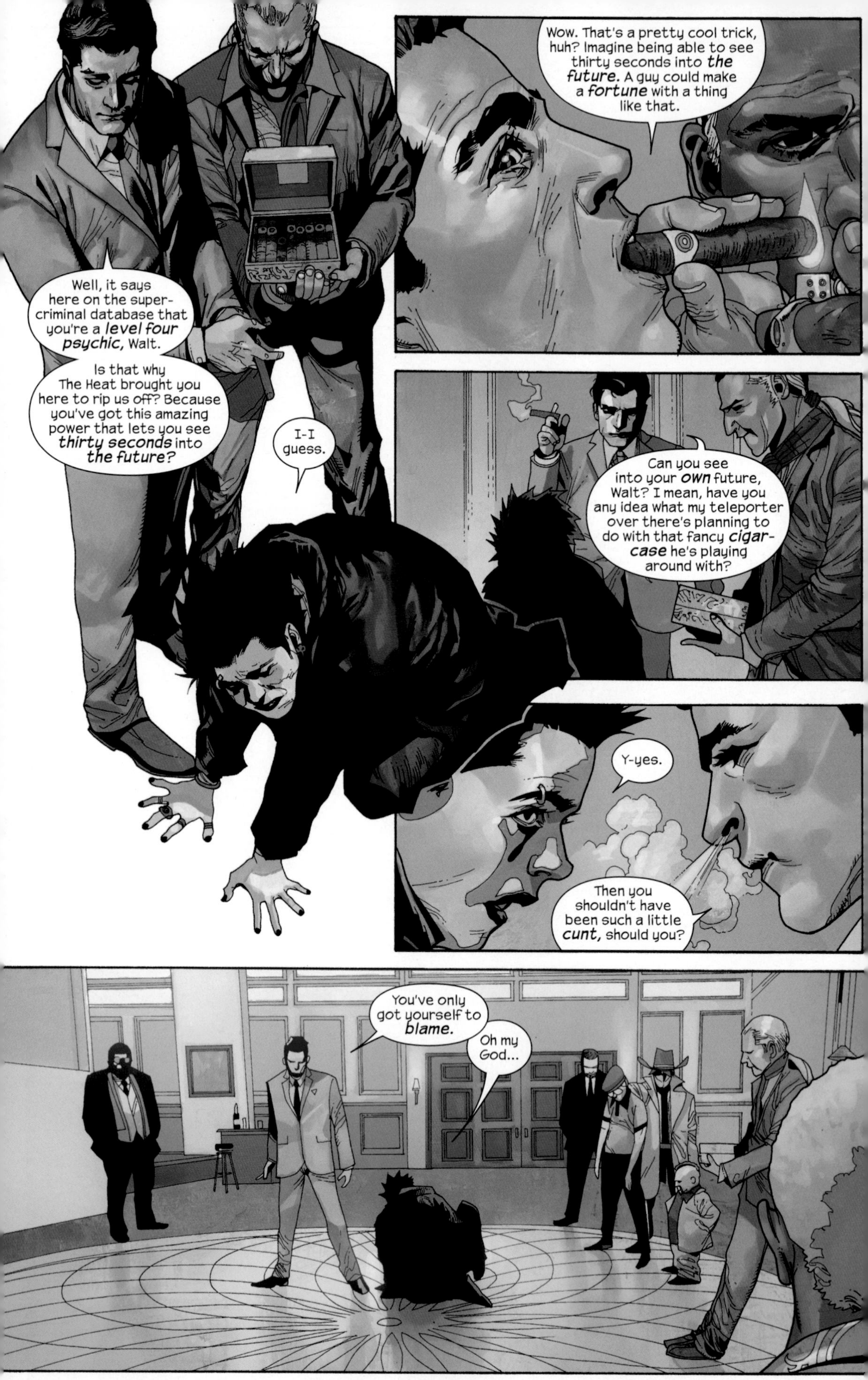
Well, it says here on the super-criminal database that you're a *level four psychic,* Walt.
Is that why The Heat brought you here to rip us off? Because you've got this amazing power that lets you see *thirty seconds* into *the future?*
I-I guess.
Wow. That's a pretty cool trick, huh? Imagine being able to see thirty seconds into *the future.* A guy could make a *fortune* with a thing like that.
Can you see into your *own* future, Walt? I mean, have you any idea what my teleporter over there's planning to do with that fancy *cigar-case* he's playing around with?
Y-yes.
Then you shouldn't have been such a little *cunt,* should you?
You've only got yourself to *blame.*
Oh my God...

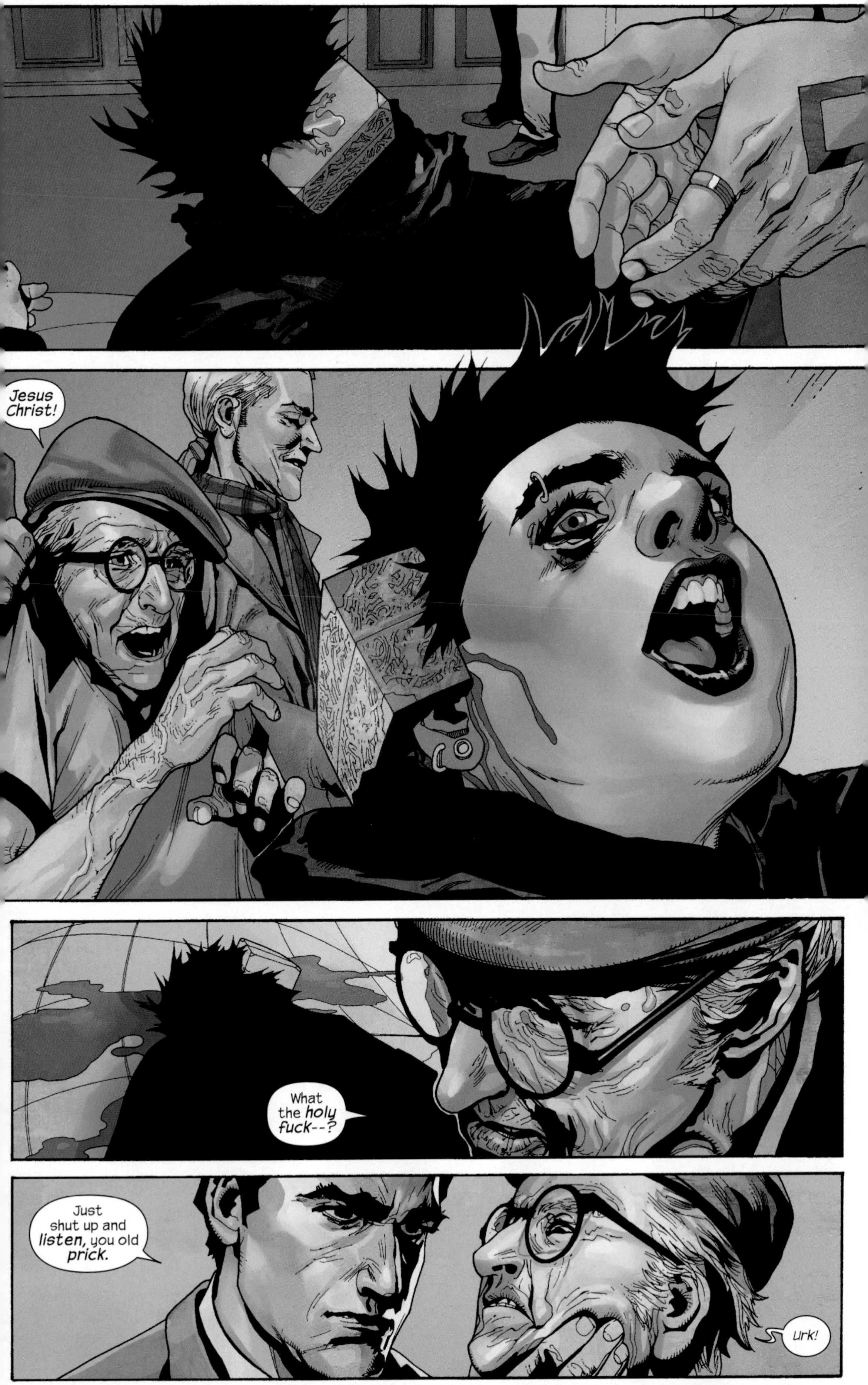
Jesus Christ!
What the holy fuck--?
Just shut up and listen, you old prick.
Urk!

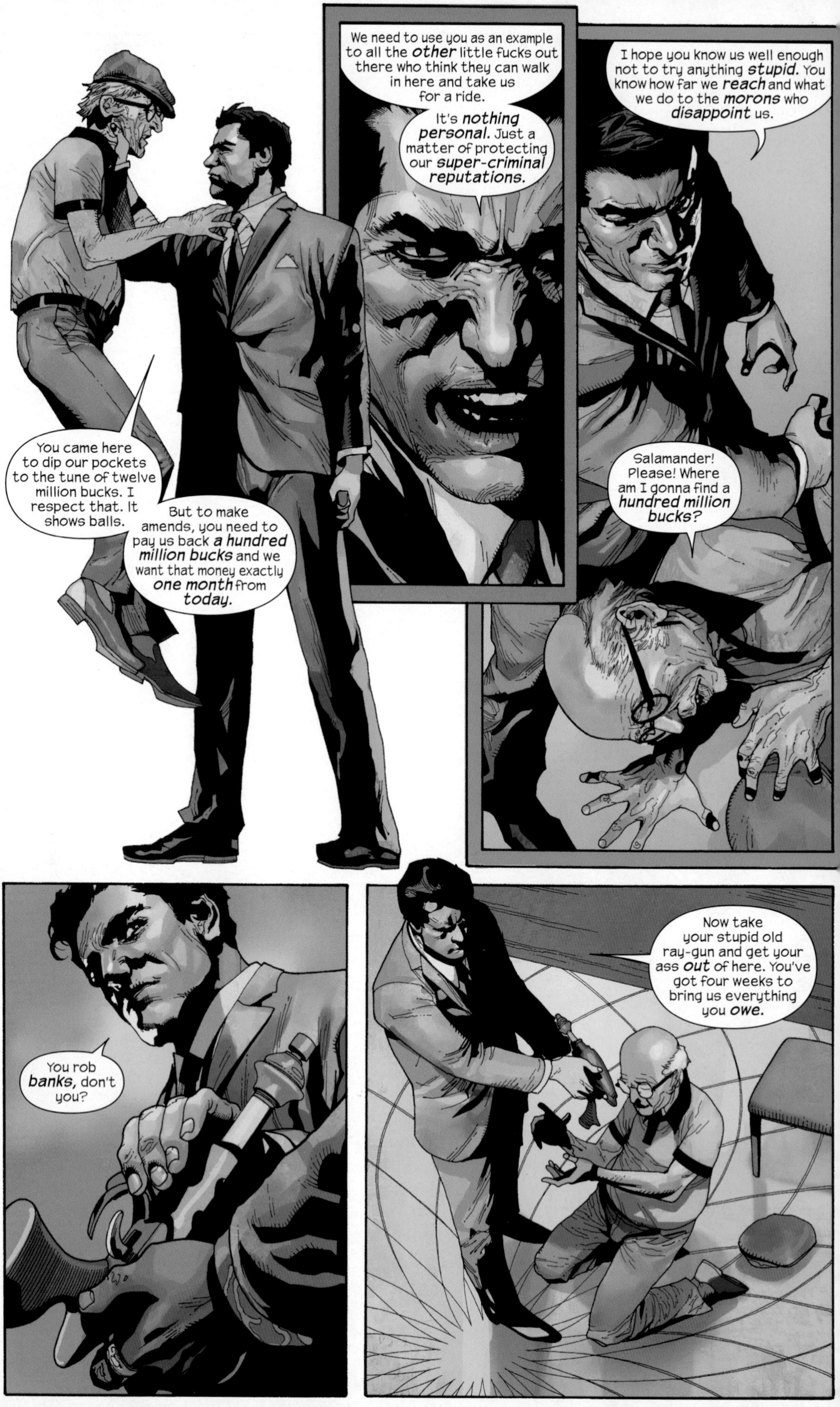
You came here to dip our pockets to the tune of twelve million bucks. I respect that. It shows balls.
But to make amends, you need to pay us back *a hundred million bucks* and we want that money exactly *one month* from *today.*
We need to use you as an example to all the *other* little fucks out there who think they can walk in here and take us for a ride.
It's *nothing personal.* Just a matter of protecting our *super-criminal reputations.*
I hope you know us well enough not to try anything *stupid.* You know how far we *reach* and what we do to the *morons* who *disappoint* us.
Salamander! Please! Where am I gonna find a *hundred million bucks?*
You rob *banks,* don't you?
Now take your stupid old ray-gun and get your ass *out* of here. You've got four weeks to bring us everything you *owe.*

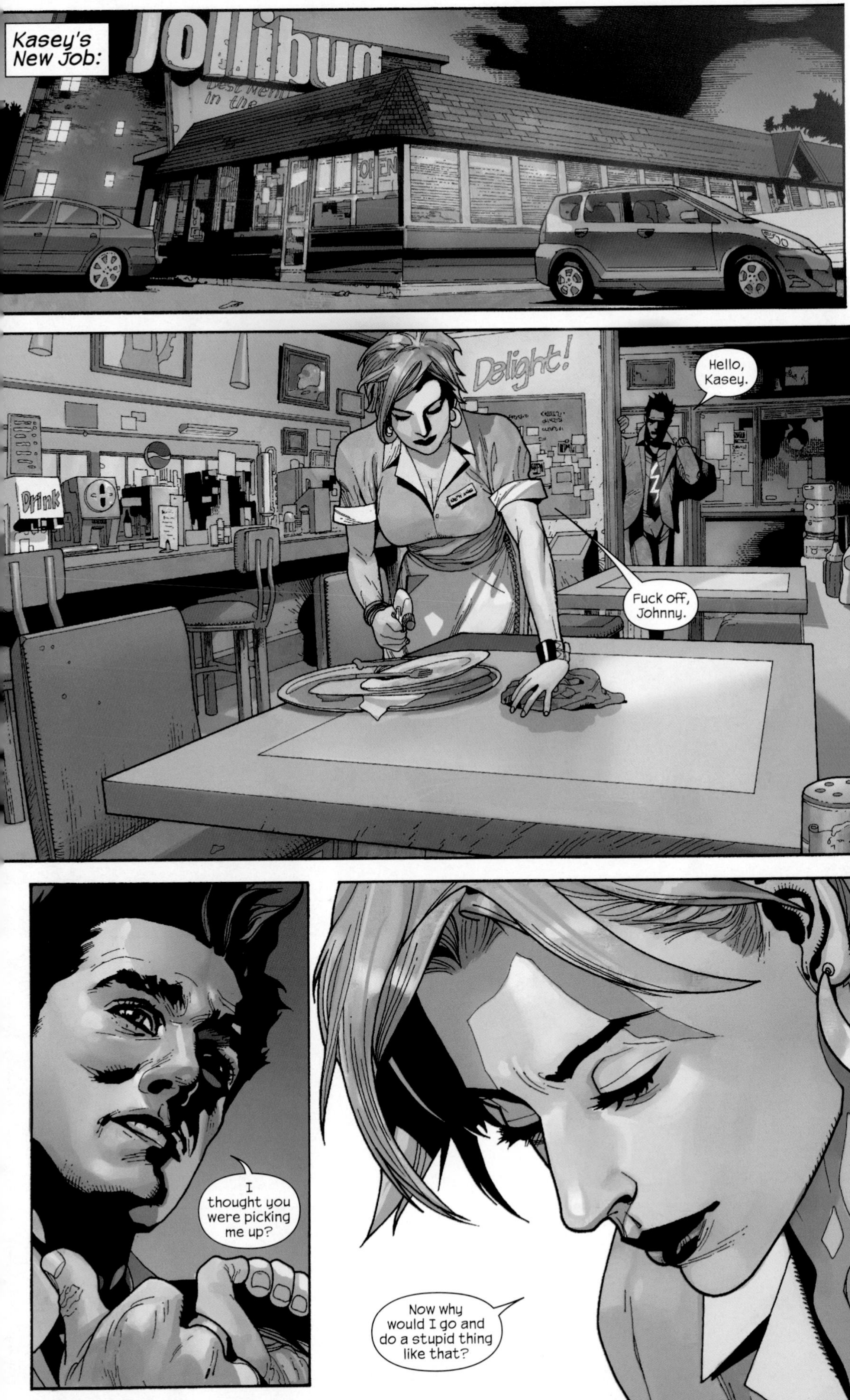
Kasey's New Job:
OPEN
Delight!
Drink
Hello, Kasey.
Fuck off, Johnny.
I thought you were picking me up?
Now why would I go and do a stupid thing like that?

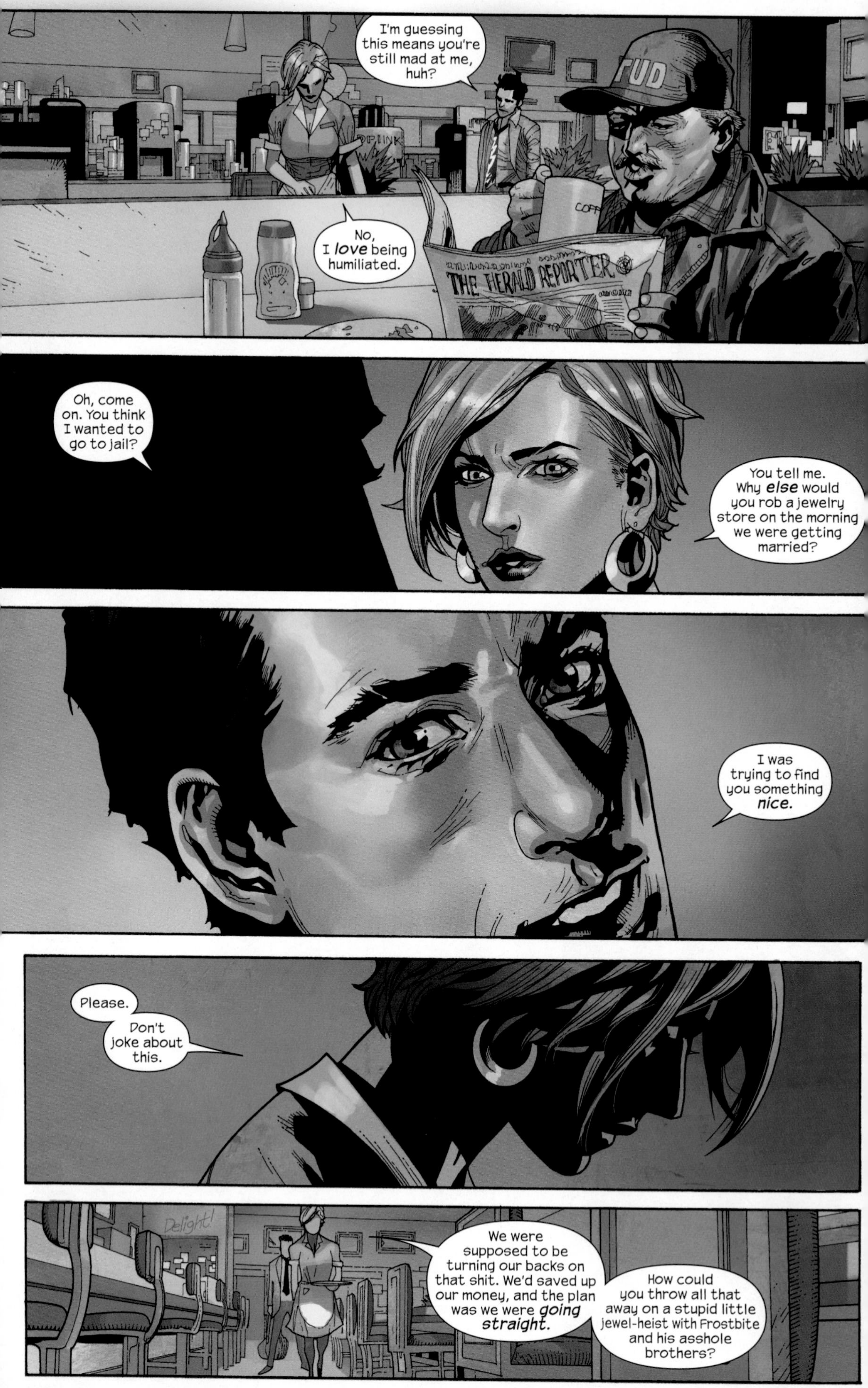

TUD
I'm guessing this means you're still mad at me, huh?
No, I *love* being humiliated.
THE HERALD REPORTER
Oh, come on. You think I wanted to go to jail?
You tell me. Why *else* would you rob a jewelry store on the morning we were getting married?
I was trying to find you something *nice*.
Please.
Don't joke about this.
Delight!
We were supposed to be turning our backs on that shit. We'd saved up our money, and the plan was we were *going straight*.
How could you throw all that away on a stupid little jewel-heist with Frostbite and his asshole brothers?

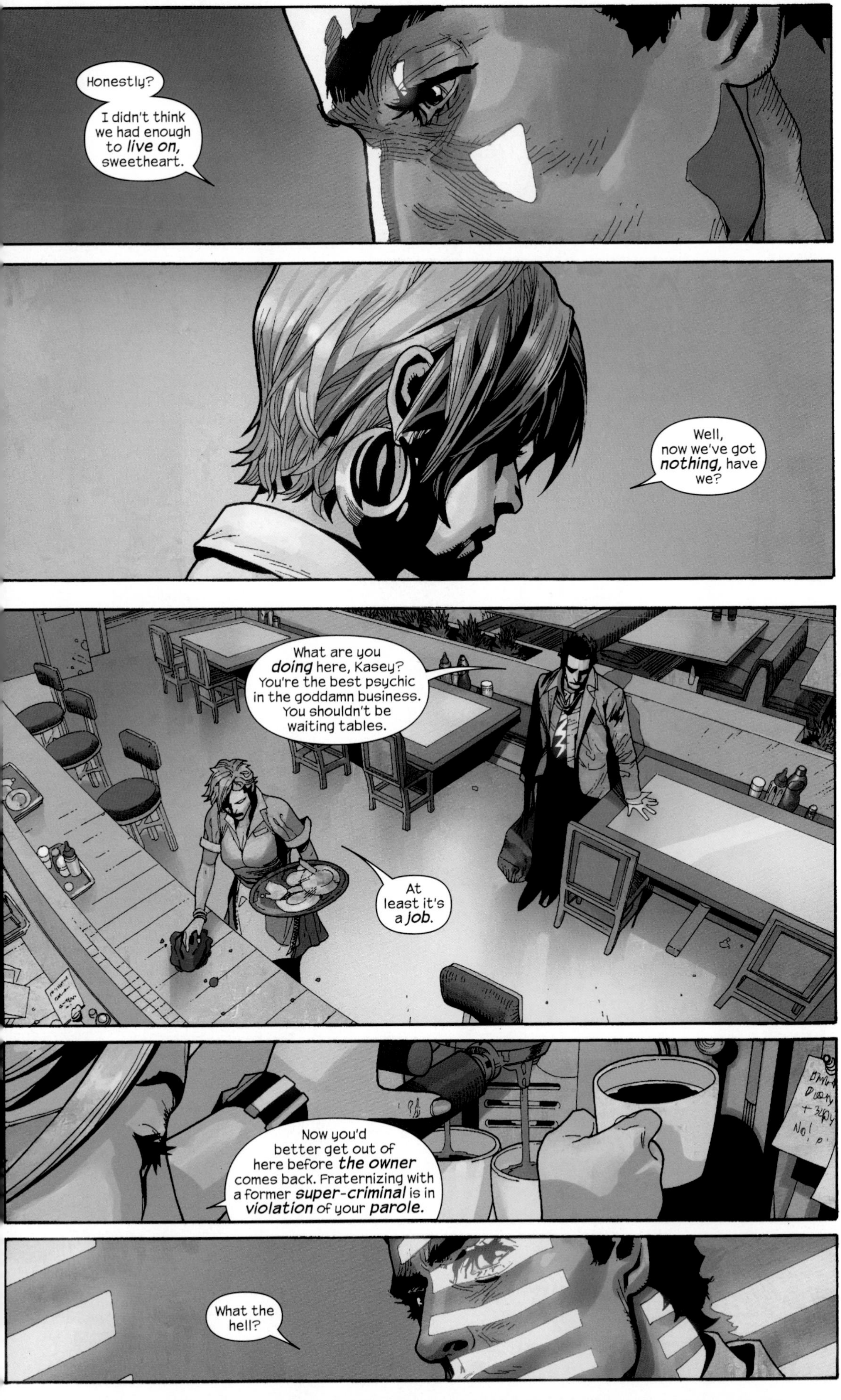
Honestly?
I didn't think we had enough to live on, sweetheart.
Well, now we've got nothing, have we?
What are you doing here, Kasey? You're the best psychic in the goddamn business. You shouldn't be waiting tables.
At least it's a job.
Now you'd better get out of here before the owner comes back. Fraternizing with a former super-criminal is in violation of your parole.
What the hell?

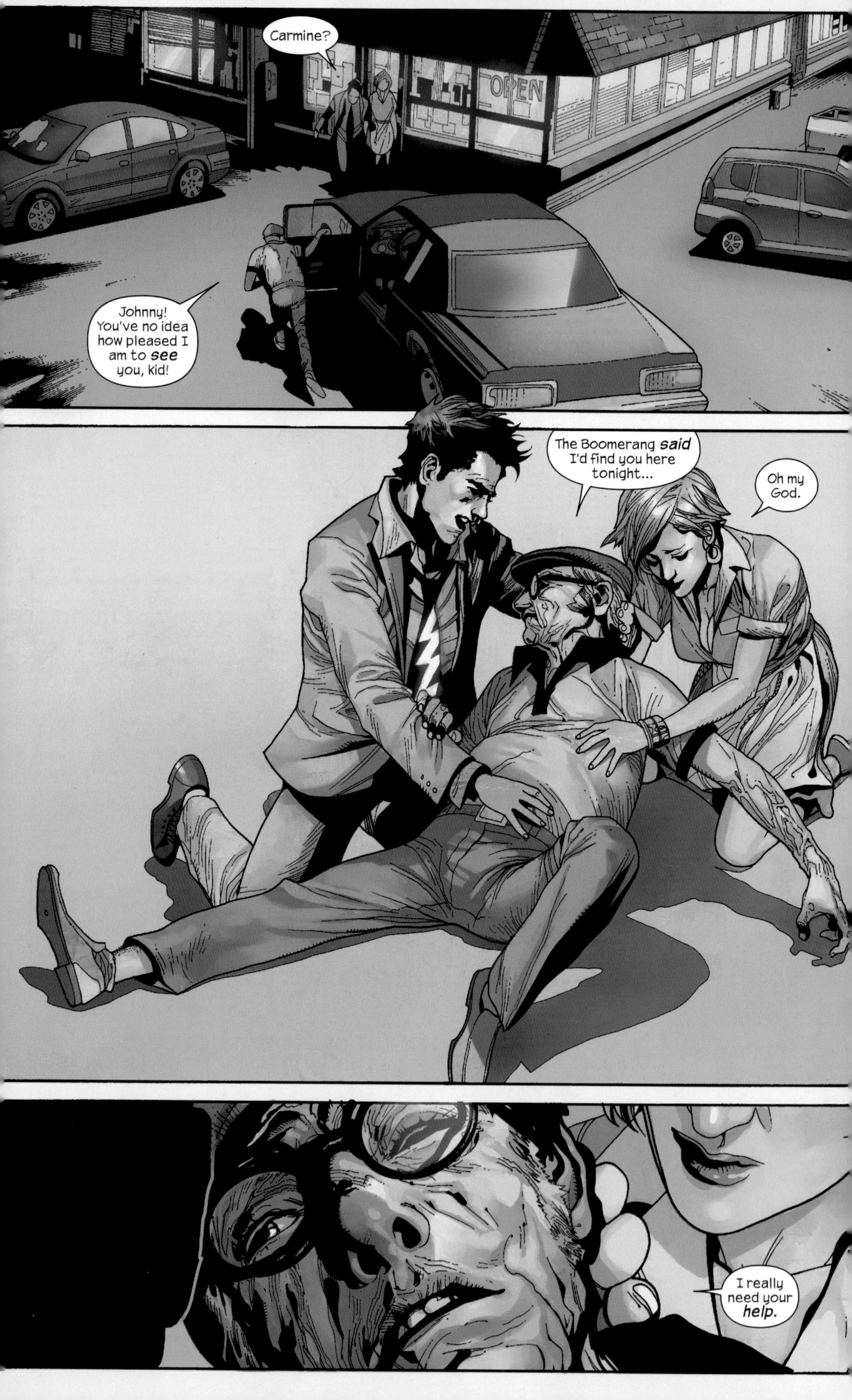
Carmine?
Johnny! You've no idea how pleased I am to *see* you, kid!
The Boomerang *said* I'd find you here tonight...
Oh my God.
I really need your *help*.

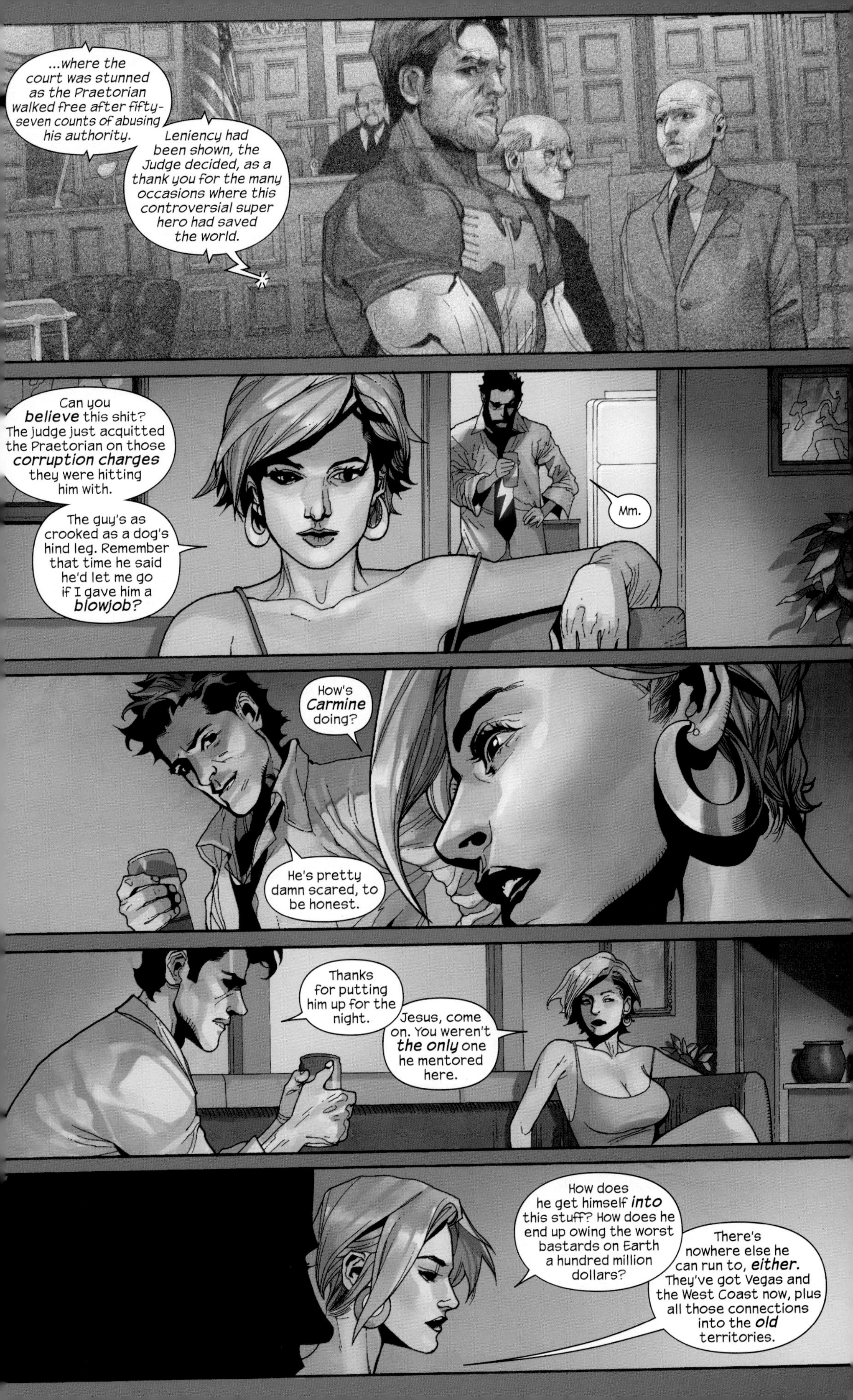
...where the court was stunned as the Praetorian walked free after fifty-seven counts of abusing his authority.
Leniency had been shown, the Judge decided, as a thank you for the many occasions where this controversial super hero had saved the world.
Can you believe this shit? The judge just acquitted the Praetorian on those corruption charges they were hitting him with.
The guy's as crooked as a dog's hind leg. Remember that time he said he'd let me go if I gave him a blowjob?
Mm.
How's Carmine doing?
He's pretty damn scared, to be honest.
Thanks for putting him up for the night.
Jesus, come on. You weren't the only one he mentored here.
How does he get himself into this stuff? How does he end up owing the worst bastards on Earth a hundred million dollars?
There's nowhere else he can run to, either. They've got Vegas and the West Coast now, plus all those connections into the old territories.

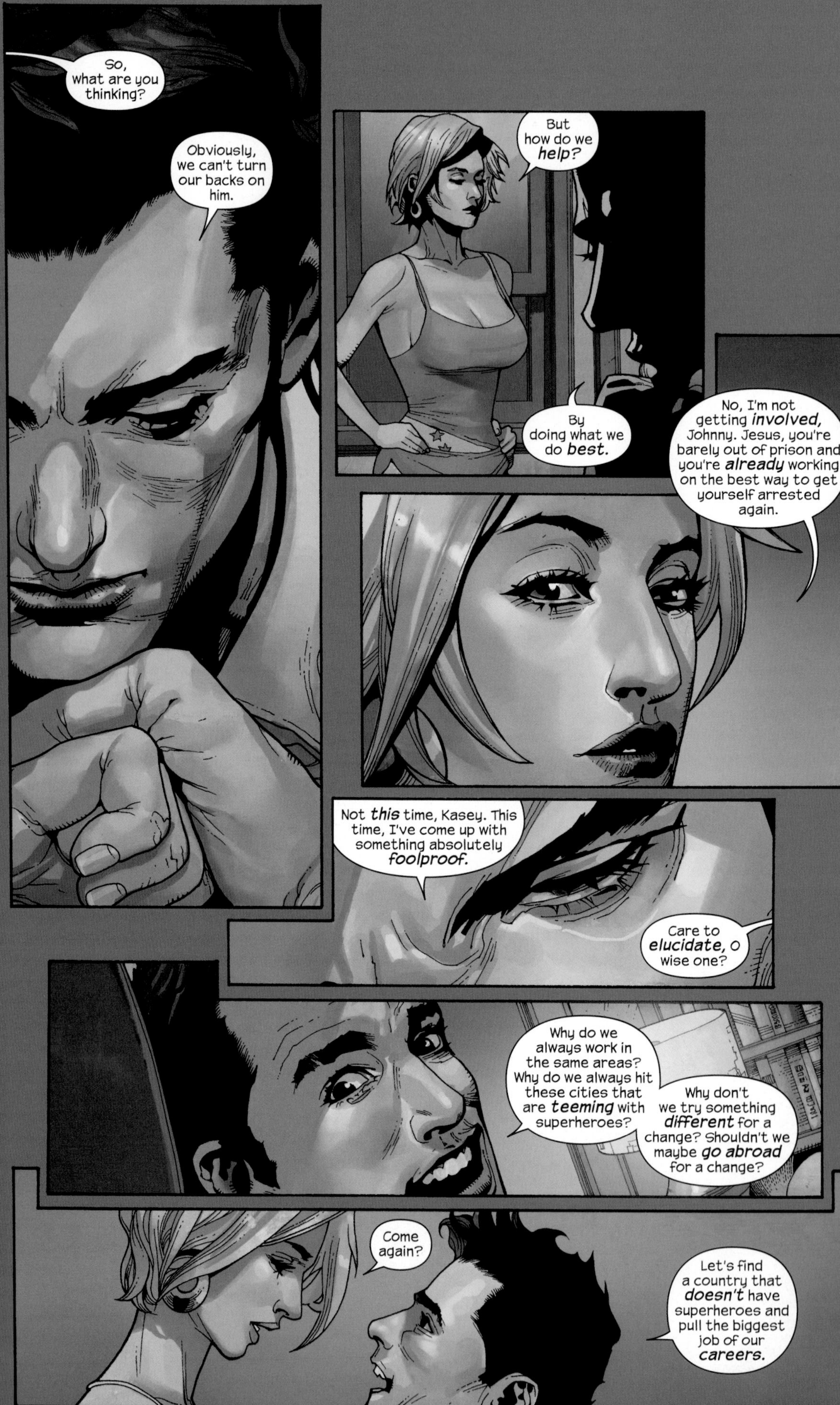

So, what are you thinking?
Obviously, we can't turn our backs on him.
But how do we help?
By doing what we do best.
No, I'm not getting involved, Johnny. Jesus, you're barely out of prison and you're already working on the best way to get yourself arrested again.
Not this time, Kasey. This time, I've come up with something absolutely foolproof.
Care to elucidate, O wise one?
Why do we always work in the same areas? Why do we always hit these cities that are teeming with superheroes?
Why don't we try something different for a change? Shouldn't we maybe go abroad for a change?
Come again?
Let's find a country that doesn't have superheroes and pull the biggest job of our careers.

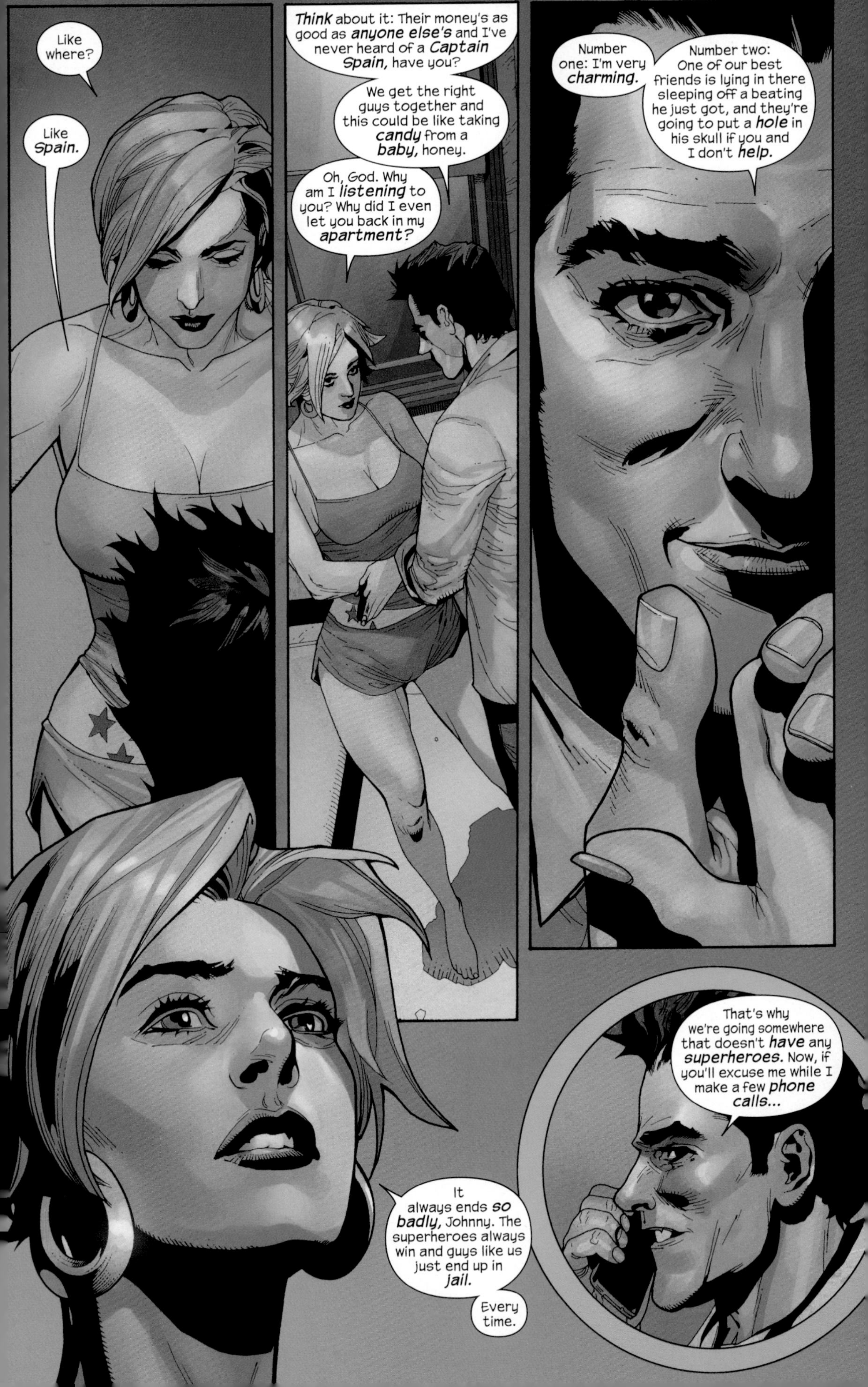
Like where?
Like Spain.
Think about it: Their money's as good as anyone else's and I've never heard of a Captain Spain, have you?
We get the right guys together and this could be like taking candy from a baby, honey.
Oh, God. Why am I listening to you? Why did I even let you back in my apartment?
Number one: I'm very charming.
Number two: One of our best friends is lying in there sleeping off a beating he just got, and they're going to put a hole in his skull if you and I don't help.
It always ends so badly, Johnny. The superheroes always win and guys like us just end up in jail.
Every time.
That's why we're going somewhere that doesn't have any superheroes. Now, if you'll excuse me while I make a few phone calls...

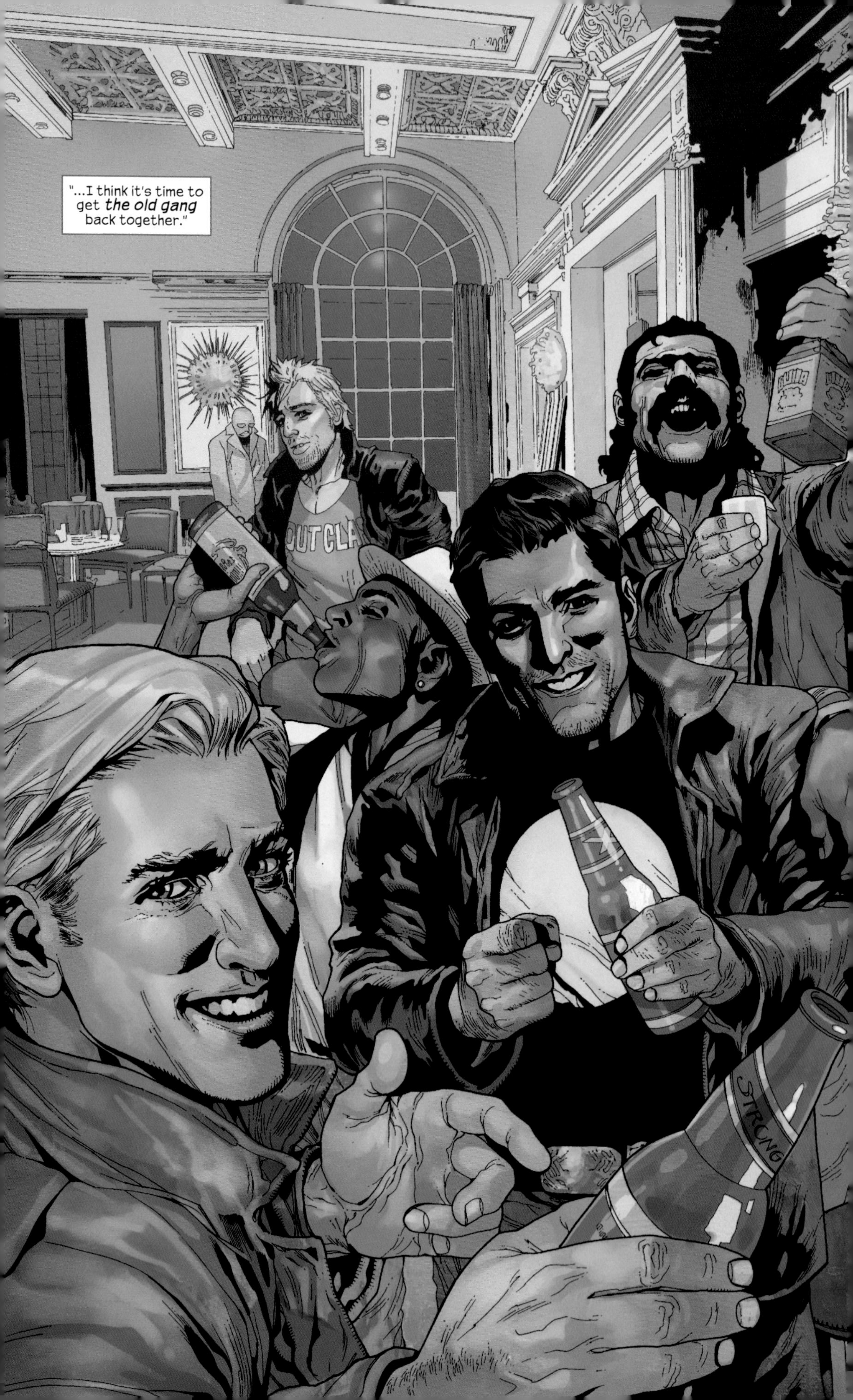
"...I think it's time to get *the old gang* back together."
OUTCLA
STRONG

# TWO

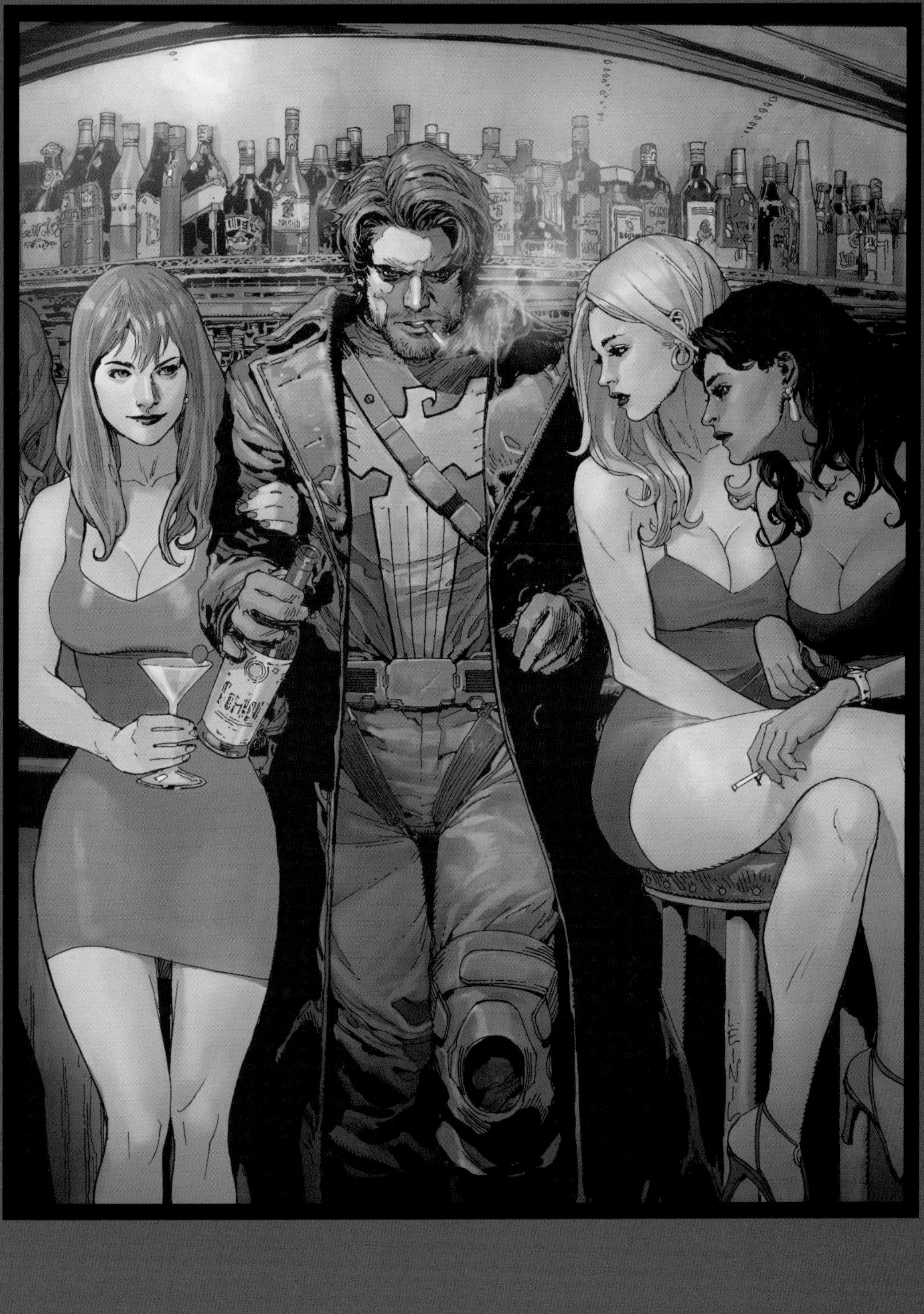

The Ghost,
*World's Greatest
Cat-Burglar:*

Not a chance.

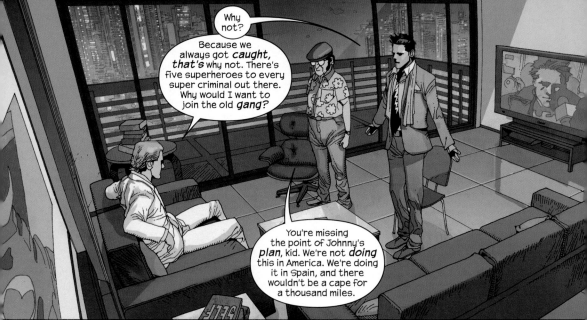

Why not?

Because we always got *caught*, *that's* why not. There's five superheroes to every super criminal out there. Why would I want to join the old *gang*?

You're missing the point of Johnny's *plan*, kid. We're not *doing* this in America. We're doing it in Spain, and there wouldn't be a cape for a thousand miles.

He's right, man. This job should be a *piece of cake.*

I'm *done* with cake. I want to be *normal.* I've been making good money with this *architect thing* and the people are really *nice.*

The people are *boring*, Josh. They haven't robbed a single bank. The Heat and I, you may recall, almost robbed *Fort Knox.*

Now c'mon! We *need* you on this! You're the best intangible in *the business*, dude.

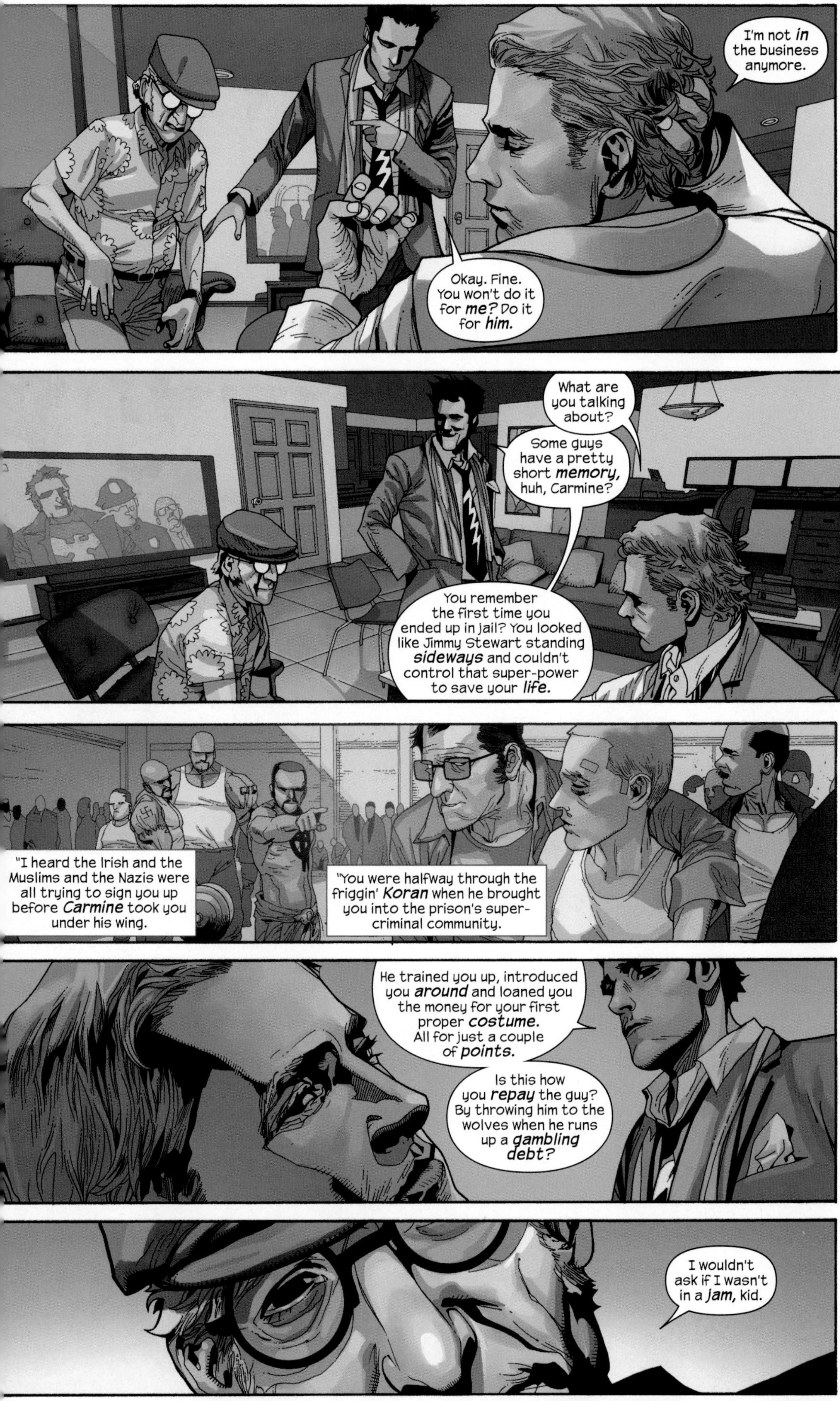
I'm not in the business anymore.
Okay. Fine. You won't do it for me? Do it for him.
What are you talking about?
Some guys have a pretty short memory, huh, Carmine?
You remember the first time you ended up in jail? You looked like Jimmy Stewart standing sideways and couldn't control that super-power to save your life.
"I heard the Irish and the Muslims and the Nazis were all trying to sign you up before Carmine took you under his wing.
"You were halfway through the friggin' Koran when he brought you into the prison's super-criminal community.
He trained you up, introduced you around and loaned you the money for your first proper costume. All for just a couple of points.
Is this how you repay the guy? By throwing him to the wolves when he runs up a gambling debt?
I wouldn't ask if I wasn't in a jam, kid.

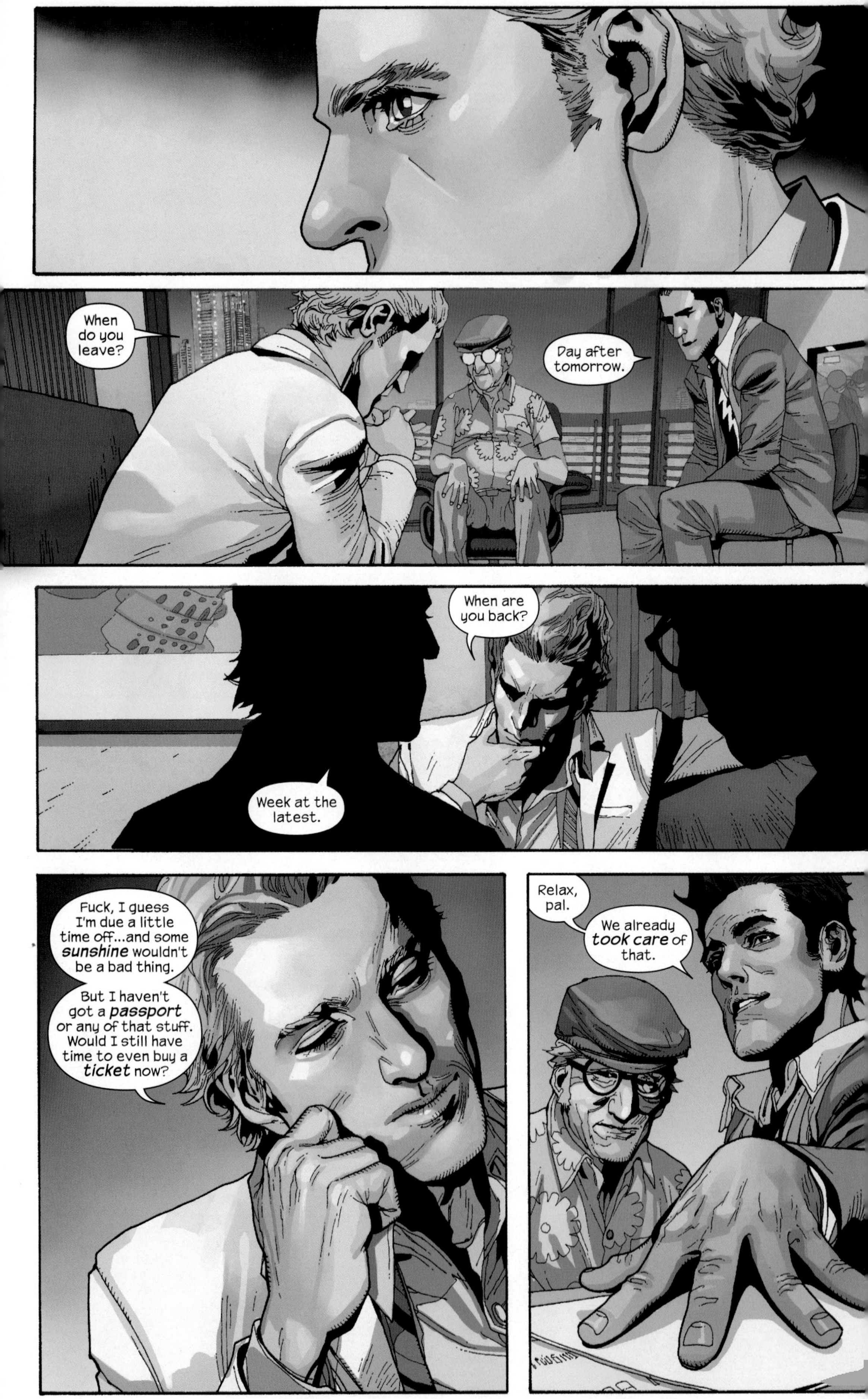

When do you leave?
Day after tomorrow.
When are you back?
Week at the latest.
Fuck, I guess I'm due a little time off...and some sunshine wouldn't be a bad thing.
But I haven't got a passport or any of that stuff. Would I still have time to even buy a ticket now?
Relax, pal.
We already took care of that.

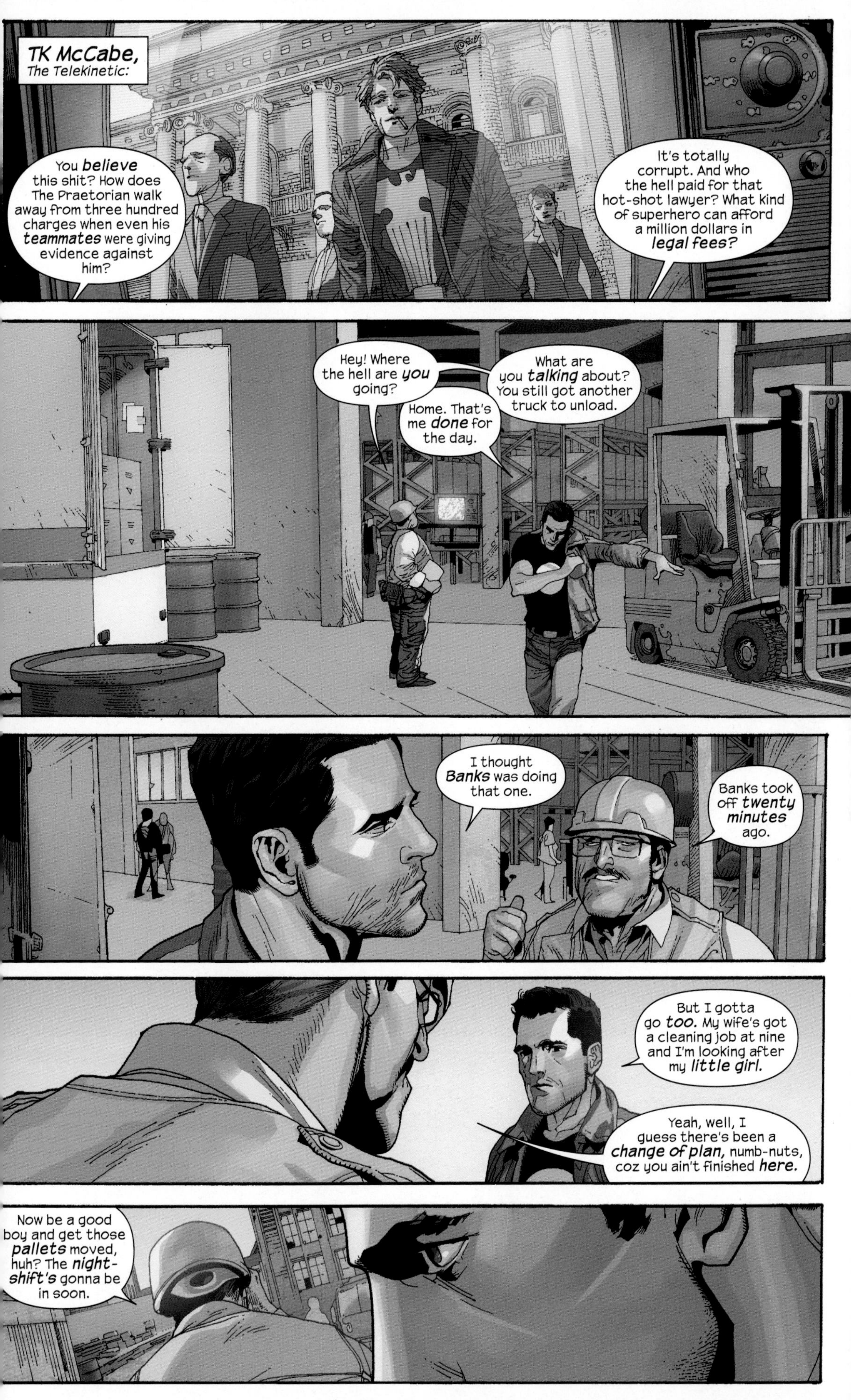
TK McCabe, The Telekinetic:
You believe this shit? How does The Praetorian walk away from three hundred charges when even his teammates were giving evidence against him?
It's totally corrupt. And who the hell paid for that hot-shot lawyer? What kind of superhero can afford a million dollars in legal fees?
Hey! Where the hell are you going?
Home. That's me done for the day.
What are you talking about? You still got another truck to unload.
I thought Banks was doing that one.
Banks took off twenty minutes ago.
But I gotta go too. My wife's got a cleaning job at nine and I'm looking after my little girl.
Yeah, well, I guess there's been a change of plan, numb-nuts, coz you ain't finished here.
Now be a good boy and get those pallets moved, huh? The night-shift's gonna be in soon.

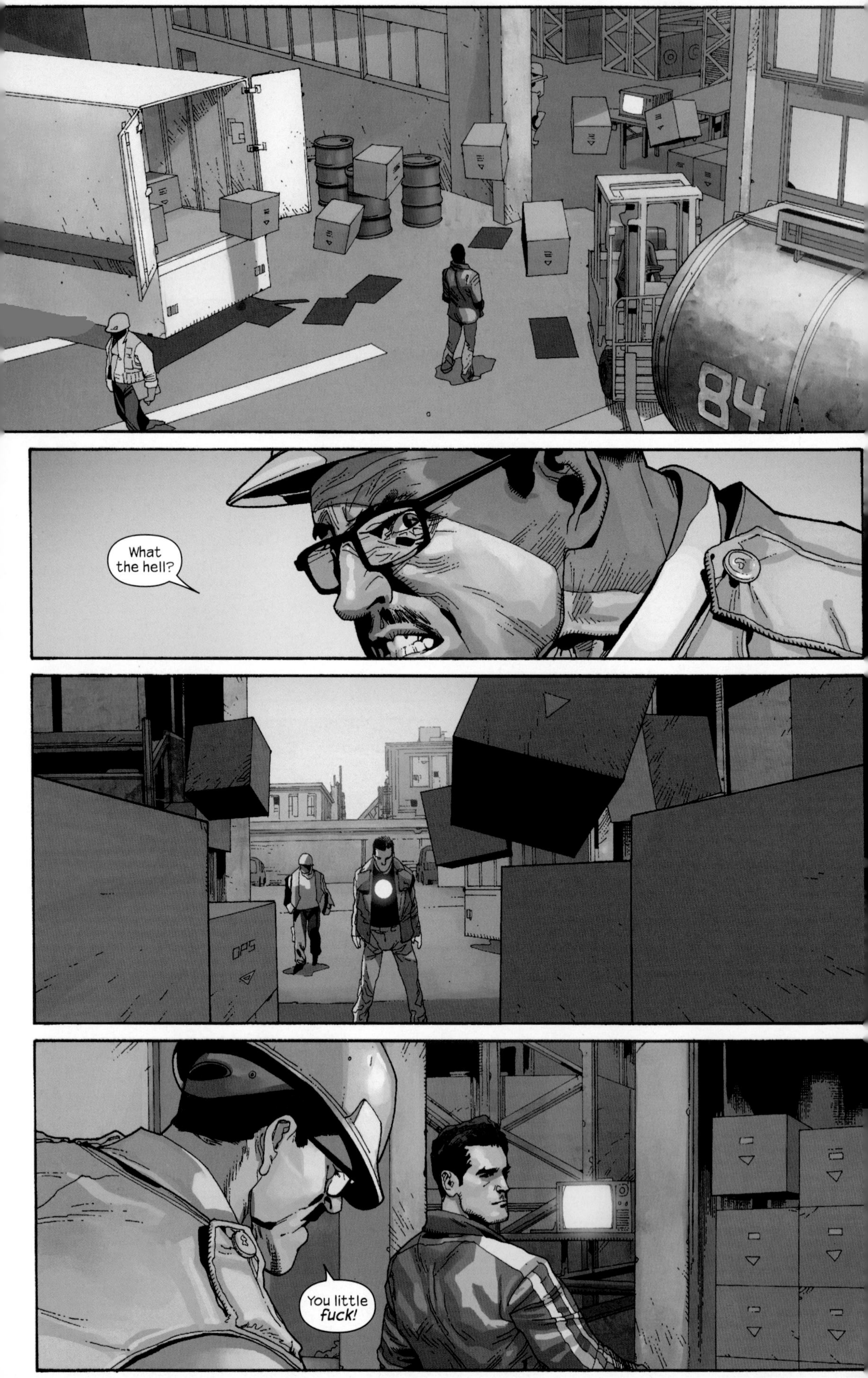
84
What the hell?
OPS
You little *fuck!*

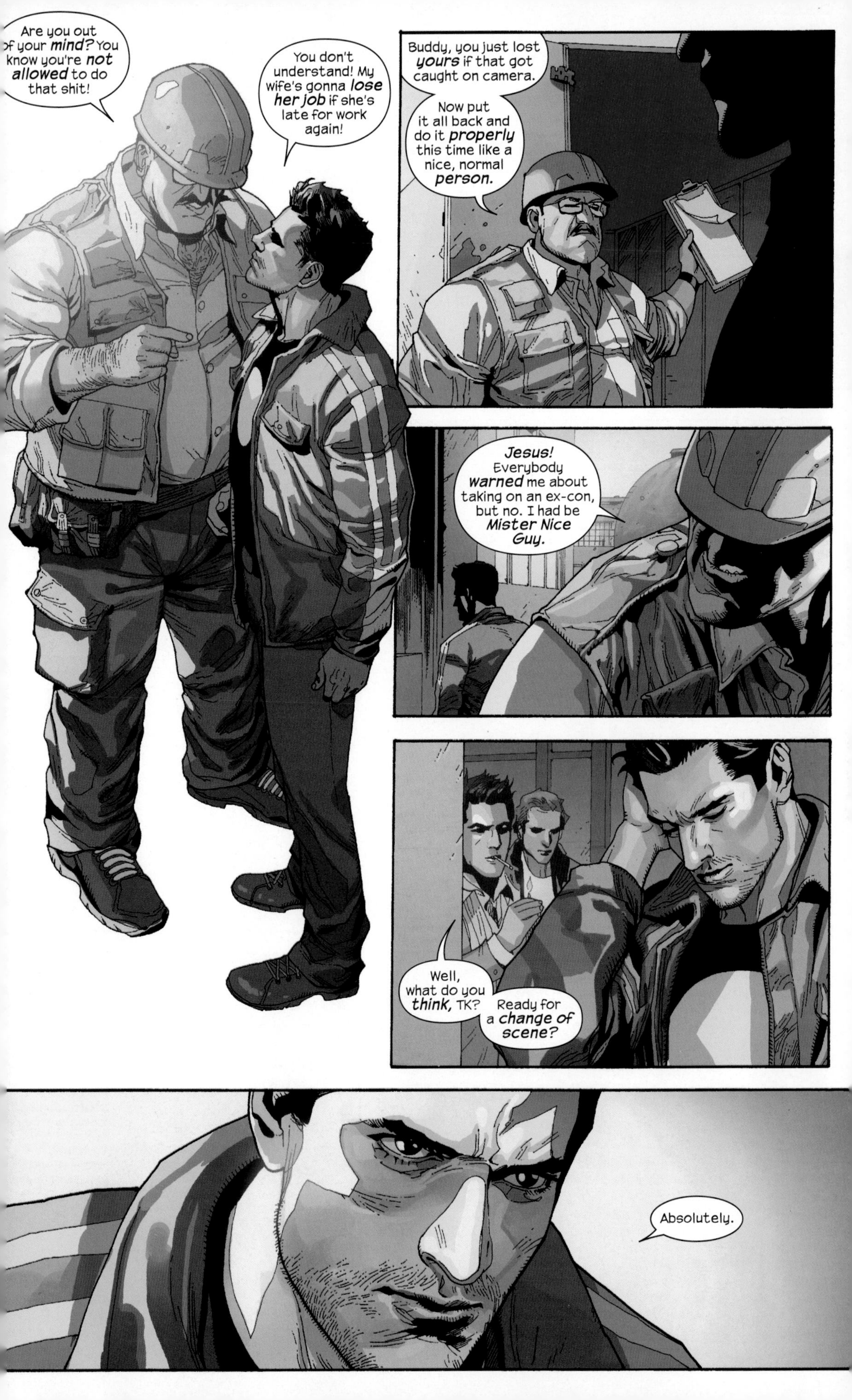
Are you out of your *mind?* You know you're *not allowed* to do that shit!
You don't understand! My wife's gonna *lose her job* if she's late for work again!
Buddy, you just lost *yours* if that got caught on camera.
Now put it all back and do it *properly* this time like a nice, normal *person.*
*Jesus!* Everybody *warned* me about taking on an ex-con, but no. I had be *Mister Nice Guy.*
Well, what do you *think,* TK?
Ready for a *change of scene?*
Absolutely.

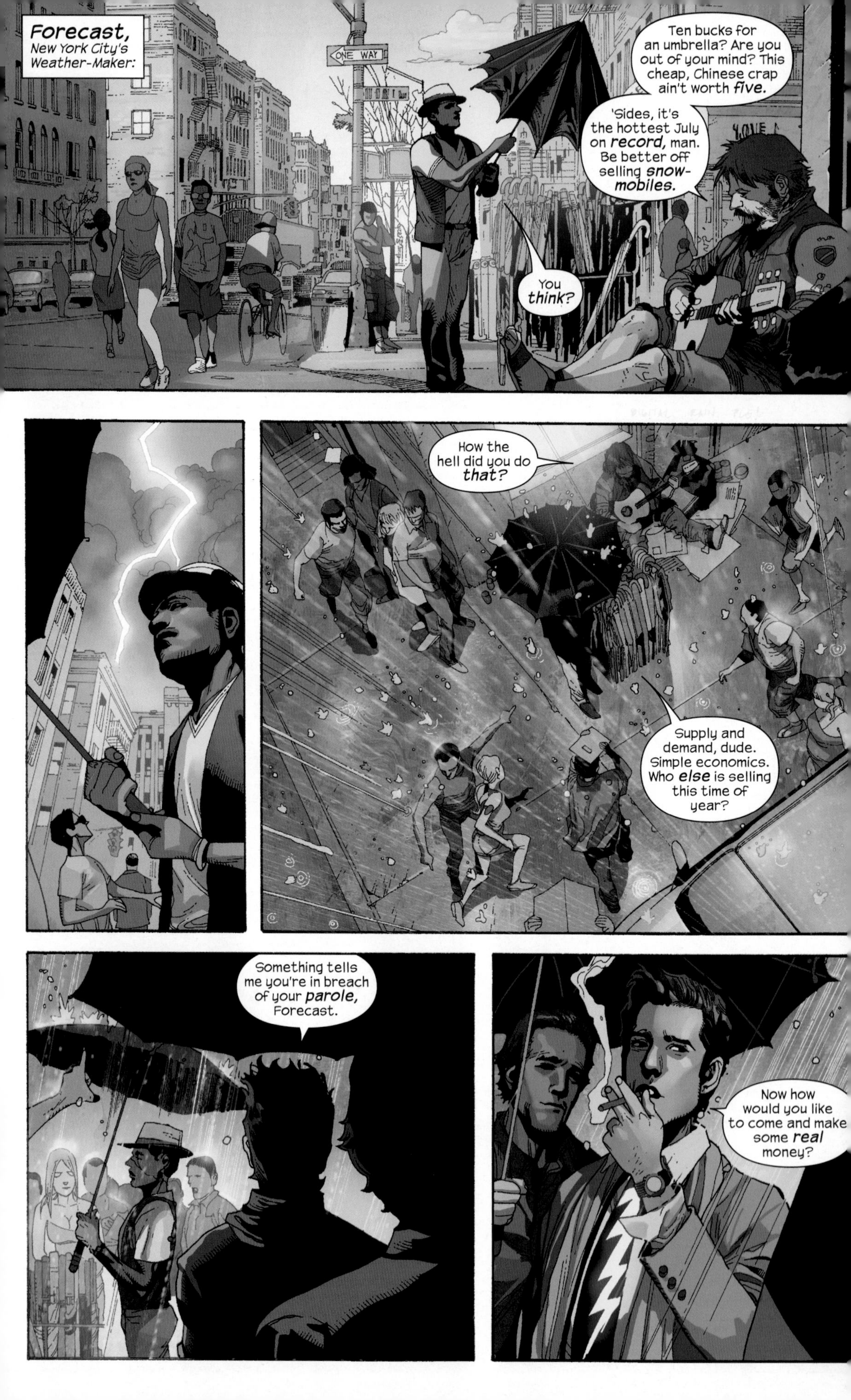
Forecast, New York City's Weather-Maker:
ONE WAY
Ten bucks for an umbrella? Are you out of your mind? This cheap, Chinese crap ain't worth five.
'Sides, it's the hottest July on record, man. Be better off selling snow-mobiles.
You think?
How the hell did you do that?
Supply and demand, dude. Simple economics. Who else is selling this time of year?
Something tells me you're in breach of your parole, Forecast.
Now how would you like to come and make some real money?

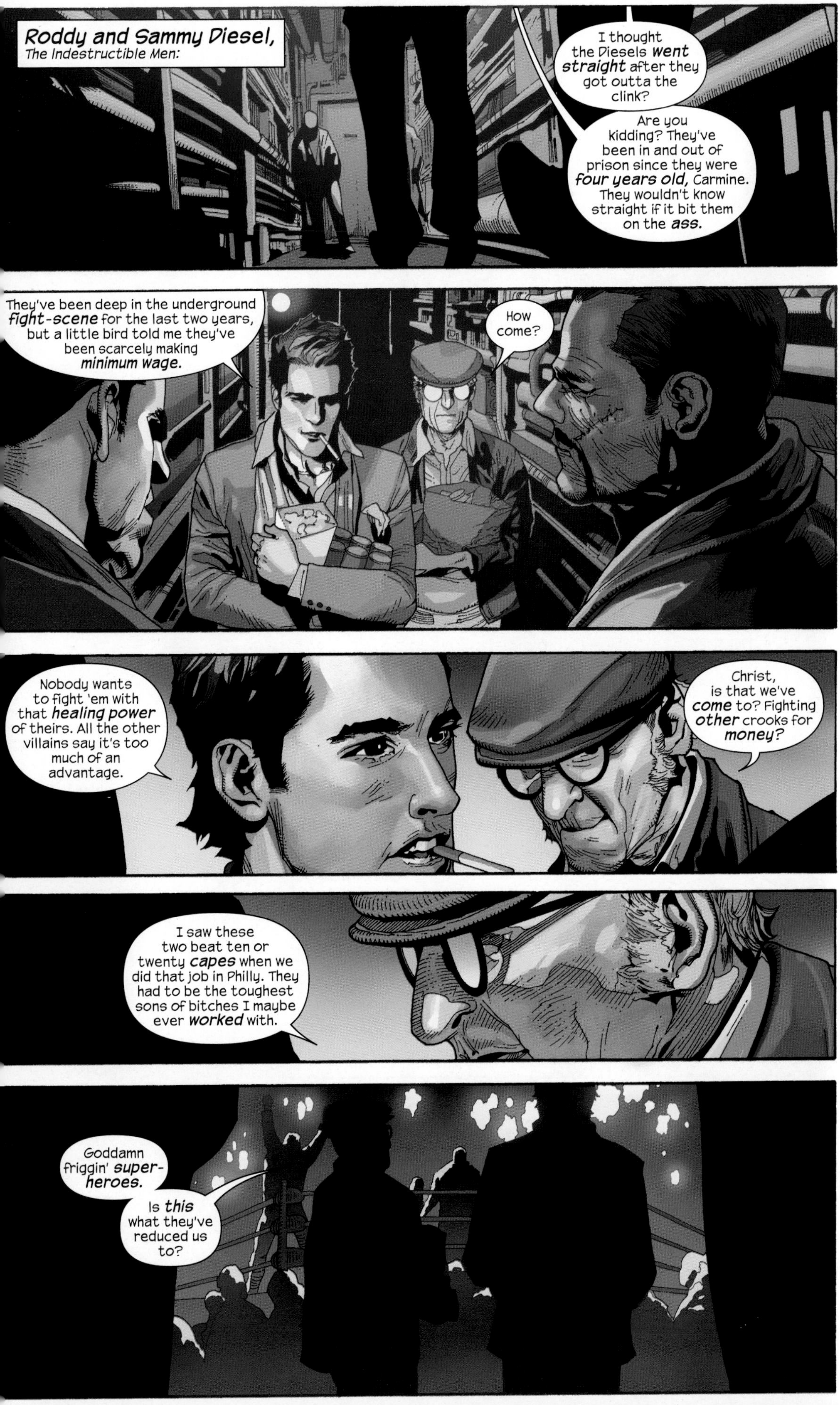
Roddy and Sammy Diesel, The Indestructible Men:
I thought the Diesels went straight after they got outta the clink?
Are you kidding? They've been in and out of prison since they were four years old, Carmine. They wouldn't know straight if it bit them on the ass.
They've been deep in the underground fight-scene for the last two years, but a little bird told me they've been scarcely making minimum wage.
How come?
Nobody wants to fight 'em with that healing power of theirs. All the other villains say it's too much of an advantage.
Christ, is that we've come to? Fighting other crooks for money?
I saw these two beat ten or twenty capes when we did that job in Philly. They had to be the toughest sons of bitches I maybe ever worked with.
Goddamn friggin' super-heroes.
Is this what they've reduced us to?

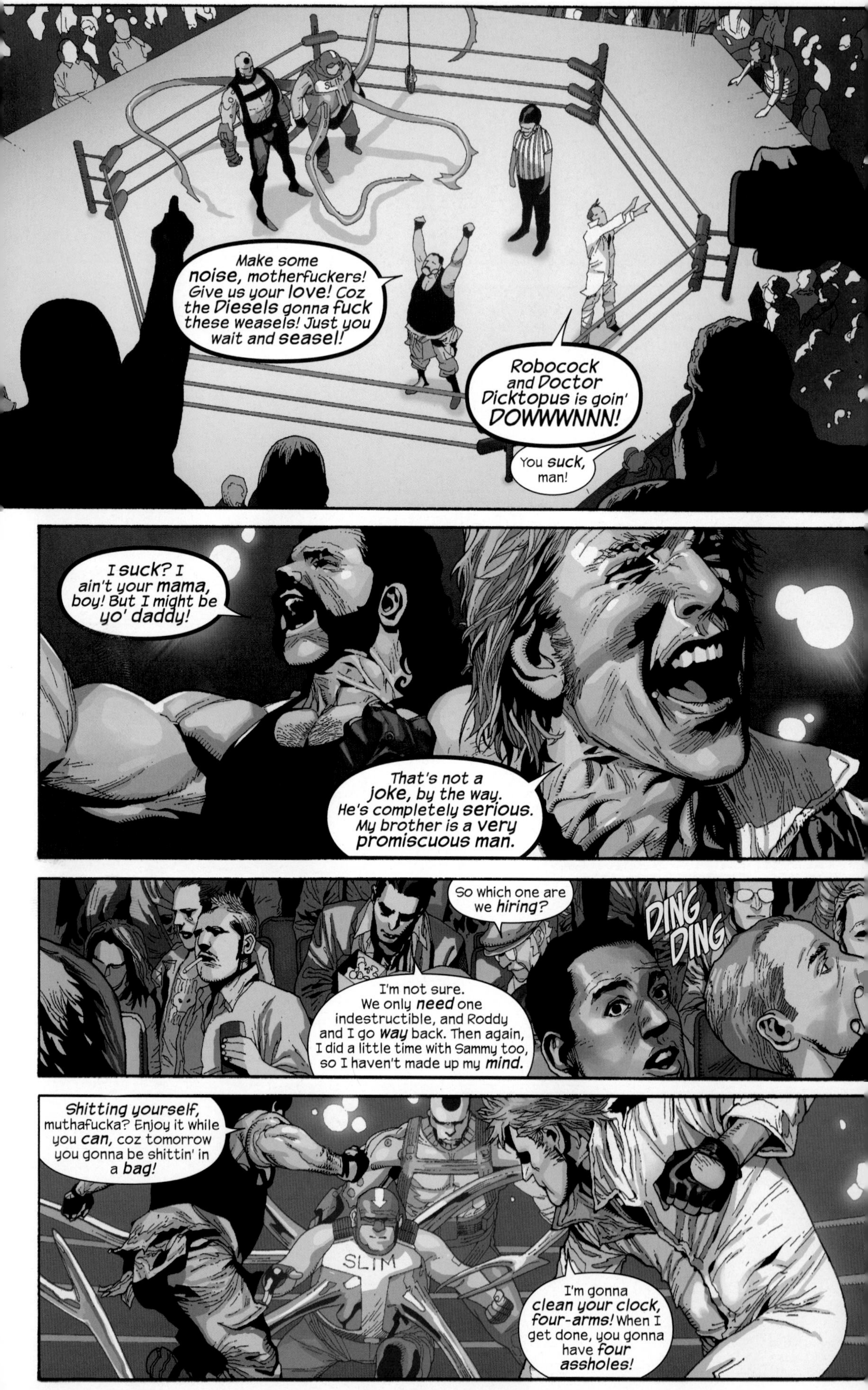

Make some noise, motherfuckers! Give us your love! Coz the Diesels gonna fuck these weasels! Just you wait and seasel!
Robocock and Doctor Dicktopus is goin' DOWWWNNN!
You suck, man!
I suck? I ain't your mama, boy! But I might be yo' daddy!
That's not a joke, by the way. He's completely serious. My brother is a very promiscuous man.
So which one are we hiring?
I'm not sure. We only need one indestructible, and Roddy and I go way back. Then again, I did a little time with Sammy too, so I haven't made up my mind.
DING DING
Shitting yourself, muthafucka? Enjoy it while you can, coz tomorrow you gonna be shittin' in a bag!
SLIM
I'm gonna clean your clock, four-arms! When I get done, you gonna have four assholes!

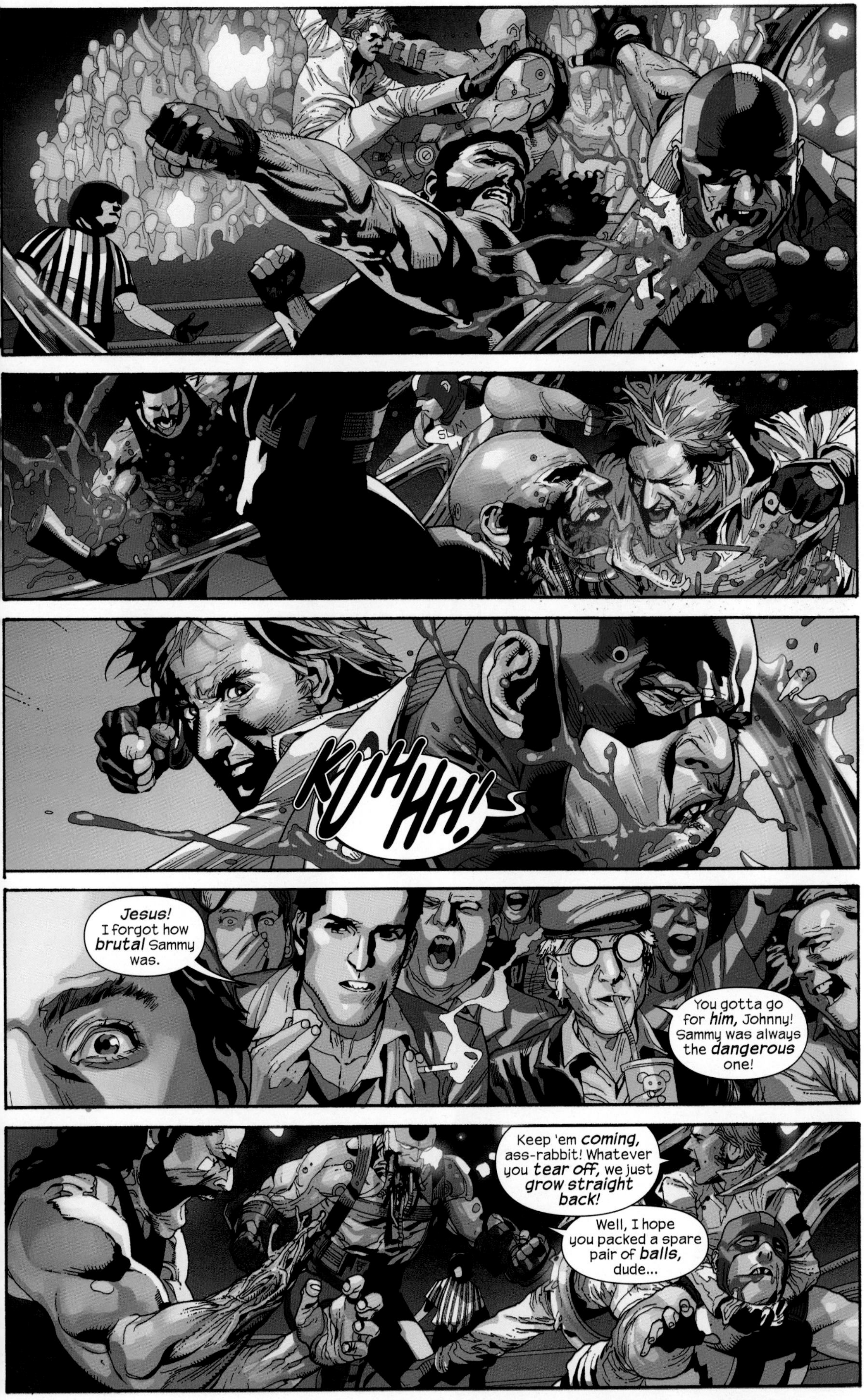

KKHHH!
Jesus! I forgot how brutal Sammy was.
You gotta go for him, Johnny! Sammy was always the dangerous one!
Keep 'em coming, ass-rabbit! Whatever you tear off, we just grow straight back!
Well, I hope you packed a spare pair of balls, dude...

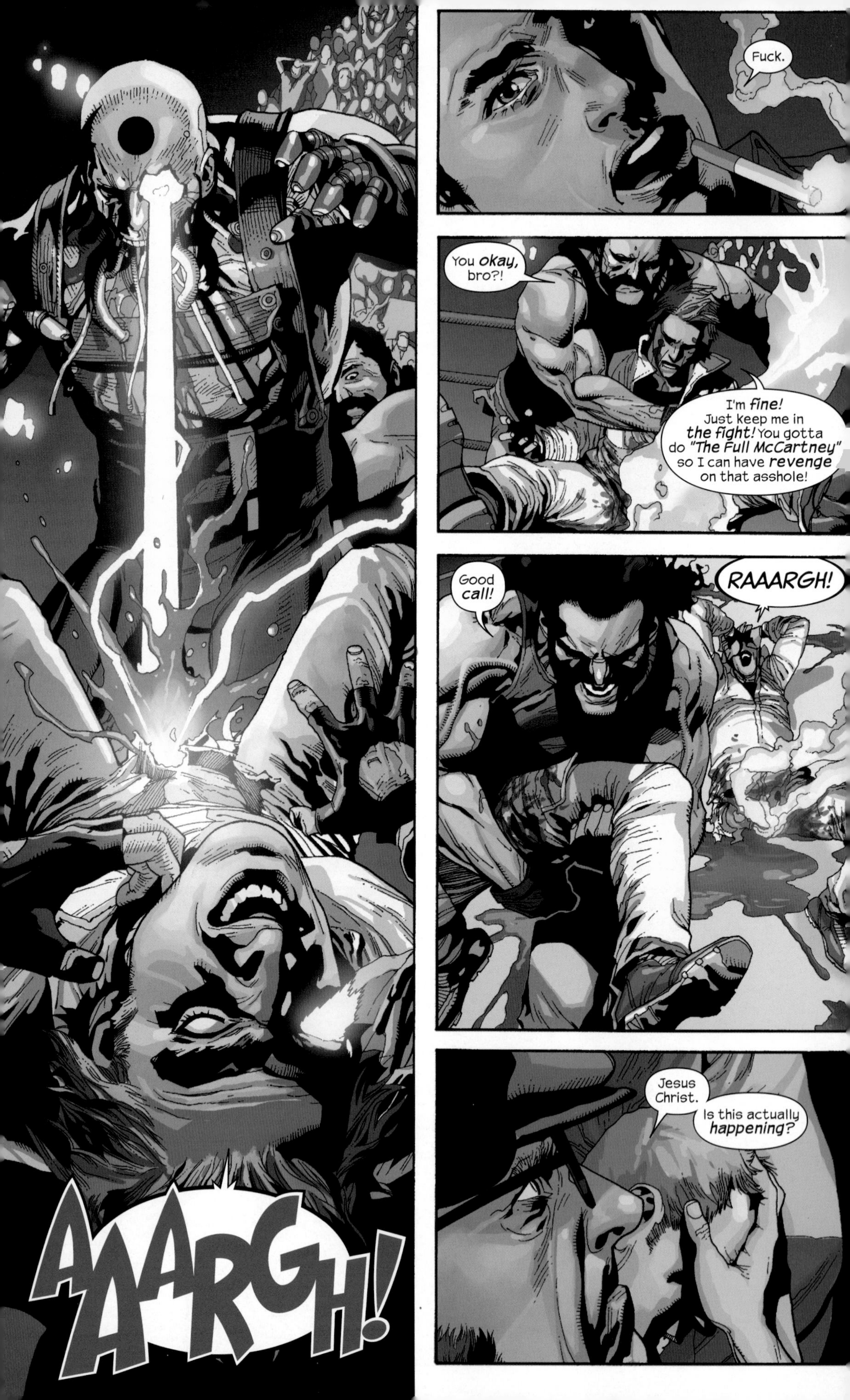
AAARGH!
Fuck.
You okay, bro?!
I'm fine! Just keep me in the fight! You gotta do "The Full McCartney" so I can have revenge on that asshole!
Good call!
RAAARGH!
Jesus Christ.
Is this actually happening?

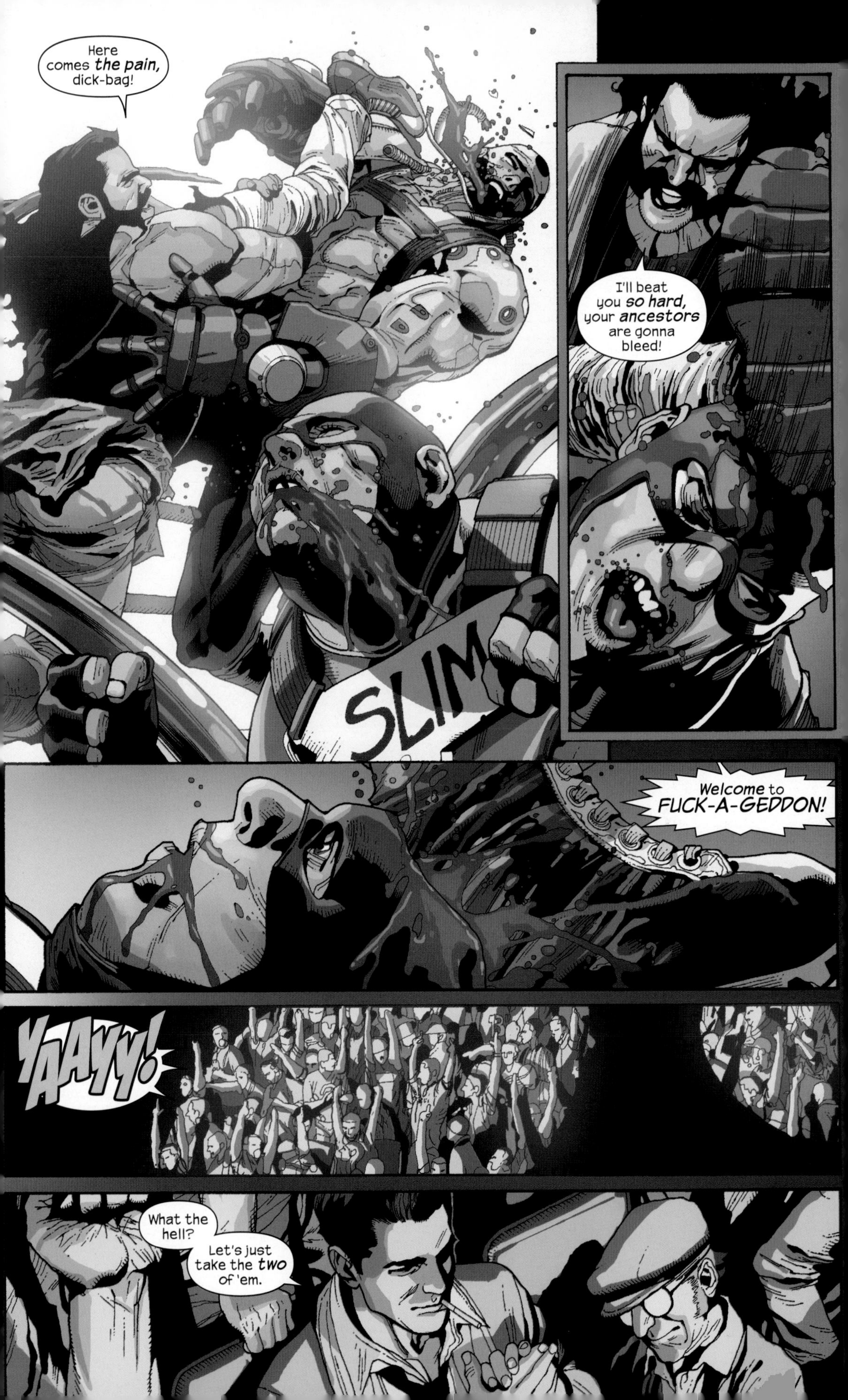
Here comes the pain, dick-bag!
I'll beat you so hard, your ancestors are gonna bleed!
SLIM
Welcome to FUCK-A-GEDDON!
YAAYY!
What the hell?
Let's just take the two of 'em.

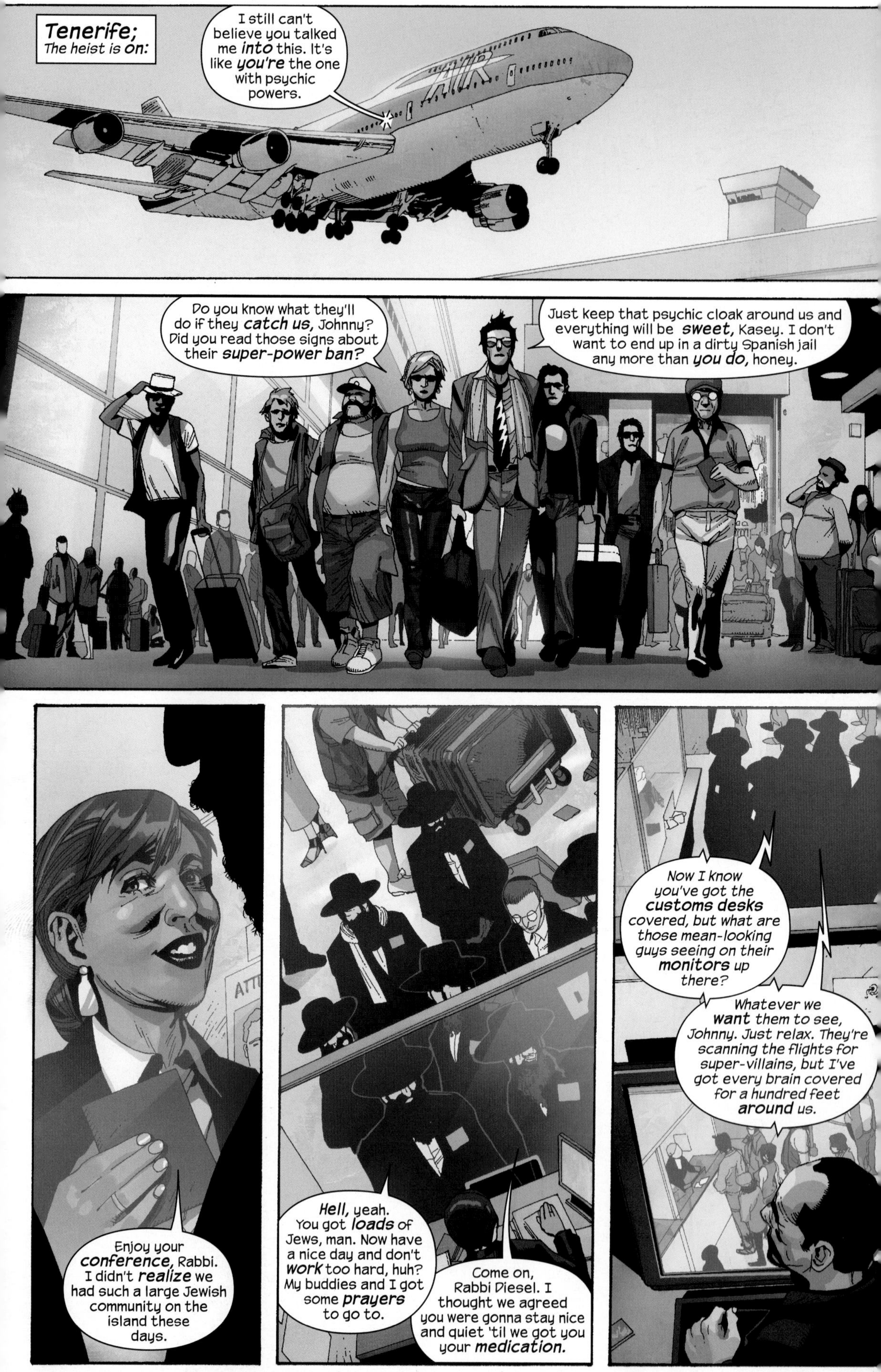

Tenerife; The heist is on:
I still can't believe you talked me into this. It's like you're the one with psychic powers.
Do you know what they'll do if they catch us, Johnny? Did you read those signs about their super-power ban?
Just keep that psychic cloak around us and everything will be sweet, Kasey. I don't want to end up in a dirty Spanish jail any more than you do, honey.
Enjoy your conference, Rabbi. I didn't realize we had such a large Jewish community on the island these days.
Hell, yeah. You got loads of Jews, man. Now have a nice day and don't work too hard, huh? My buddies and I got some prayers to go to.
Come on, Rabbi Diesel. I thought we agreed you were gonna stay nice and quiet 'til we got you your medication.
Now I know you've got the customs desks covered, but what are those mean-looking guys seeing on their monitors up there?
Whatever we want them to see, Johnny. Just relax. They're scanning the flights for super-villains, but I've got every brain covered for a hundred feet around us.

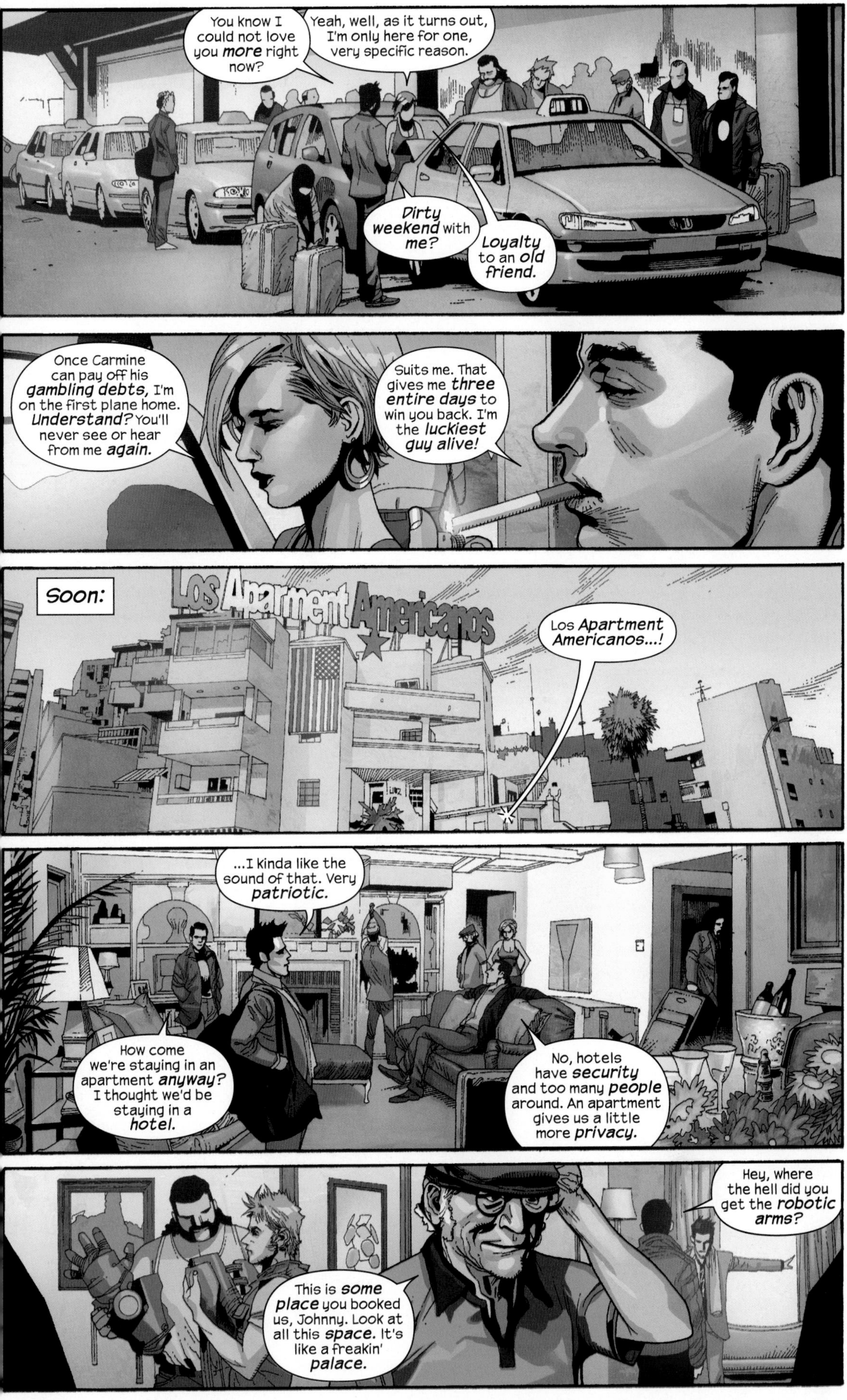

You know I could not love you *more* right now?
Yeah, well, as it turns out, I'm only here for one, very specific reason.
*Dirty weekend* with *me?*
*Loyalty* to an *old friend.*
Once Carmine can pay off his *gambling debts,* I'm on the first plane home. *Understand?* You'll never see or hear from me *again.*
Suits me. That gives me *three entire days* to win you back. I'm the *luckiest guy alive!*
Soon:
Los Apartment Americanos
Los *Apartment Americanos...!*
...I kinda like the sound of that. Very *patriotic.*
How come we're staying in an apartment *anyway?* I thought we'd be staying in a *hotel.*
No, hotels have *security* and too many *people* around. An apartment gives us a little more *privacy.*
This is *some place* you booked us, Johnny. Look at all this *space.* It's like a freakin' *palace.*
Hey, where the hell did you get the *robotic arms?*

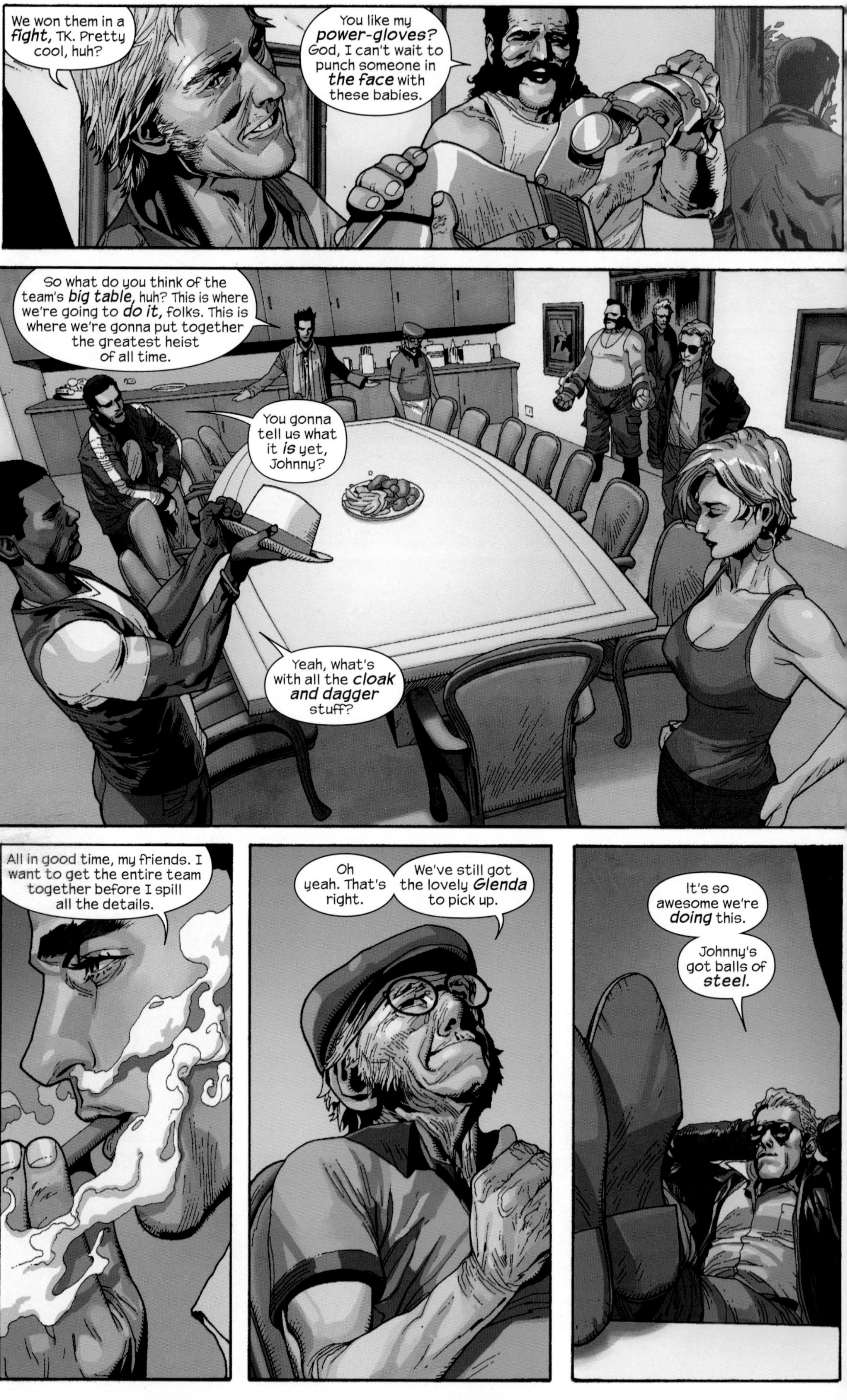
We won them in a *fight,* TK. Pretty cool, huh?
You like my *power-gloves?* God, I can't wait to punch someone in *the face* with these babies.
So what do you think of the team's *big table,* huh? This is where we're going to *do it,* folks. This is where we're gonna put together the greatest heist of all time.
You gonna tell us what it *is* yet, Johnny?
Yeah, what's with all the *cloak and dagger* stuff?
All in good time, my friends. I want to get the entire team together before I spill all the details.
Oh yeah. That's right.
We've still got the lovely *Glenda* to pick up.
It's so awesome we're *doing* this.
Johnny's got balls of *steel.*

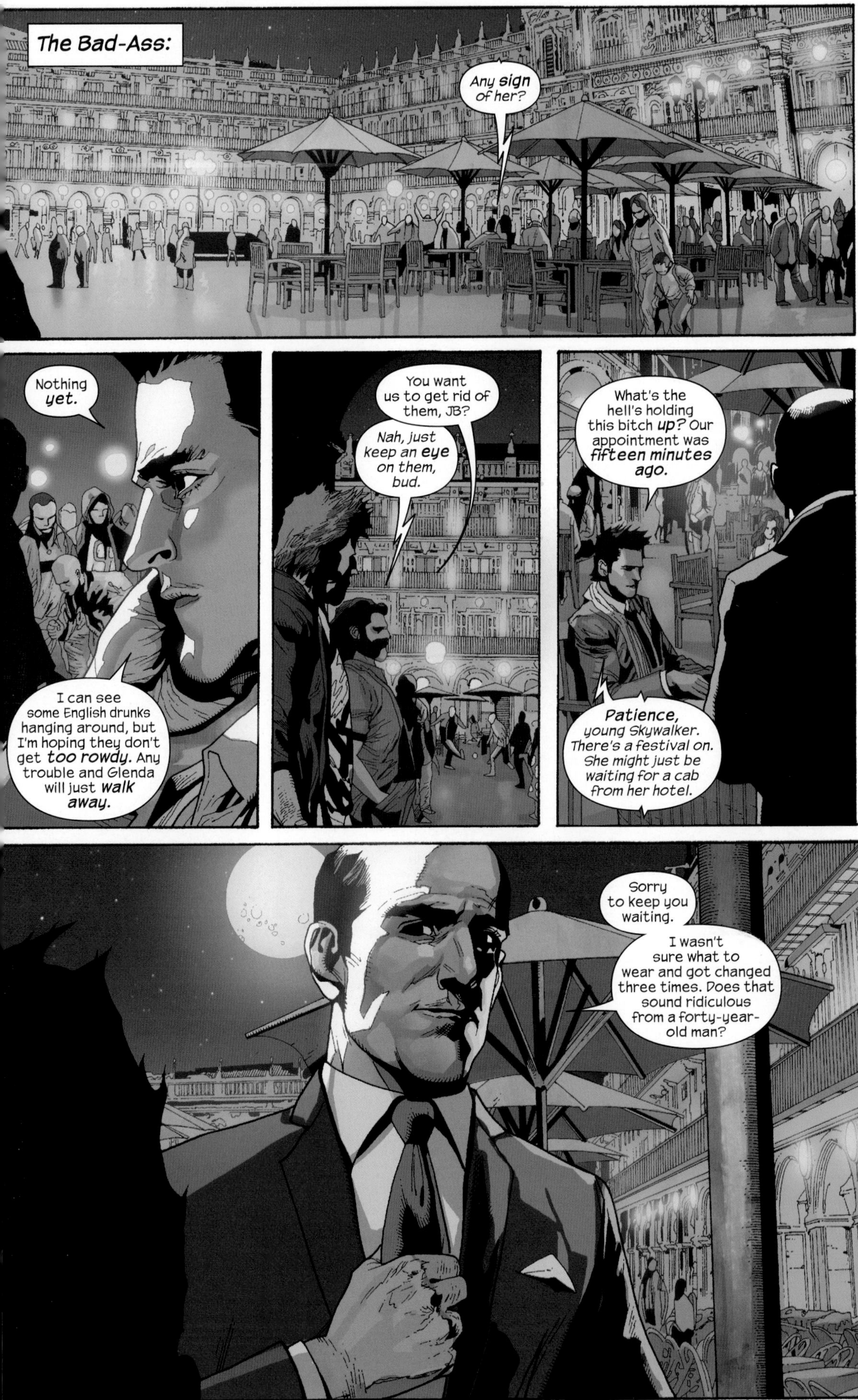
The Bad-Ass:
Any sign of her?
Nothing yet.
I can see some English drunks hanging around, but I'm hoping they don't get too rowdy. Any trouble and Glenda will just walk away.
You want us to get rid of them, JB?
Nah, just keep an eye on them, bud.
What's the hell's holding this bitch up? Our appointment was fifteen minutes ago.
Patience, young Skywalker. There's a festival on. She might just be waiting for a cab from her hotel.
Sorry to keep you waiting.
I wasn't sure what to wear and got changed three times. Does that sound ridiculous from a forty-year-old man?

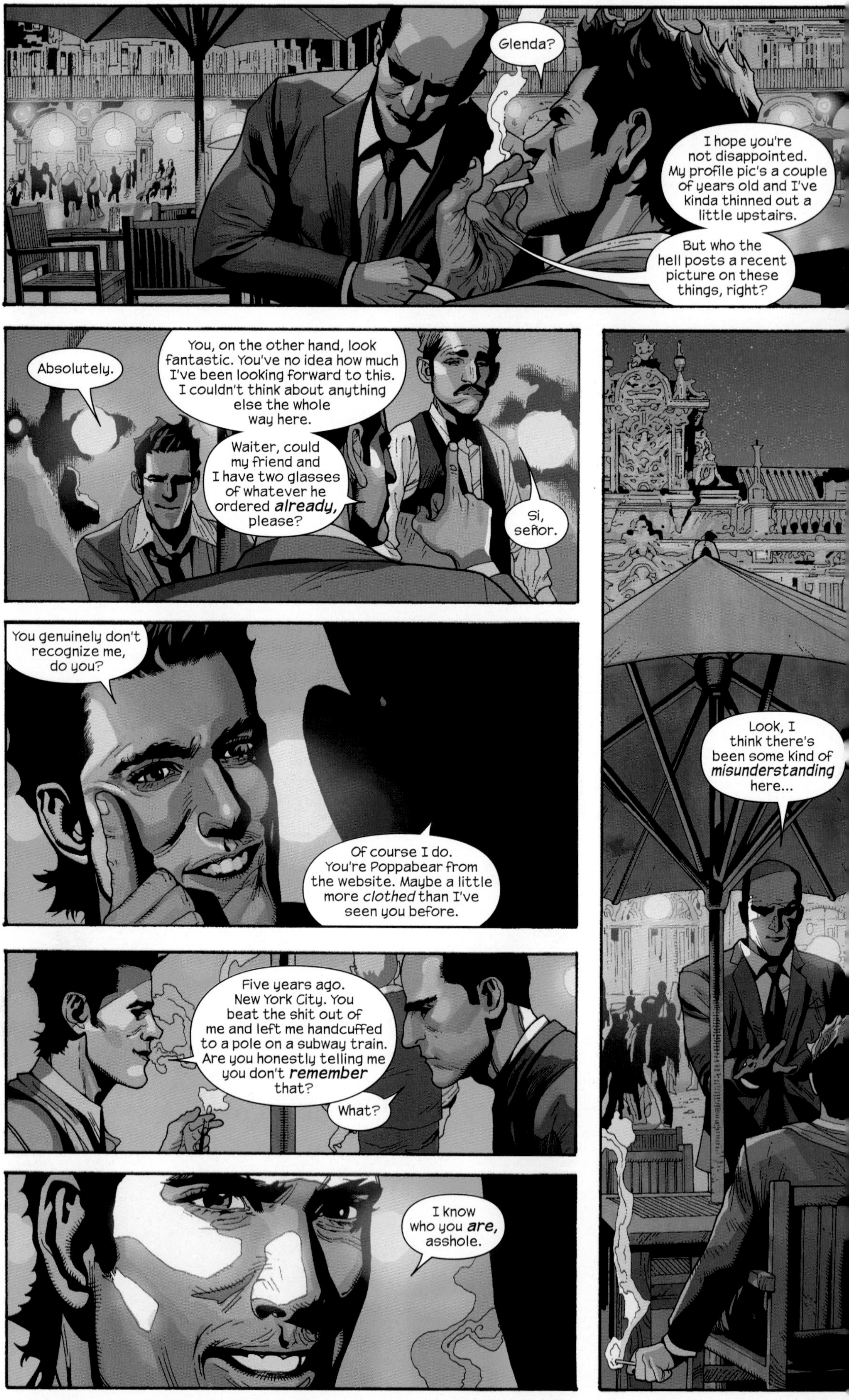
Glenda?
I hope you're not disappointed. My profile pic's a couple of years old and I've kinda thinned out a little upstairs.
But who the hell posts a recent picture on these things, right?
Absolutely.
You, on the other hand, look fantastic. You've no idea how much I've been looking forward to this. I couldn't think about anything else the whole way here.
Waiter, could my friend and I have two glasses of whatever he ordered *already,* please?
Si, señor.
Look, I think there's been some kind of *misunderstanding* here...
You genuinely don't recognize me, do you?
Of course I do. You're Poppabear from the website. Maybe a little more *clothed* than I've seen you before.
Five years ago. New York City. You beat the shit out of me and left me handcuffed to a pole on a subway train. Are you honestly telling me you don't *remember* that?
What?
I know who you *are,* asshole.

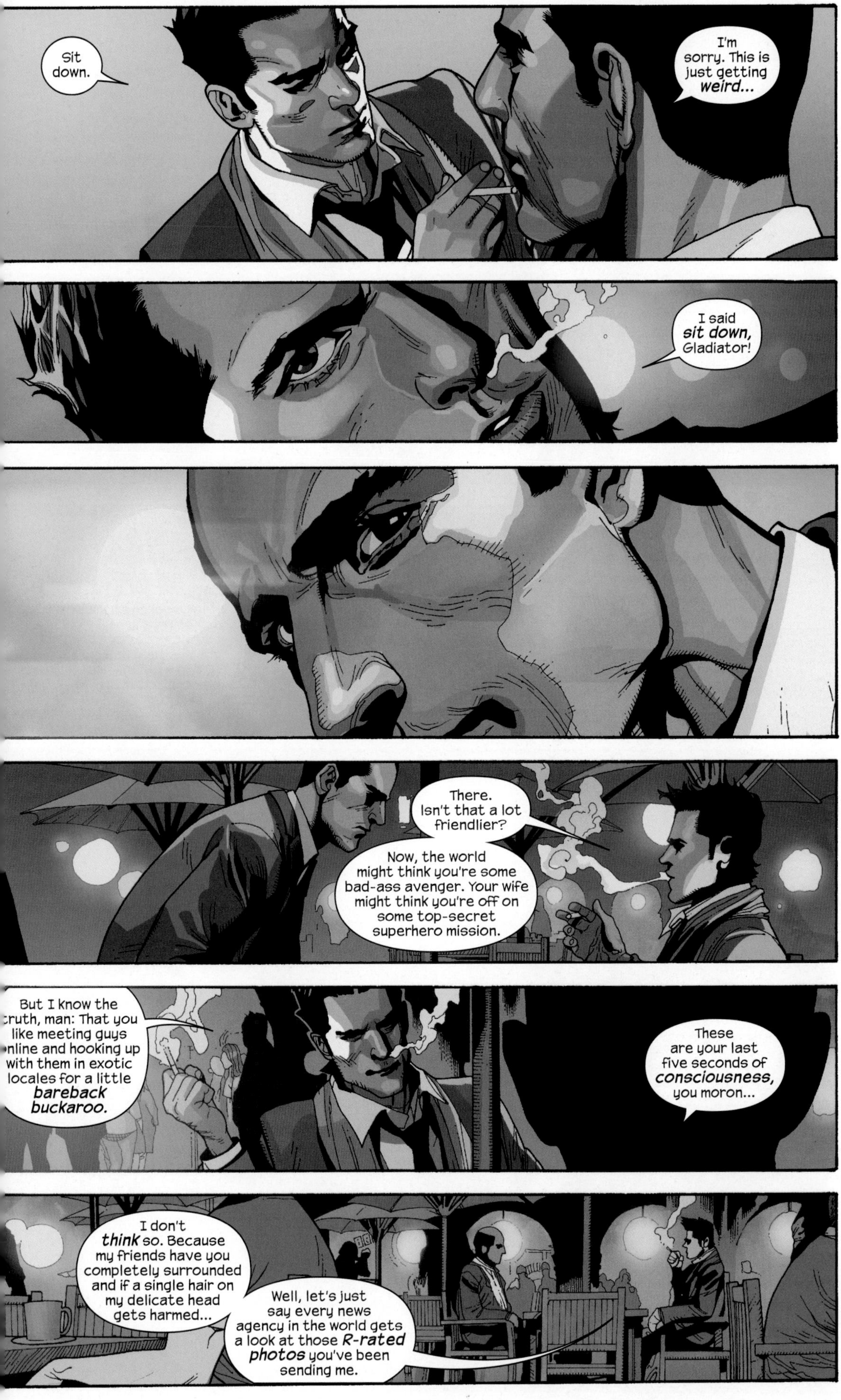
Sit down.
I'm sorry. This is just getting weird...
I said sit down, Gladiator!
There. Isn't that a lot friendlier?
Now, the world might think you're some bad-ass avenger. Your wife might think you're off on some top-secret superhero mission.
But I know the truth, man: That you like meeting guys online and hooking up with them in exotic locales for a little bareback buckaroo.
These are your last five seconds of consciousness, you moron...
I don't think so. Because my friends have you completely surrounded and if a single hair on my delicate head gets harmed...
Well, let's just say every news agency in the world gets a look at those R-rated photos you've been sending me.

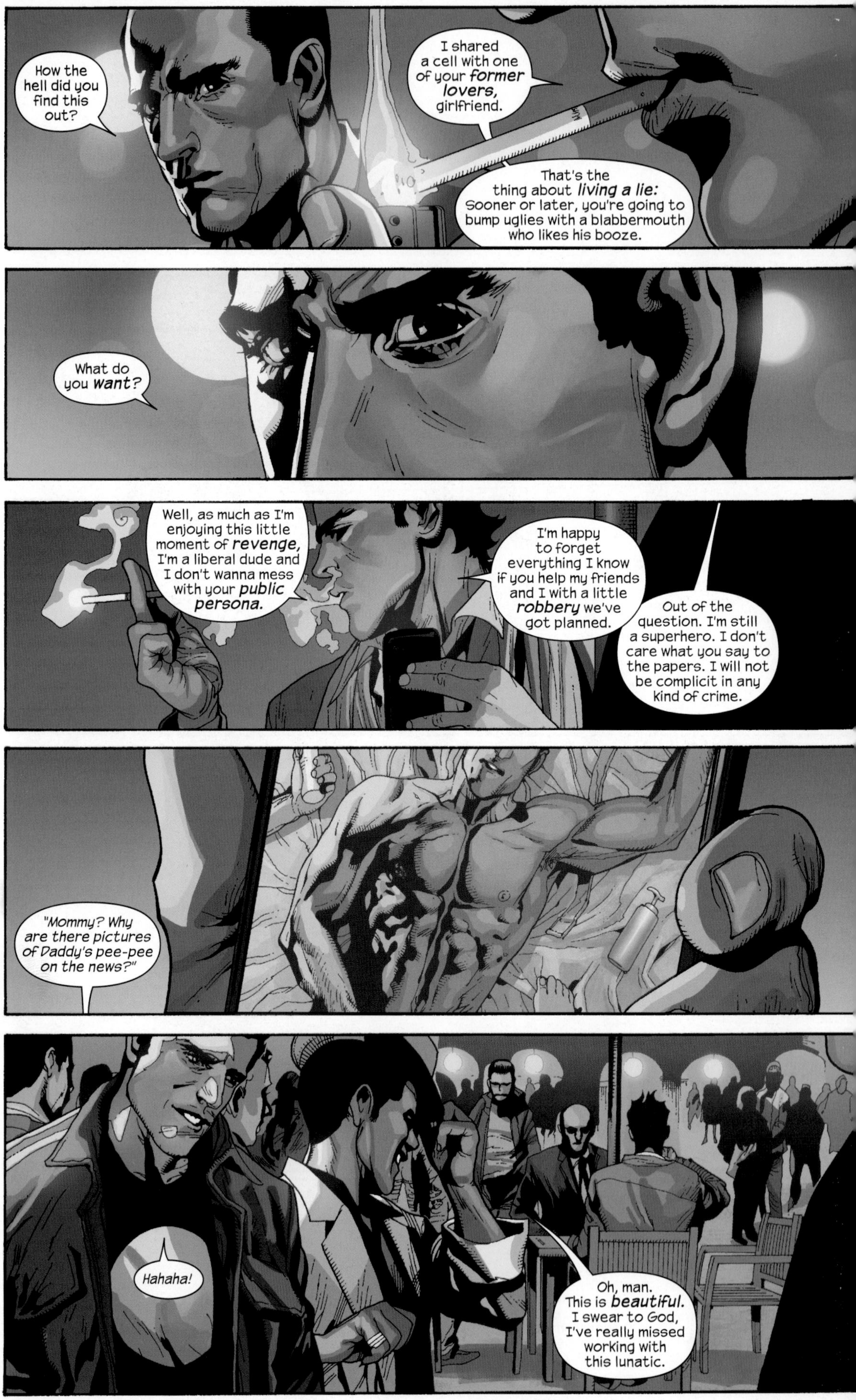

How the hell did you find this out?
I shared a cell with one of your *former lovers,* girlfriend.
That's the thing about *living a lie:* Sooner or later, you're going to bump uglies with a blabbermouth who likes his booze.
What do you *want?*
Well, as much as I'm enjoying this little moment of *revenge,* I'm a liberal dude and I don't wanna mess with your *public persona.*
I'm happy to forget everything I know if you help my friends and I with a little *robbery* we've got planned.
Out of the question. I'm still a superhero. I don't care what you say to the papers. I will not be complicit in any kind of crime.
"Mommy? Why are there pictures of Daddy's pee-pee on the news?"
*Hahaha!*
Oh, man. This is *beautiful.* I swear to God, I've really missed working with this lunatic.

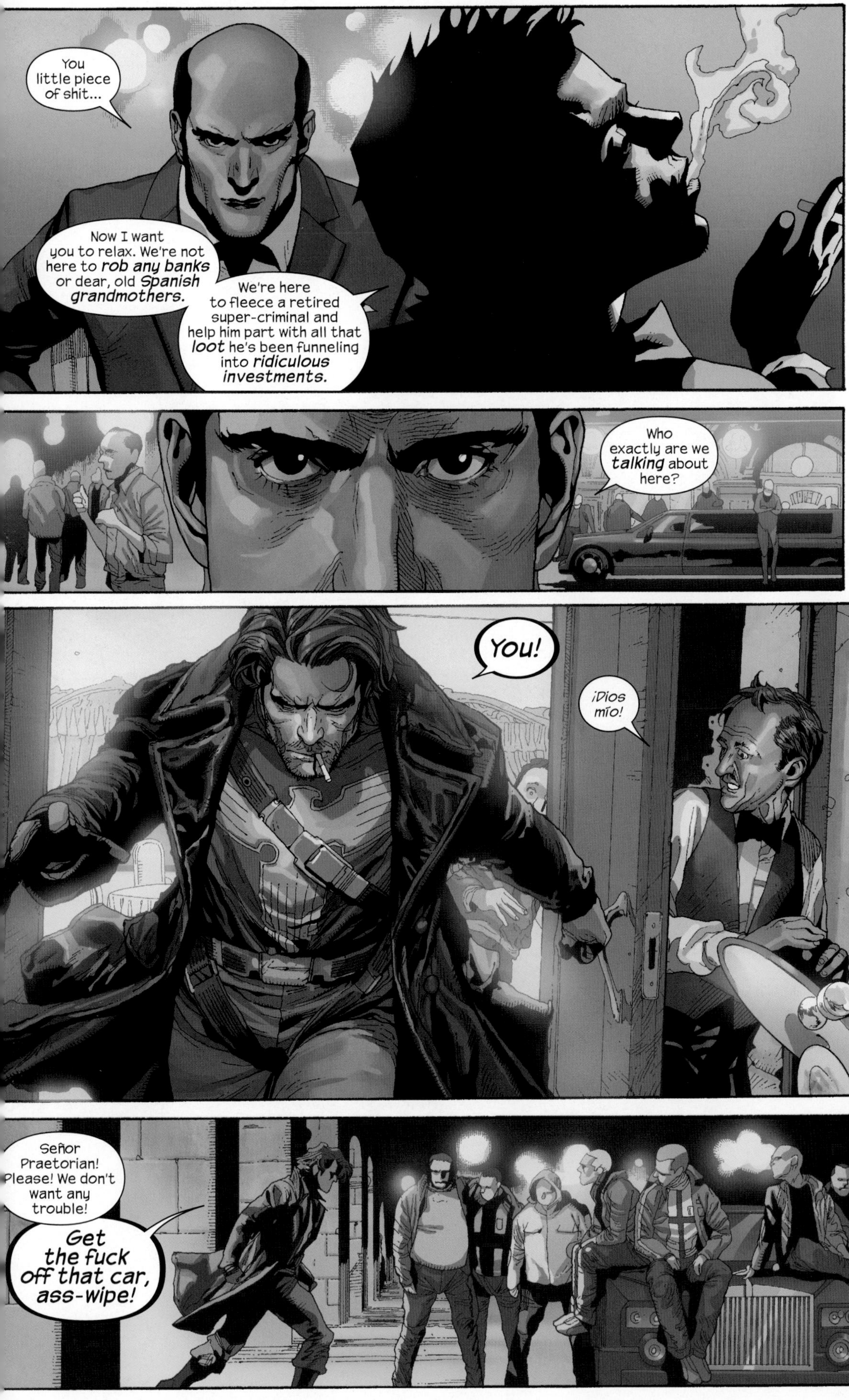
You little piece of shit...
Now I want you to relax. We're not here to rob any banks or dear, old Spanish grandmothers.
We're here to fleece a retired super-criminal and help him part with all that loot he's been funneling into ridiculous investments.
Who exactly are we talking about here?
You!
¡Dios mío!
Señor Praetorian! Please! We don't want any trouble!
Get the fuck off that car, ass-wipe!

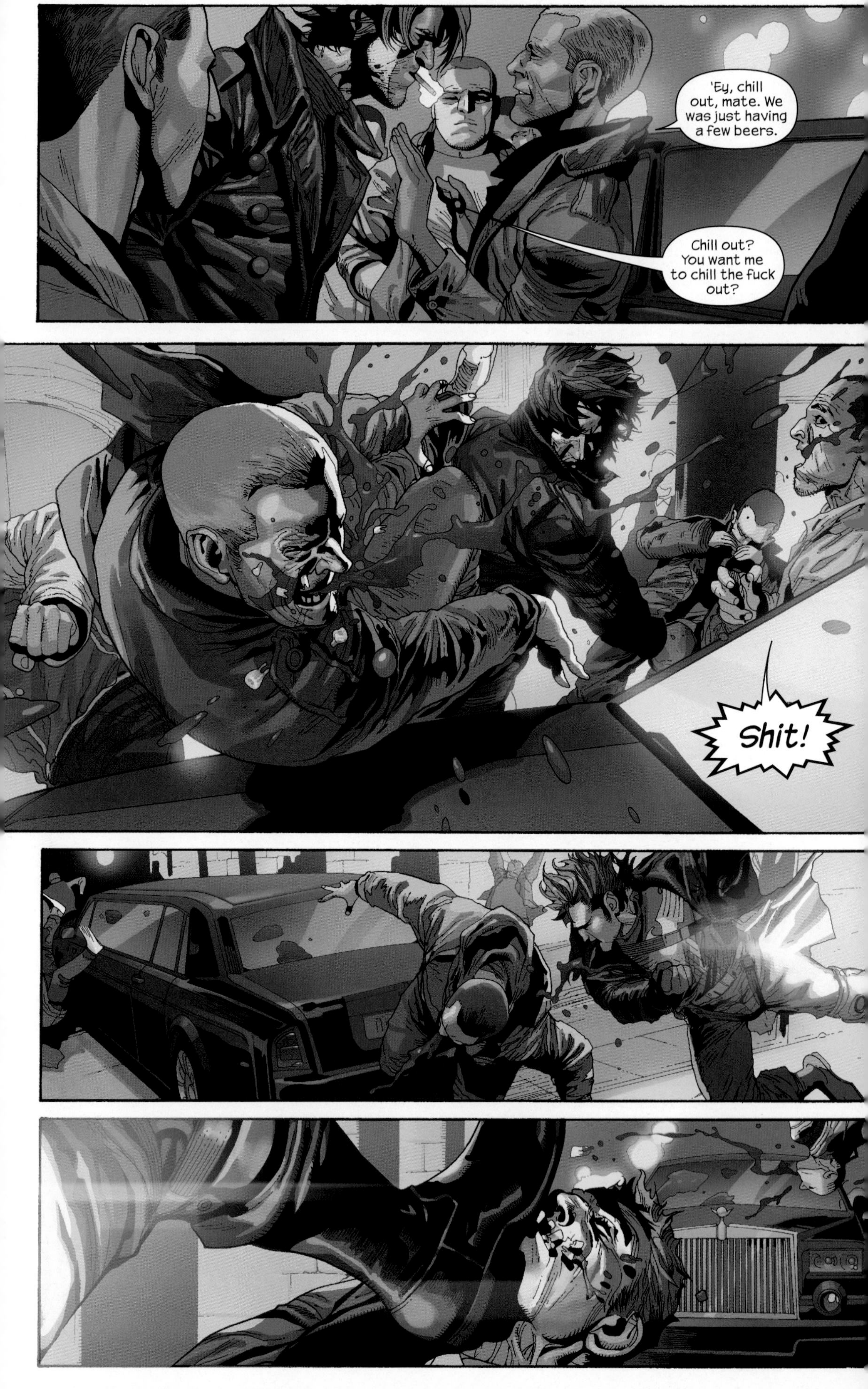
'Ey, chill out, mate. We was just having a few beers.
Chill out? You want me to chill the fuck out?
Shit!

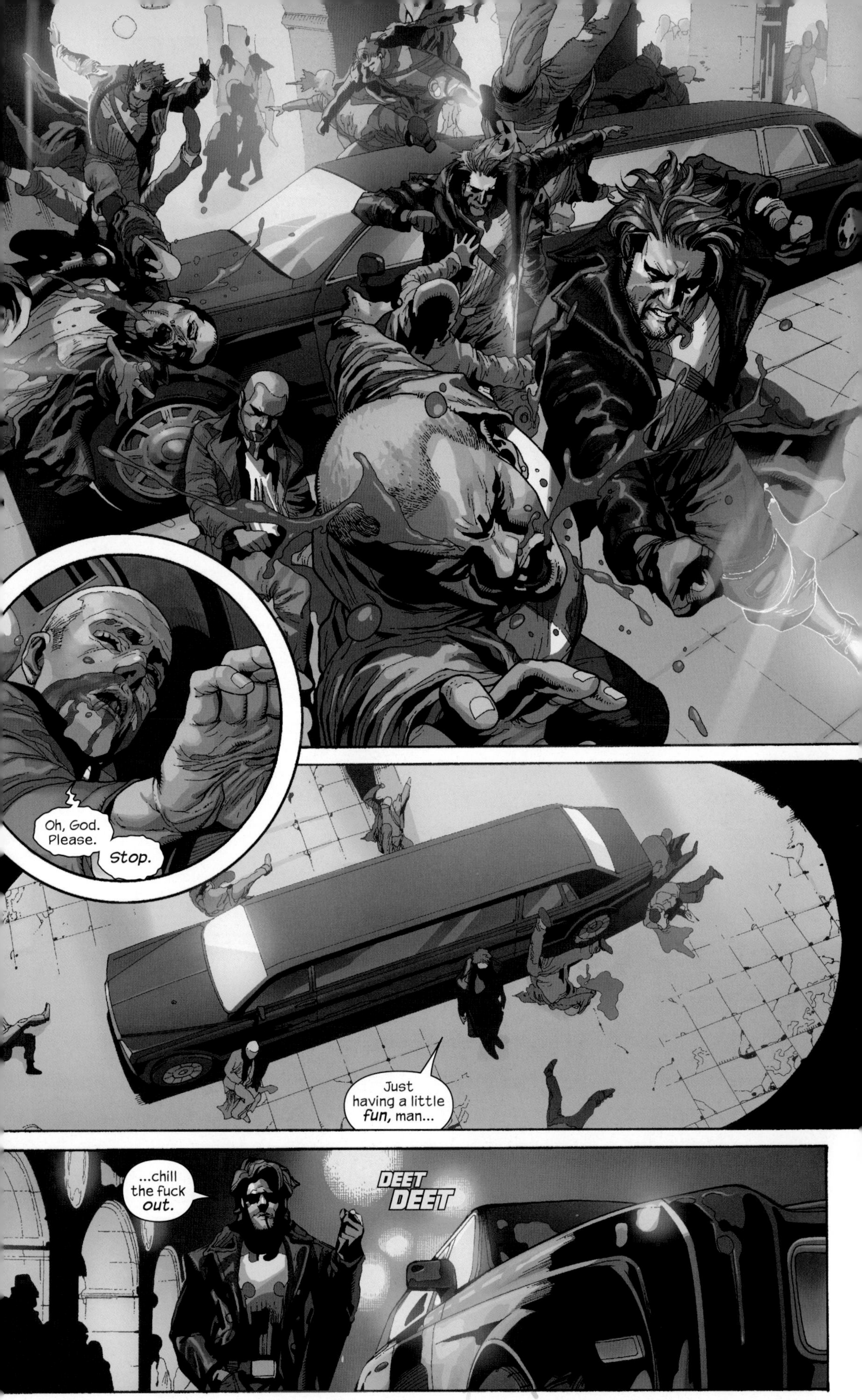
Oh, God. Please.
Stop.
Just having a little fun, man...
...chill the fuck out.
DEET DEET

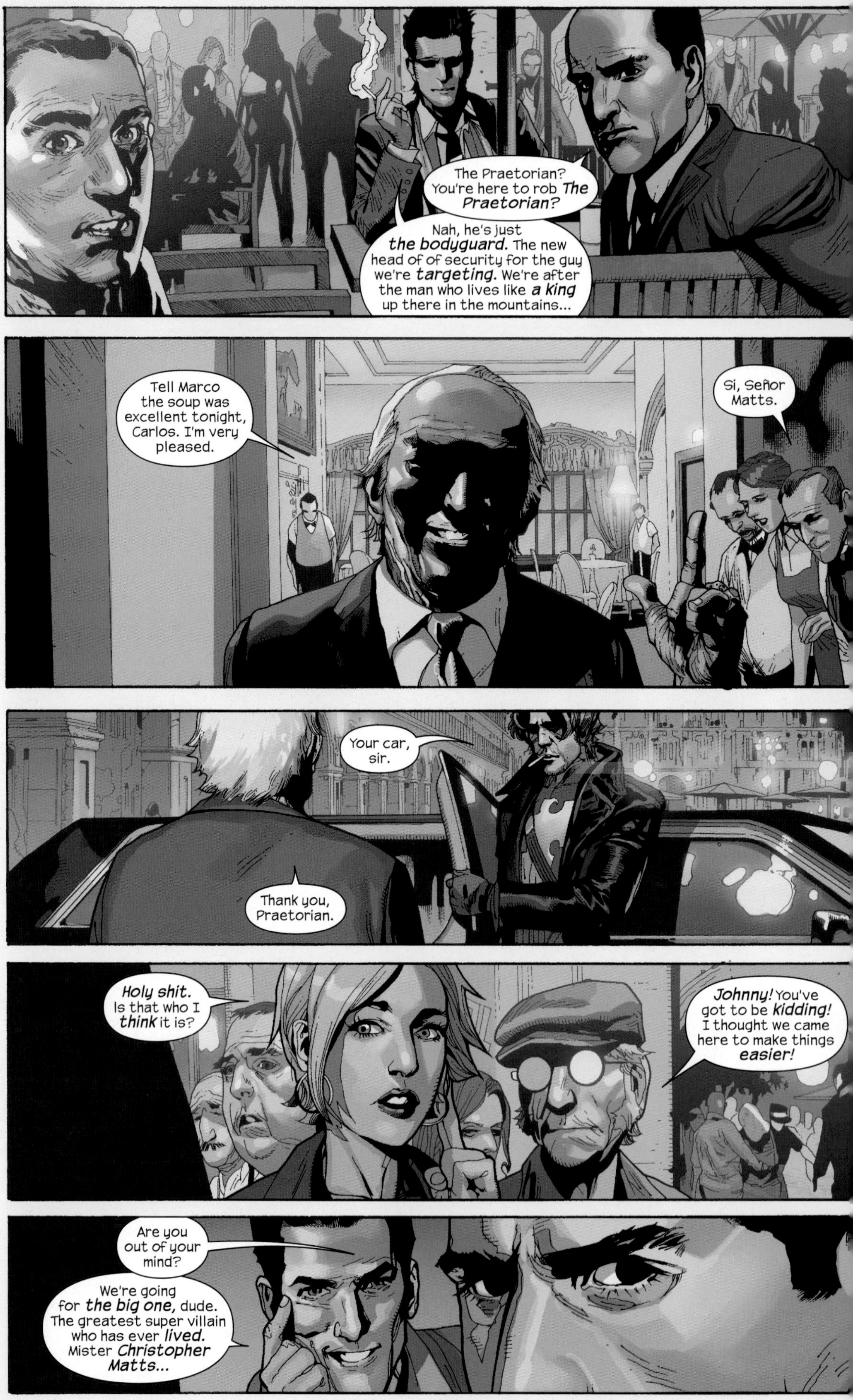

The Praetorian? You're here to rob The Praetorian?
Nah, he's just the bodyguard. The new head of of security for the guy we're targeting. We're after the man who lives like a king up there in the mountains...
Tell Marco the soup was excellent tonight, Carlos. I'm very pleased.
Si, Señor Matts.
Your car, sir.
Thank you, Praetorian.
Holy shit. Is that who I think it is?
Johnny! You've got to be kidding! I thought we came here to make things easier!
Are you out of your mind?
We're going for the big one, dude. The greatest super villain who has ever lived. Mister Christopher Matts...

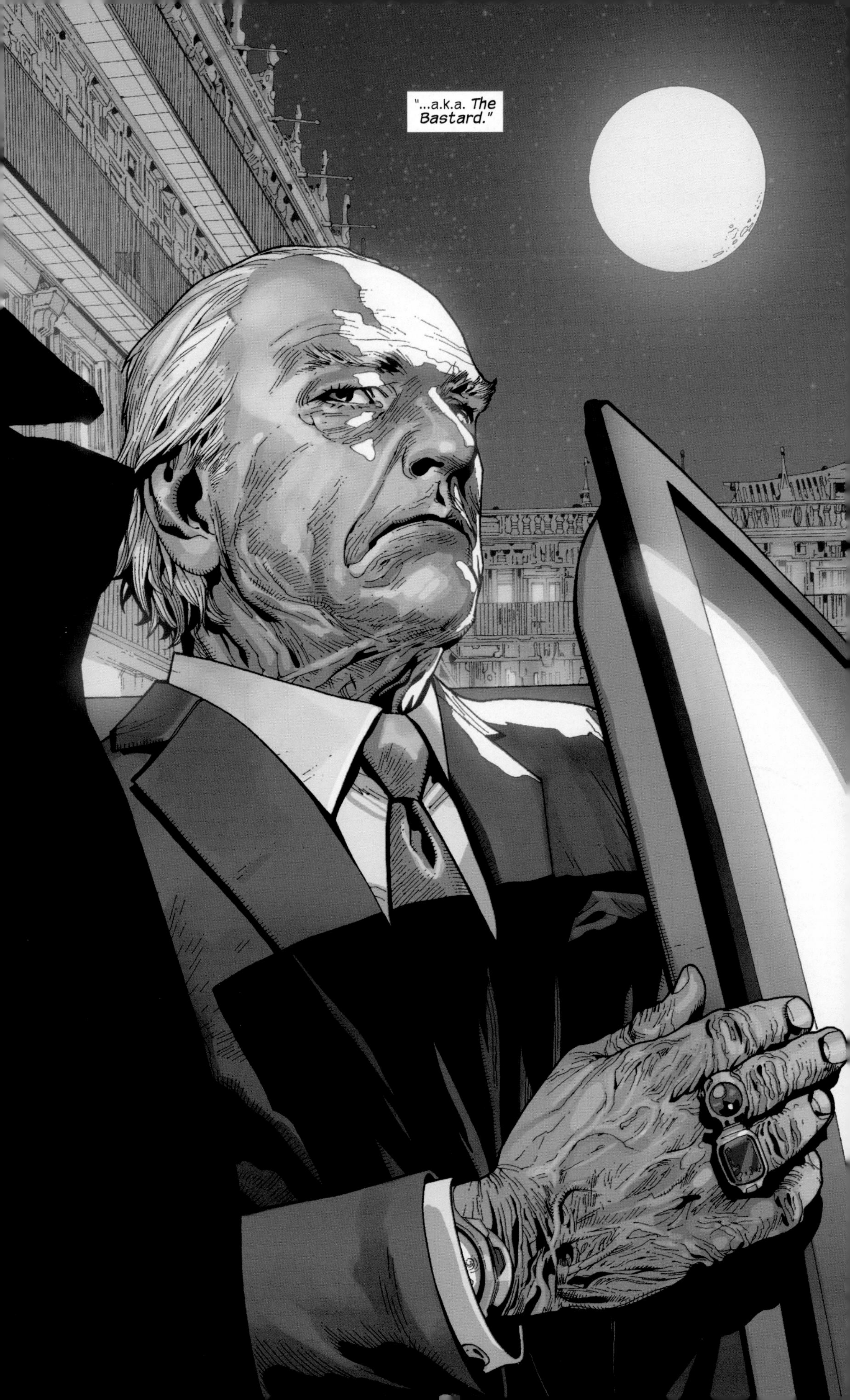
"...a.k.a. *The Bastard.*"

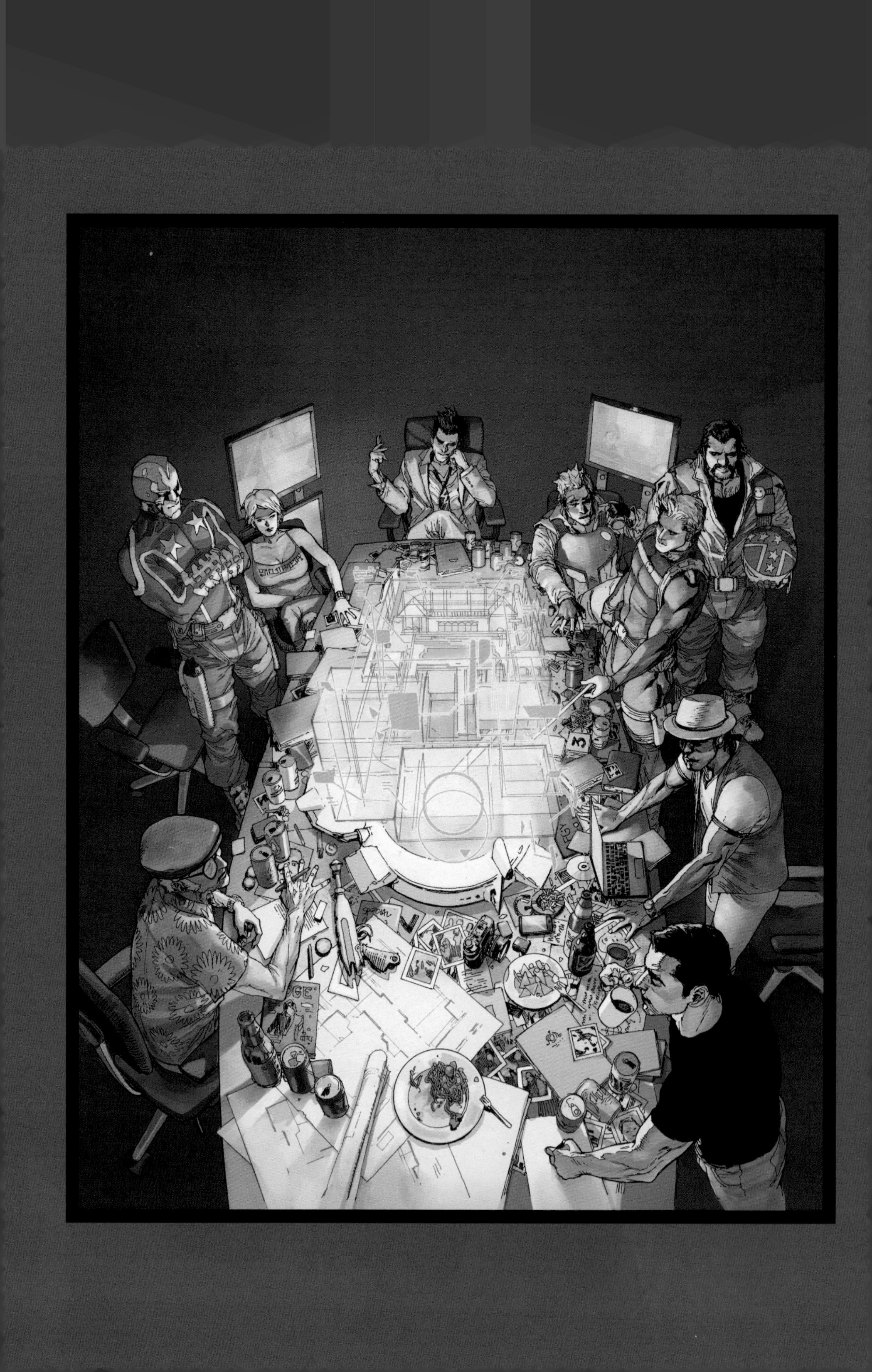

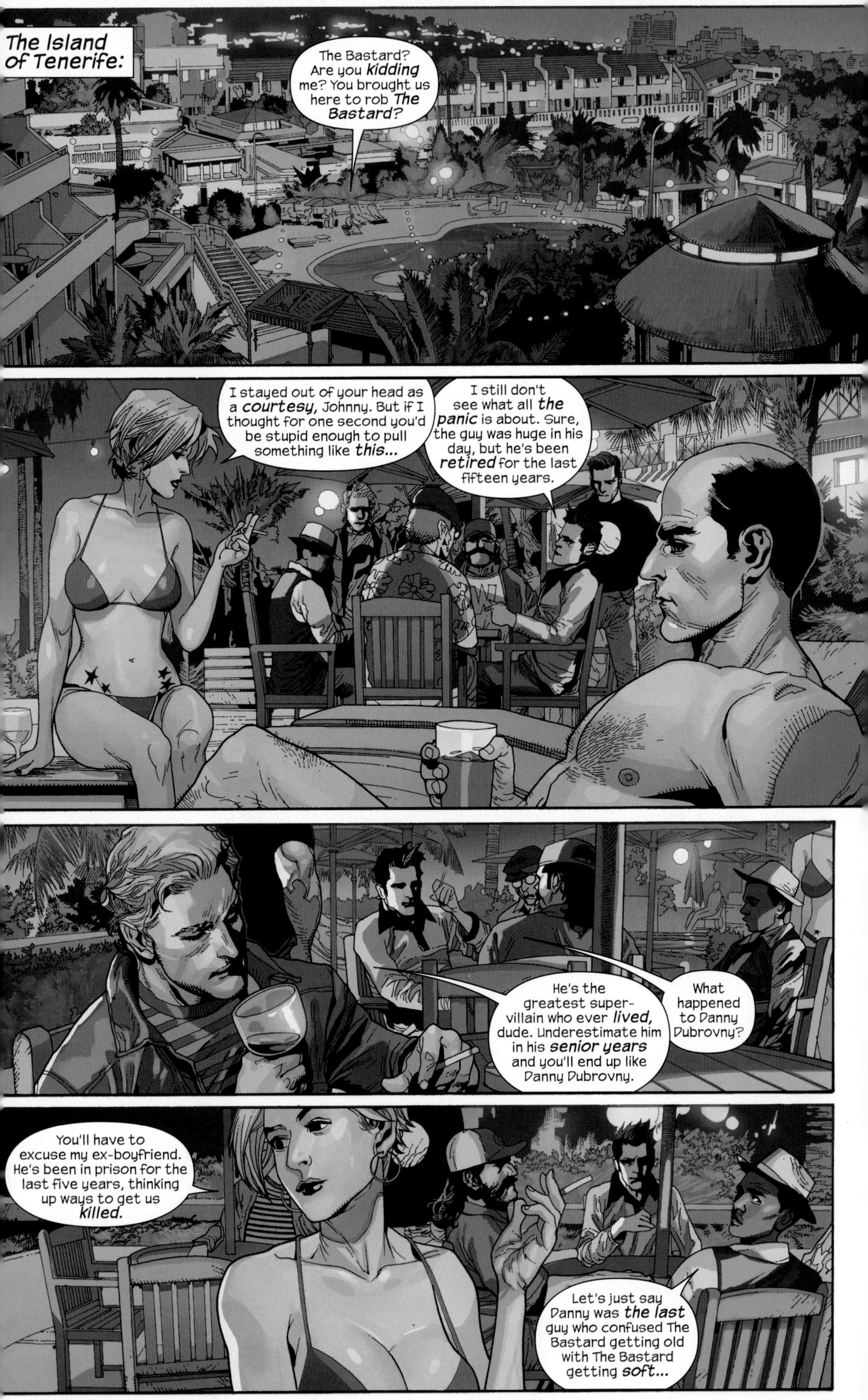
The Island of Tenerife:
The Bastard? Are you kidding me? You brought us here to rob The Bastard?
I stayed out of your head as a courtesy, Johnny. But if I thought for one second you'd be stupid enough to pull something like this...
I still don't see what all the panic is about. Sure, the guy was huge in his day, but he's been retired for the last fifteen years.
He's the greatest super-villain who ever lived, dude. Underestimate him in his senior years and you'll end up like Danny Dubrovny.
What happened to Danny Dubrovny?
You'll have to excuse my ex-boyfriend. He's been in prison for the last five years, thinking up ways to get us killed.
Let's just say Danny was the last guy who confused The Bastard getting old with The Bastard getting soft...

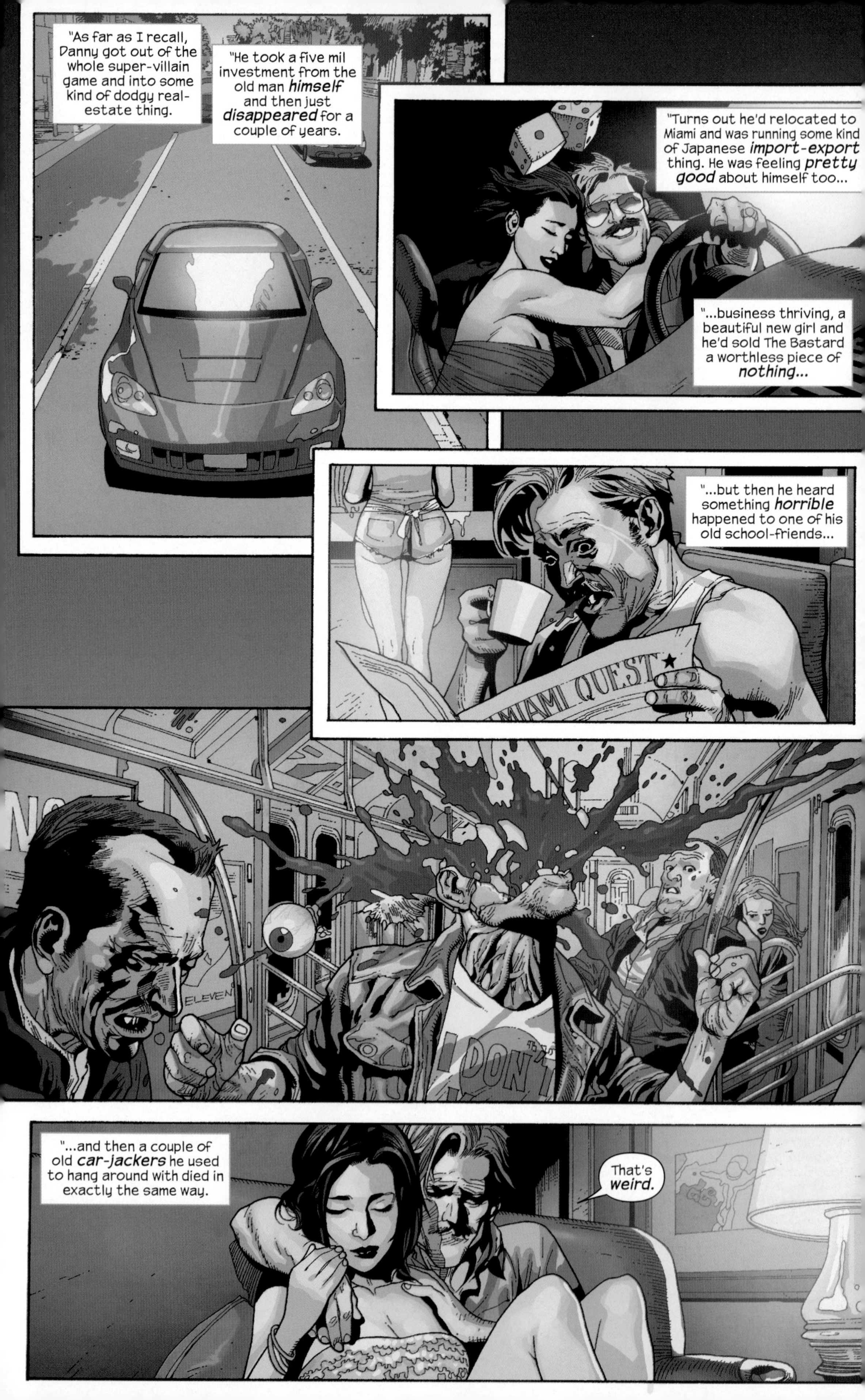

"As far as I recall, Danny got out of the whole super-villain game and into some kind of dodgy real-estate thing.
"He took a five mil investment from the old man *himself* and then just *disappeared* for a couple of years.
"Turns out he'd relocated to Miami and was running some kind of Japanese *import-export* thing. He was feeling *pretty good* about himself too...
"...business thriving, a beautiful new girl and he'd sold The Bastard a worthless piece of *nothing*...
"...but then he heard something *horrible* happened to one of his old school-friends...
MIAMI QUEST
ELEVEN
"...and then a couple of old *car-jackers* he used to hang around with died in exactly the same way.
That's *weird.*

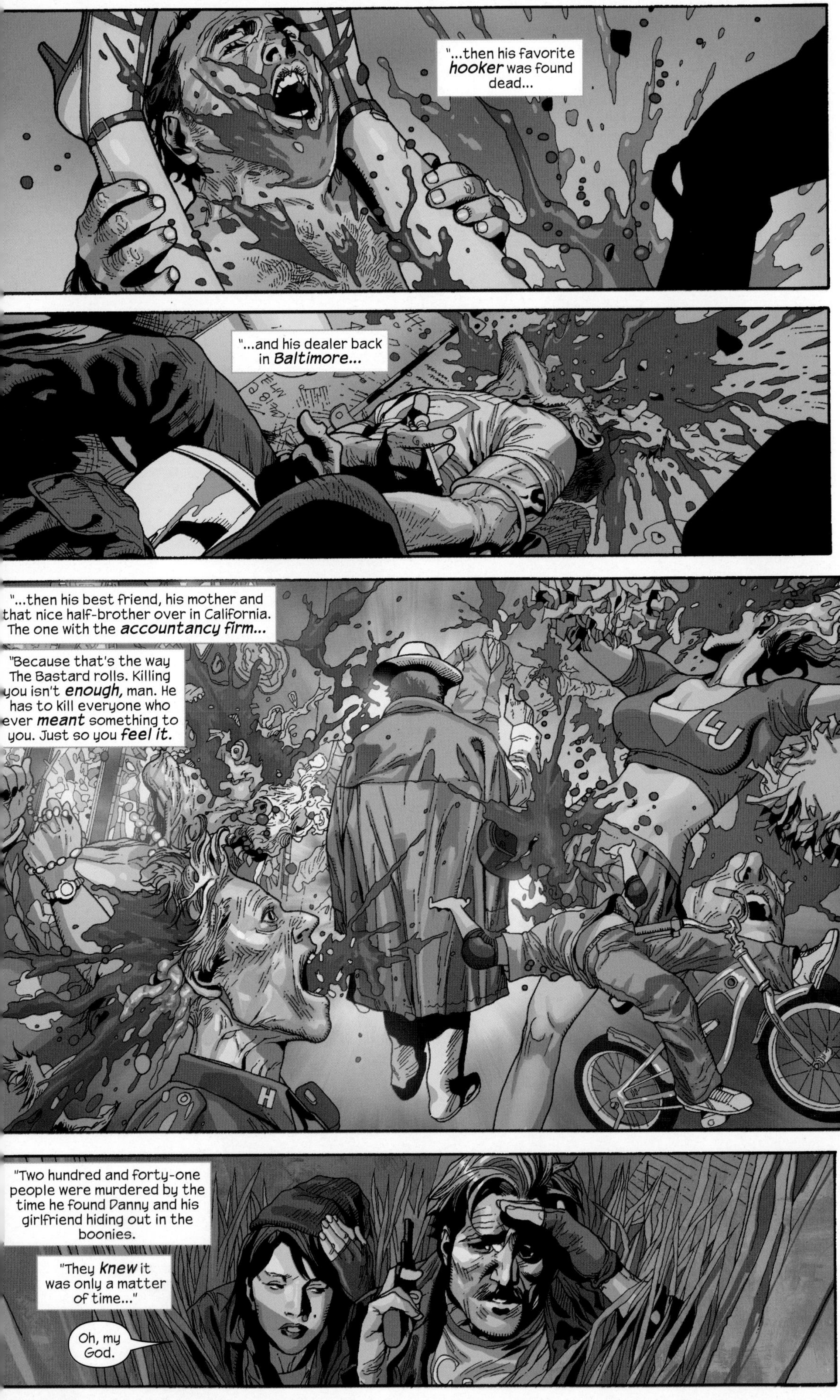
"...then his favorite hooker was found dead...
"...and his dealer back in Baltimore...
"...then his best friend, his mother and that nice half-brother over in California. The one with the accountancy firm...
"Because that's the way The Bastard rolls. Killing you isn't enough, man. He has to kill everyone who ever meant something to you. Just so you feel it.
"Two hundred and forty-one people were murdered by the time he found Danny and his girlfriend hiding out in the boonies.
"They knew it was only a matter of time..."
Oh, my God.

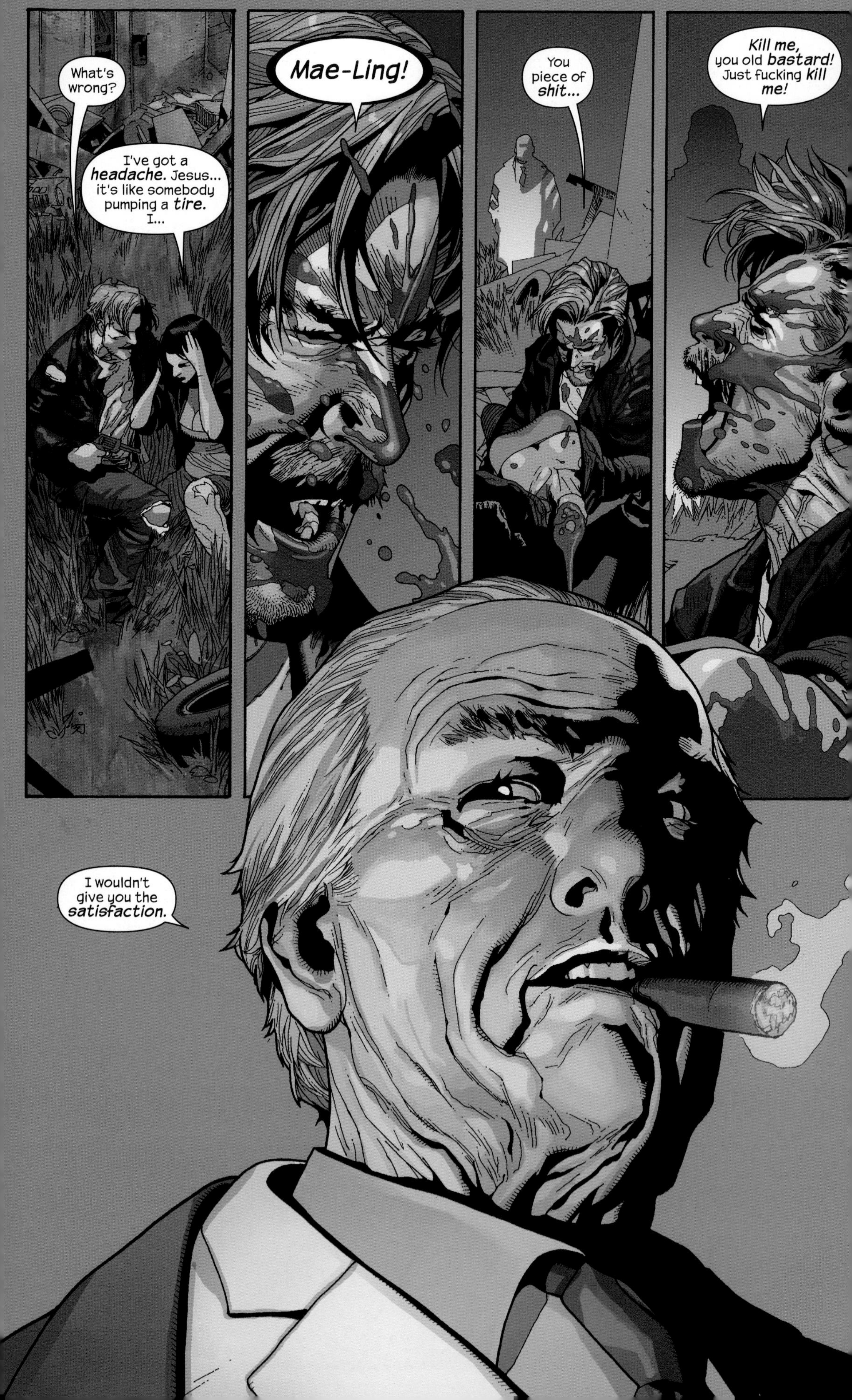
What's wrong?
I've got a headache. Jesus... it's like somebody pumping a tire. I...
Mae-Ling!
You piece of shit...
Kill me, you old bastard! Just fucking kill me!
I wouldn't give you the satisfaction.

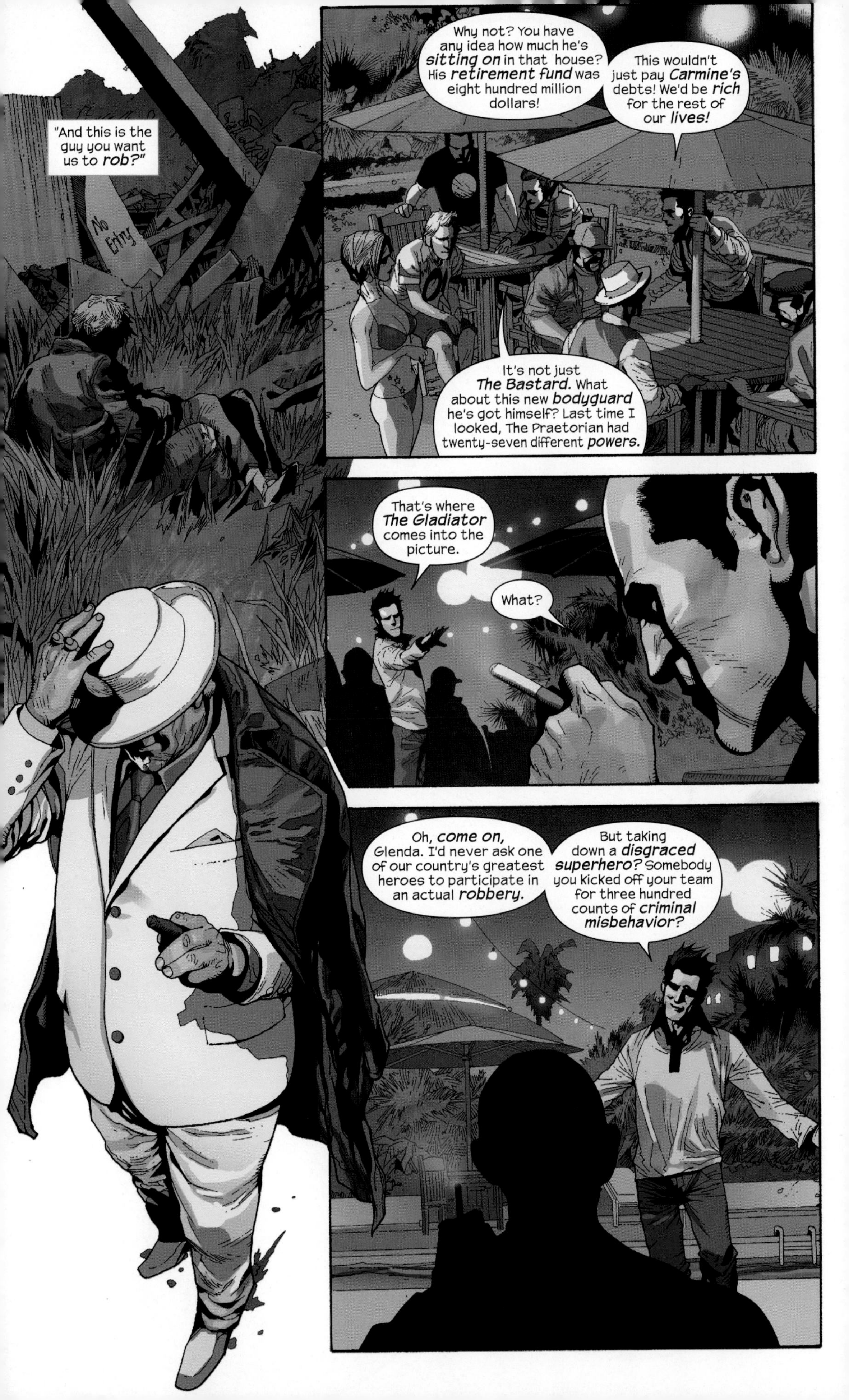
"And this is the guy you want us to rob?"
No Entry
Why not? You have any idea how much he's sitting on in that house? His retirement fund was eight hundred million dollars!
This wouldn't just pay Carmine's debts! We'd be rich for the rest of our lives!
It's not just The Bastard. What about this new bodyguard he's got himself? Last time I looked, The Praetorian had twenty-seven different powers.
That's where The Gladiator comes into the picture.
What?
Oh, come on, Glenda. I'd never ask one of our country's greatest heroes to participate in an actual robbery.
But taking down a disgraced superhero? Somebody you kicked off your team for three hundred counts of criminal misbehavior?

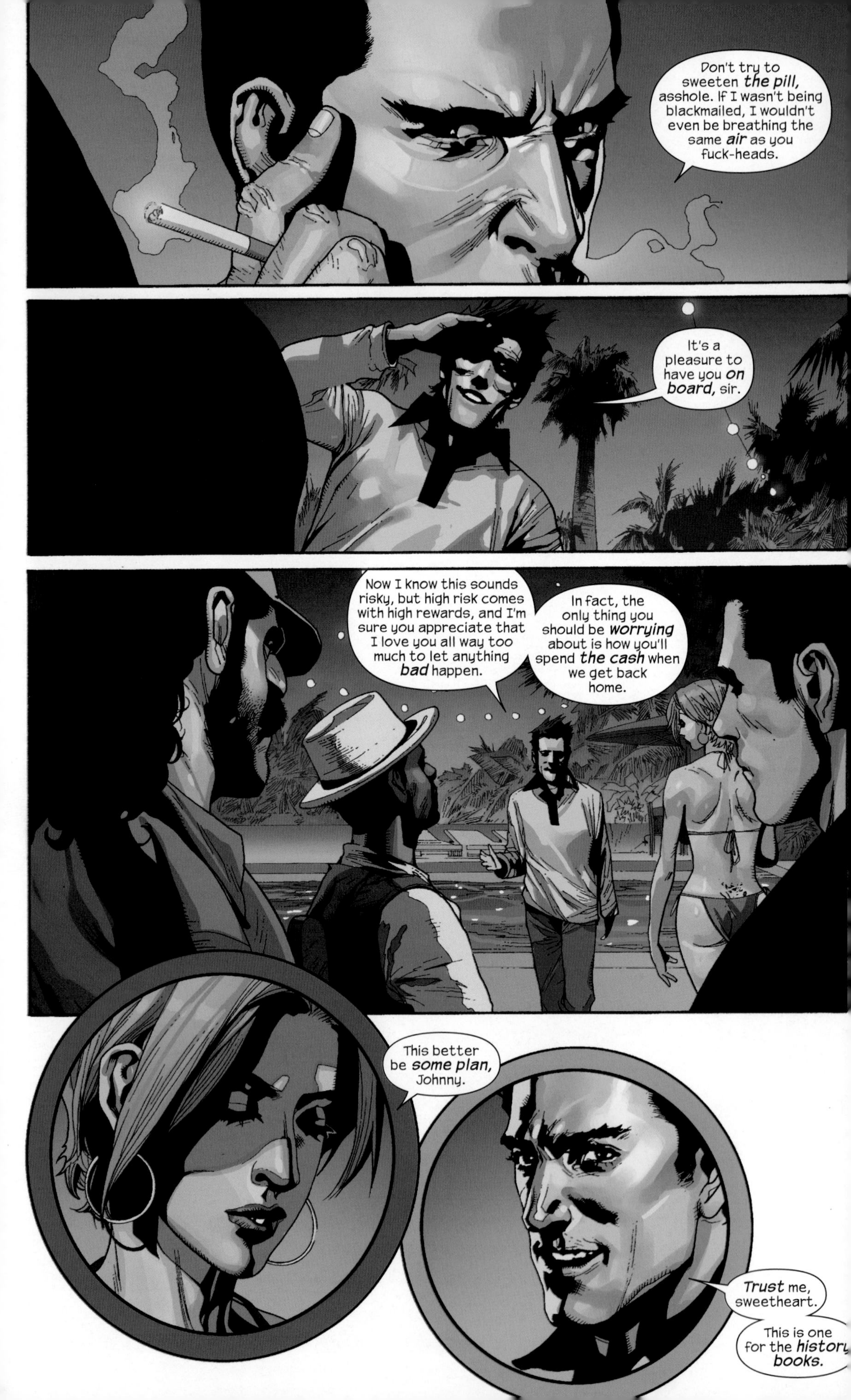

Don't try to sweeten *the pill,* asshole. If I wasn't being blackmailed, I wouldn't even be breathing the same *air* as you fuck-heads.
It's a pleasure to have you *on board,* sir.
Now I know this sounds risky, but high risk comes with high rewards, and I'm sure you appreciate that I love you all way too much to let anything *bad* happen.
In fact, the only thing you should be *worrying* about is how you'll spend *the cash* when we get back home.
This better be *some plan,* Johnny.
*Trust* me, sweetheart.
This is one for the *history books.*

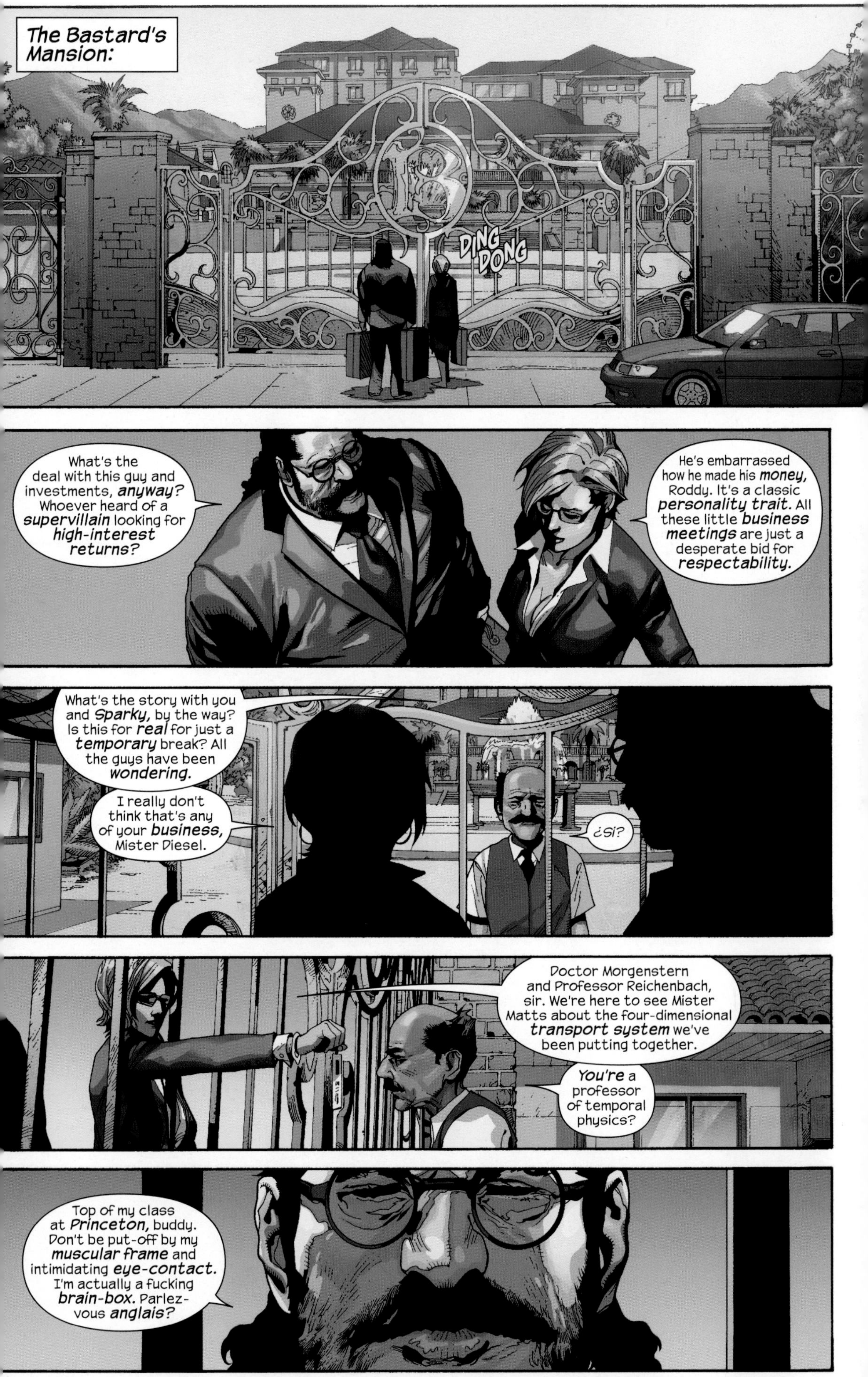

The Bastard's Mansion:
DING DONG
What's the deal with this guy and investments, anyway? Whoever heard of a supervillain looking for high-interest returns?
He's embarrassed how he made his money, Roddy. It's a classic personality trait. All these little business meetings are just a desperate bid for respectability.
What's the story with you and Sparky, by the way? Is this for real for just a temporary break? All the guys have been wondering.
I really don't think that's any of your business, Mister Diesel.
¿Si?
Doctor Morgenstern and Professor Reichenbach, sir. We're here to see Mister Matts about the four-dimensional transport system we've been putting together.
You're a professor of temporal physics?
Top of my class at Princeton, buddy. Don't be put-off by my muscular frame and intimidating eye-contact. I'm actually a fucking brain-box. Parlez-vous anglais?

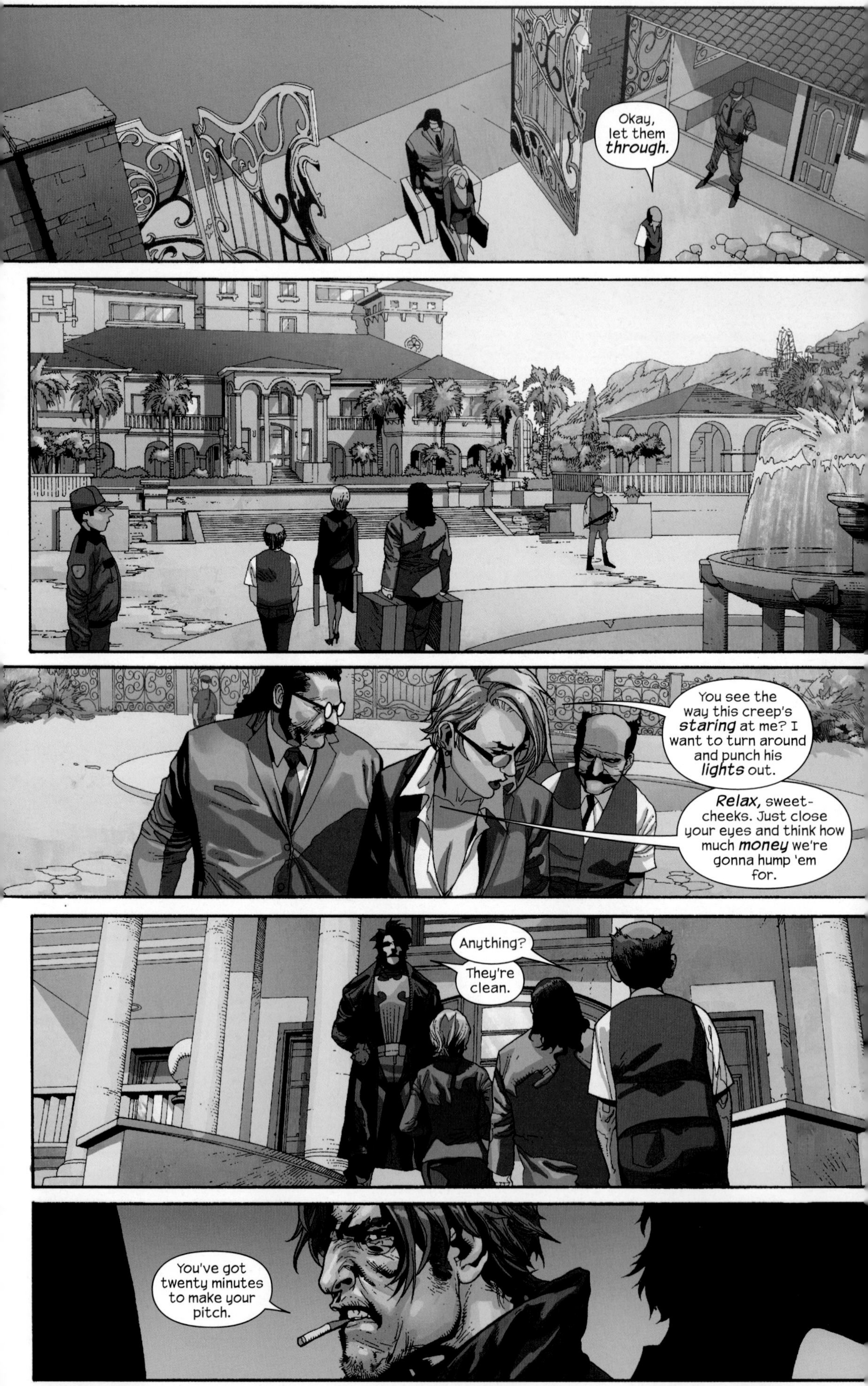
Okay, let them through.
You see the way this creep's staring at me? I want to turn around and punch his lights out.
Relax, sweet-cheeks. Just close your eyes and think how much money we're gonna hump 'em for.
Anything?
They're clean.
You've got twenty minutes to make your pitch.

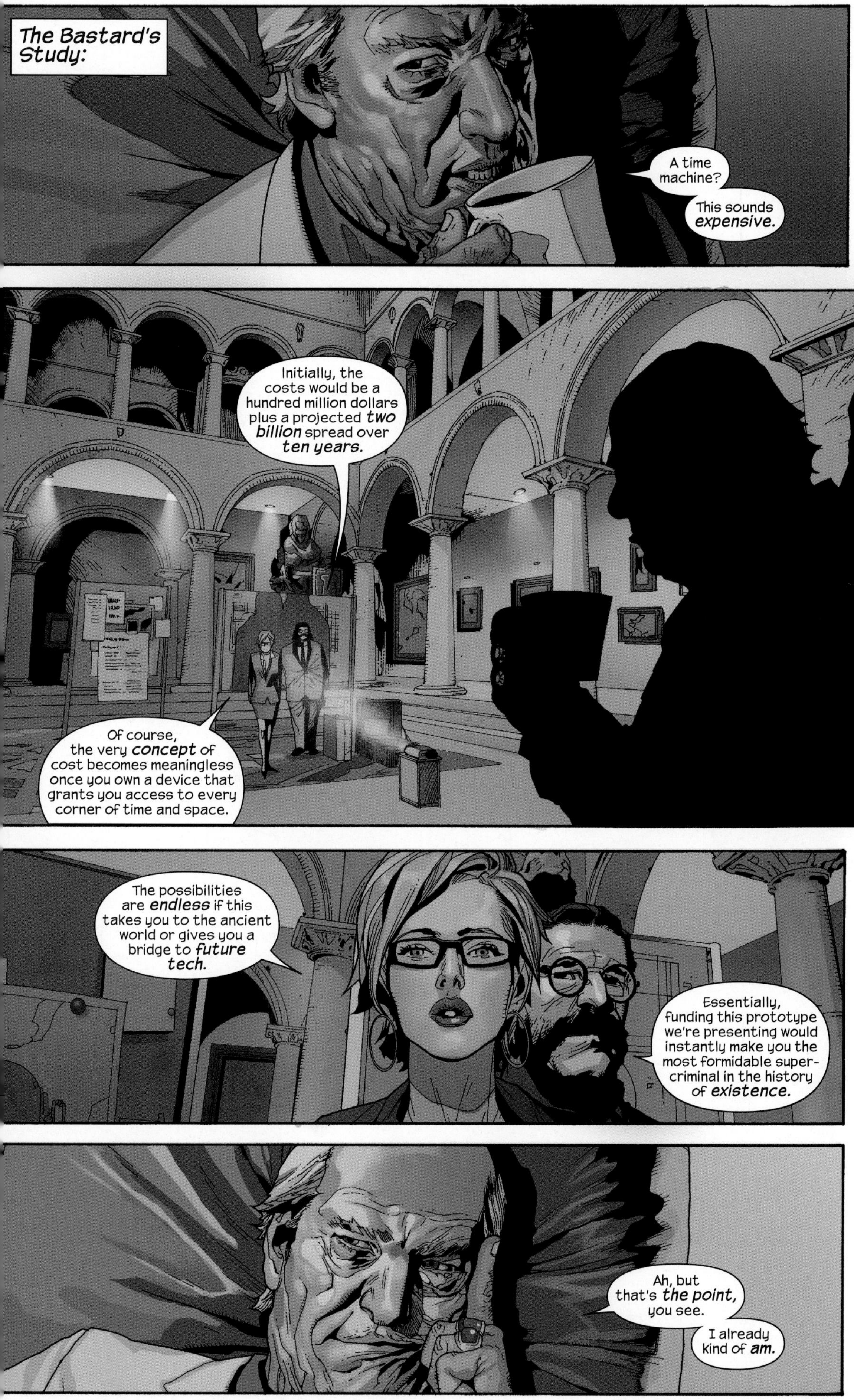

The Bastard's Study:
A time machine?
This sounds *expensive.*
Initially, the costs would be a hundred million dollars plus a projected *two billion* spread over *ten years.*
Of course, the very *concept* of cost becomes meaningless once you own a device that grants you access to every corner of time and space.
The possibilities are *endless* if this takes you to the ancient world or gives you a bridge to *future tech.*
Essentially, funding this prototype we're presenting would instantly make you the most formidable super-criminal in the history of *existence.*
Ah, but that's *the point,* you see.
I already kind of *am.*

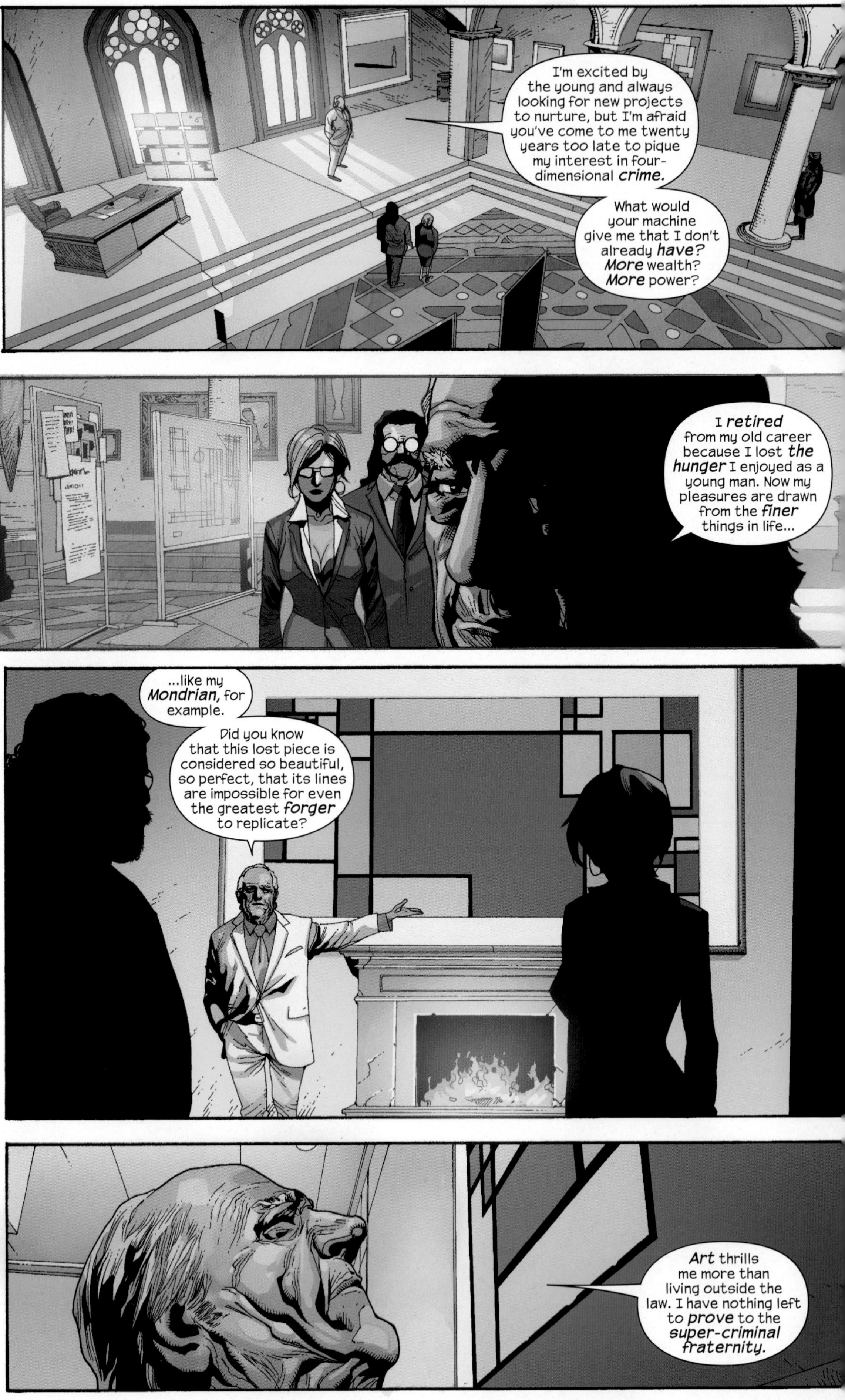
I'm excited by the young and always looking for new projects to nurture, but I'm afraid you've come to me twenty years too late to pique my interest in four-dimensional *crime.*
What would your machine give me that I don't already *have? More* wealth? *More* power?
I *retired* from my old career because I lost *the hunger* I enjoyed as a young man. Now my pleasures are drawn from the *finer* things in life...
...like my *Mondrian,* for example.
Did you know that this lost piece is considered so beautiful, so perfect, that its lines are impossible for even the greatest *forger* to replicate?
*Art* thrills me more than living outside the law. I have nothing left to *prove* to the *super-criminal fraternity.*

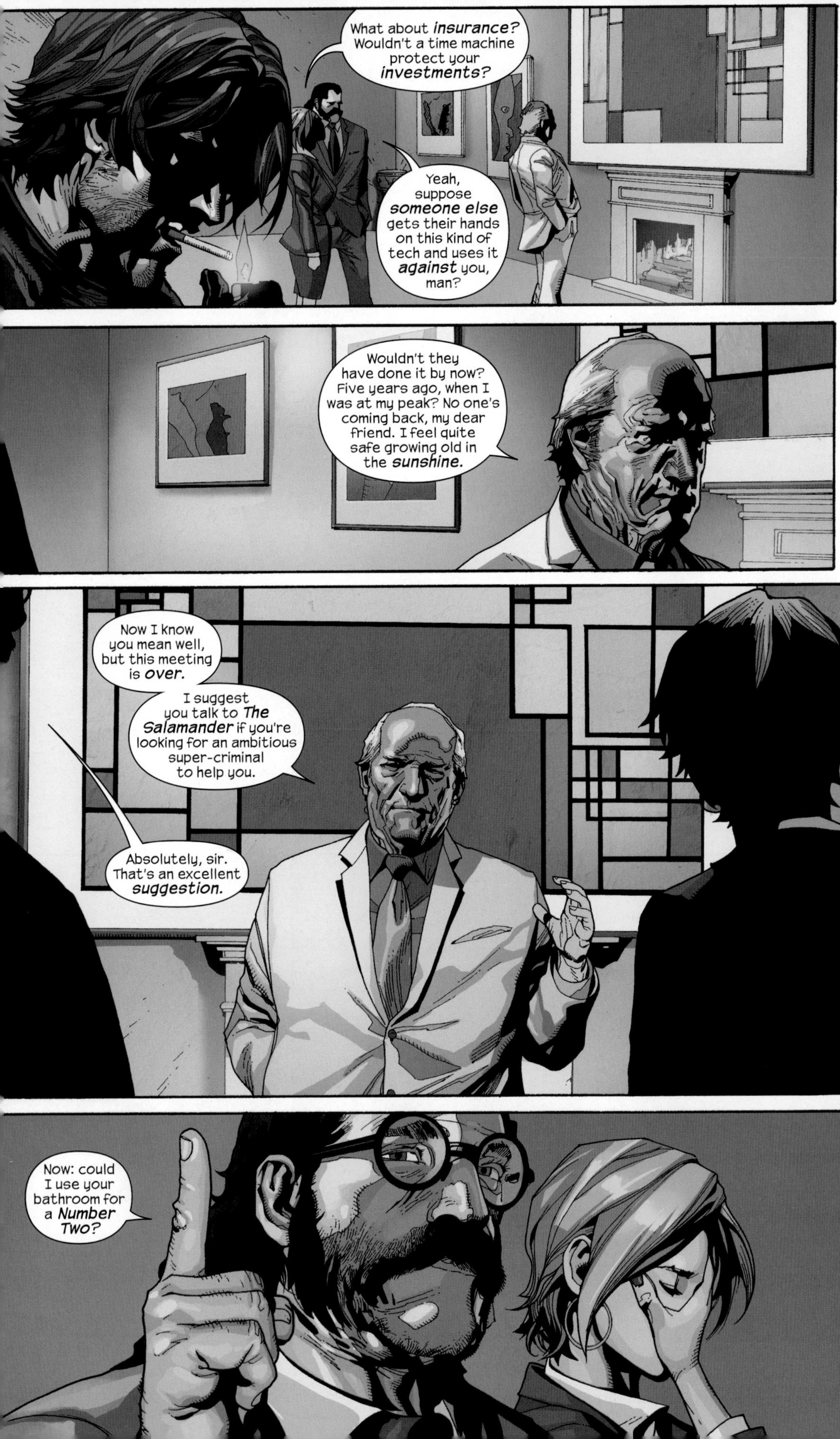

What about insurance? Wouldn't a time machine protect your investments?
Yeah, suppose someone else gets their hands on this kind of tech and uses it against you, man?
Wouldn't they have done it by now? Five years ago, when I was at my peak? No one's coming back, my dear friend. I feel quite safe growing old in the sunshine.
Now I know you mean well, but this meeting is over.
I suggest you talk to The Salamander if you're looking for an ambitious super-criminal to help you.
Absolutely, sir. That's an excellent suggestion.
Now: could I use your bathroom for a Number Two?

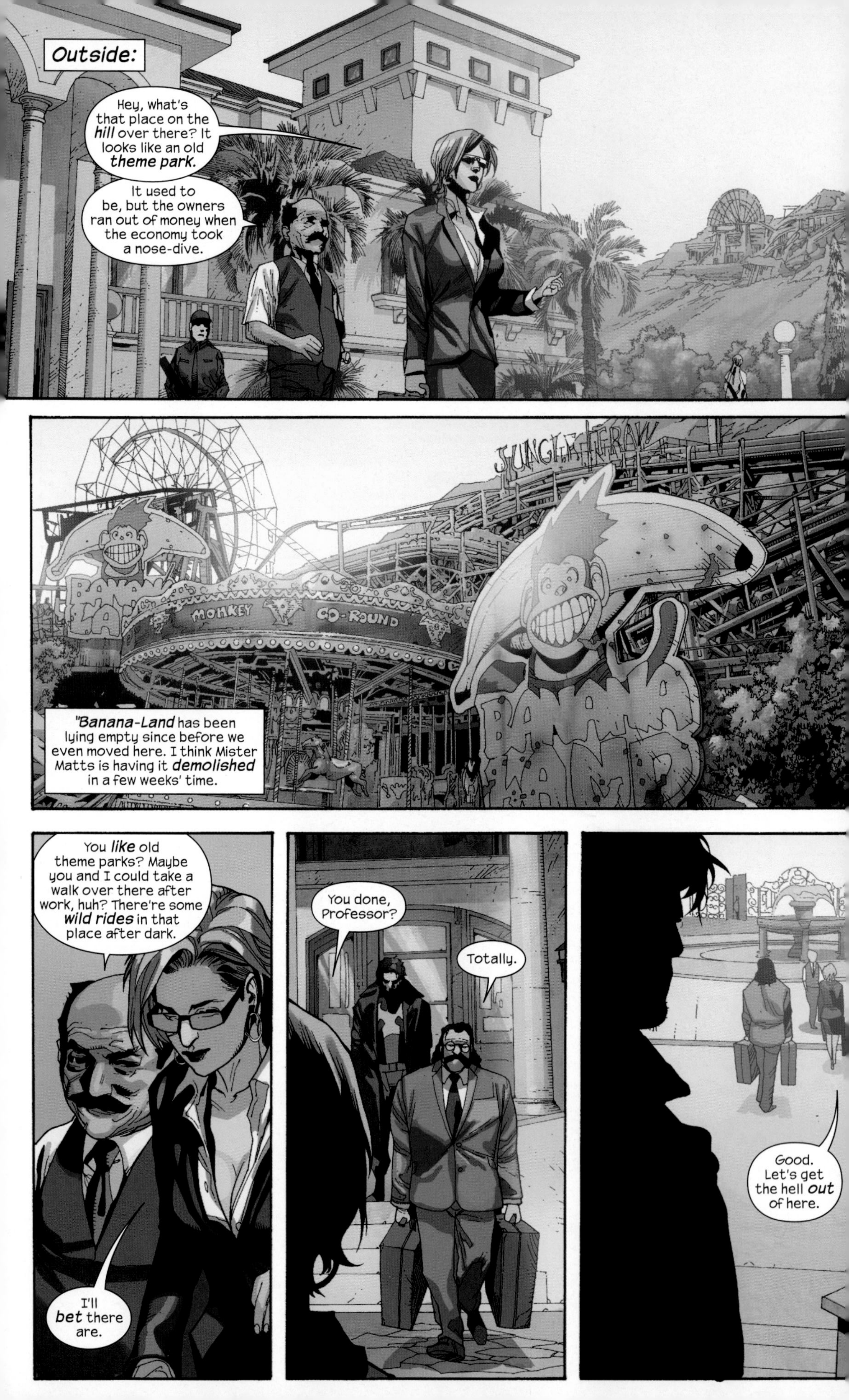
Outside:
Hey, what's that place on the *hill* over there? It looks like an old *theme park.*
It used to be, but the owners ran out of money when the economy took a nose-dive.
"*Banana-Land* has been lying empty since before we even moved here. I think Mister Matts is having it *demolished* in a few weeks' time.
You *like* old theme parks? Maybe you and I could take a walk over there after work, huh? There're some *wild rides* in that place after dark.
I'll *bet* there are.
You done, Professor?
Totally.
Good. Let's get the hell *out* of here.

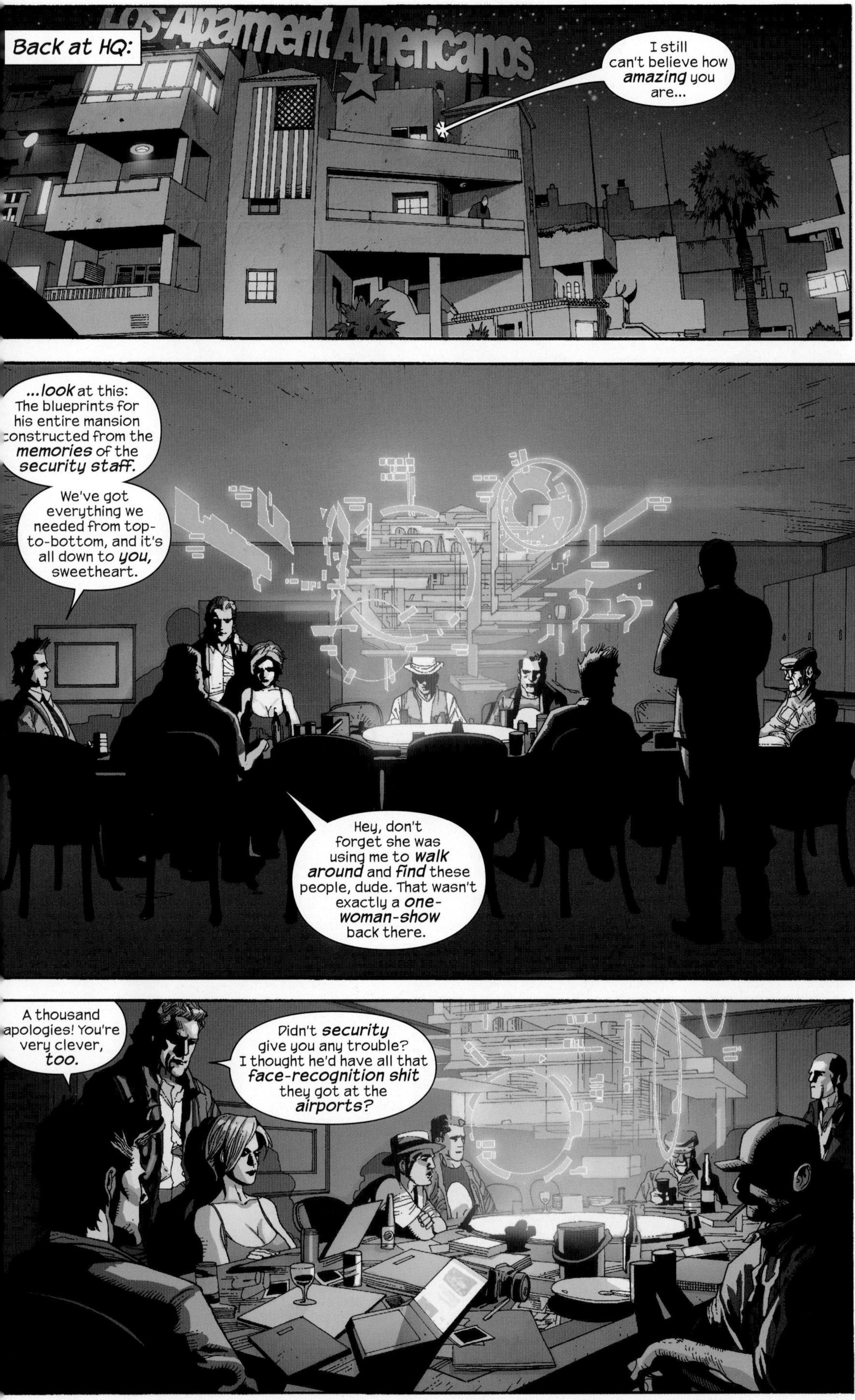
Back at HQ:
I still can't believe how amazing you are...
...look at this: The blueprints for his entire mansion constructed from the memories of the security staff.
We've got everything we needed from top-to-bottom, and it's all down to you, sweetheart.
Hey, don't forget she was using me to walk around and find these people, dude. That wasn't exactly a one-woman-show back there.
A thousand apologies! You're very clever, too.
Didn't security give you any trouble? I thought he'd have all that face-recognition shit they got at the airports?

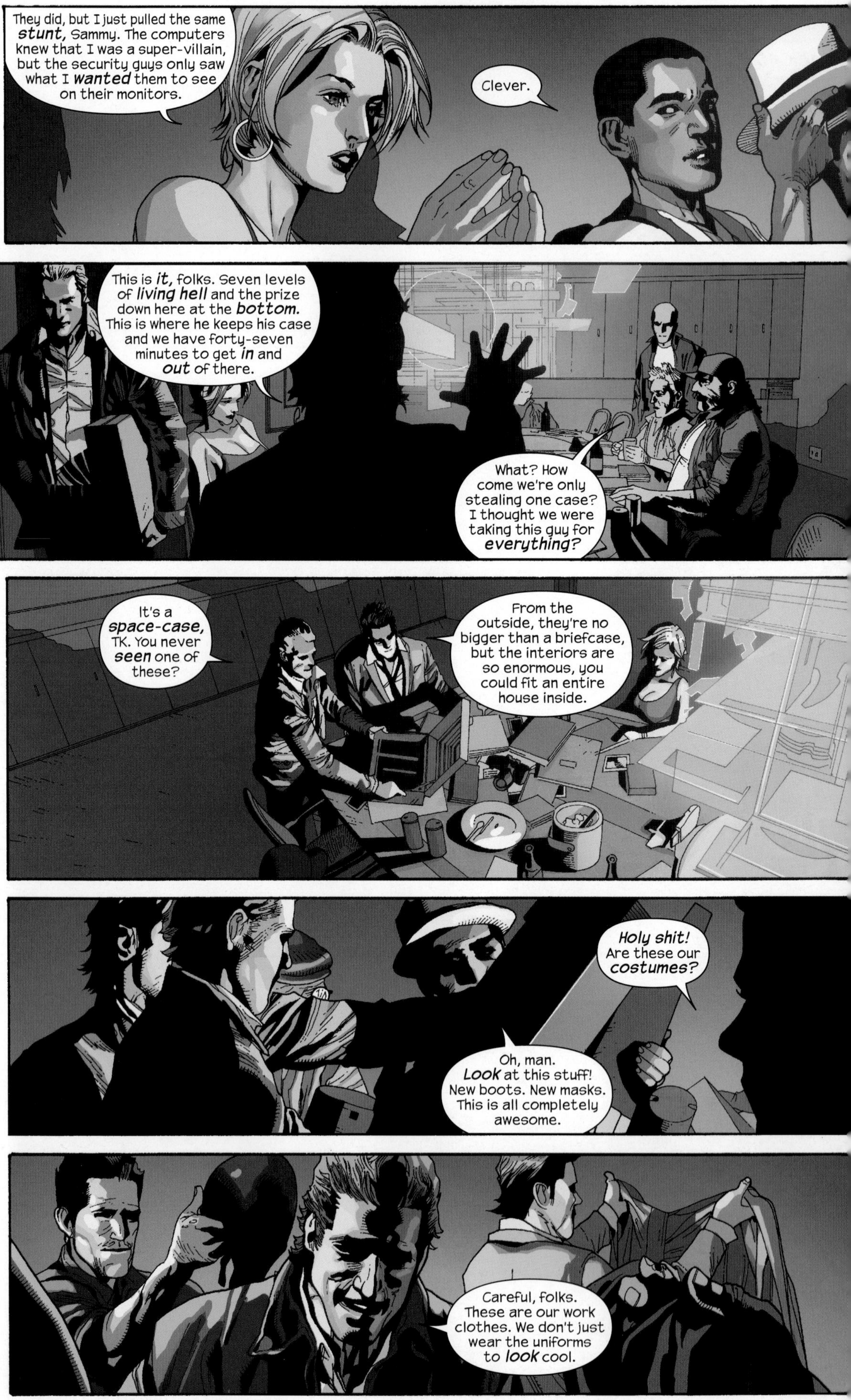
They did, but I just pulled the same *stunt,* Sammy. The computers knew that I was a super-villain, but the security guys only saw what I *wanted* them to see on their monitors.
Clever.
This is *it,* folks. Seven levels of *living hell* and the prize down here at the *bottom.* This is where he keeps his case and we have forty-seven minutes to get *in* and *out* of there.
What? How come we're only stealing one case? I thought we were taking this guy for *everything?*
It's a *space-case,* TK. You never *seen* one of these?
From the outside, they're no bigger than a briefcase, but the interiors are so enormous, you could fit an entire house inside.
*Holy shit!* Are these our *costumes?*
Oh, man. *Look* at this stuff! New boots. New masks. This is all completely awesome.
Careful, folks. These are our work clothes. We don't just wear the uniforms to *look* cool.

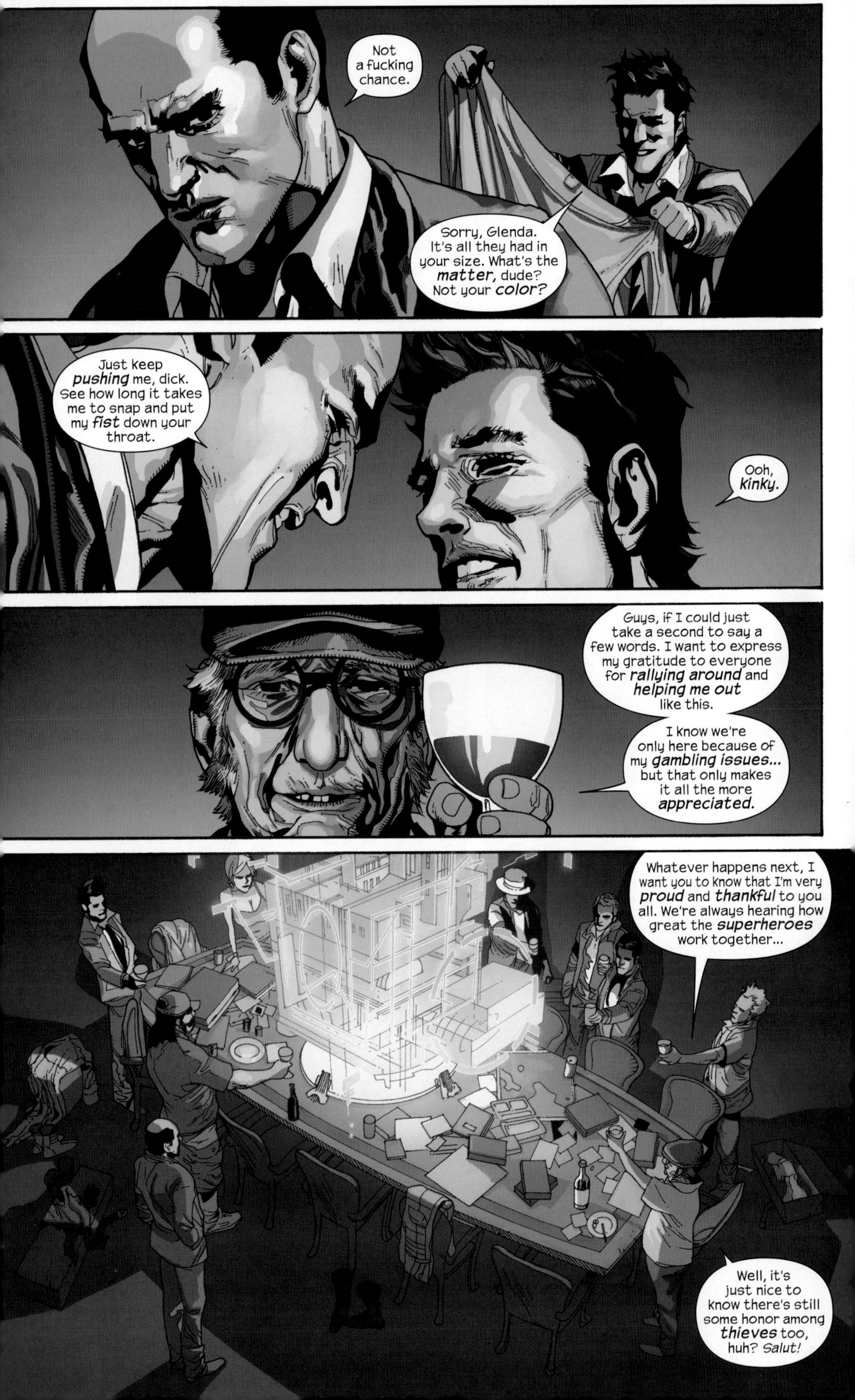
Not a fucking chance.
Sorry, Glenda. It's all they had in your size. What's the matter, dude? Not your color?
Just keep pushing me, dick. See how long it takes me to snap and put my fist down your throat.
Ooh, kinky.
Guys, if I could just take a second to say a few words. I want to express my gratitude to everyone for rallying around and helping me out like this.
I know we're only here because of my gambling issues... but that only makes it all the more appreciated.
Whatever happens next, I want you to know that I'm very proud and thankful to you all. We're always hearing how great the superheroes work together...
Well, it's just nice to know there's still some honor among thieves too, huh? Salut!

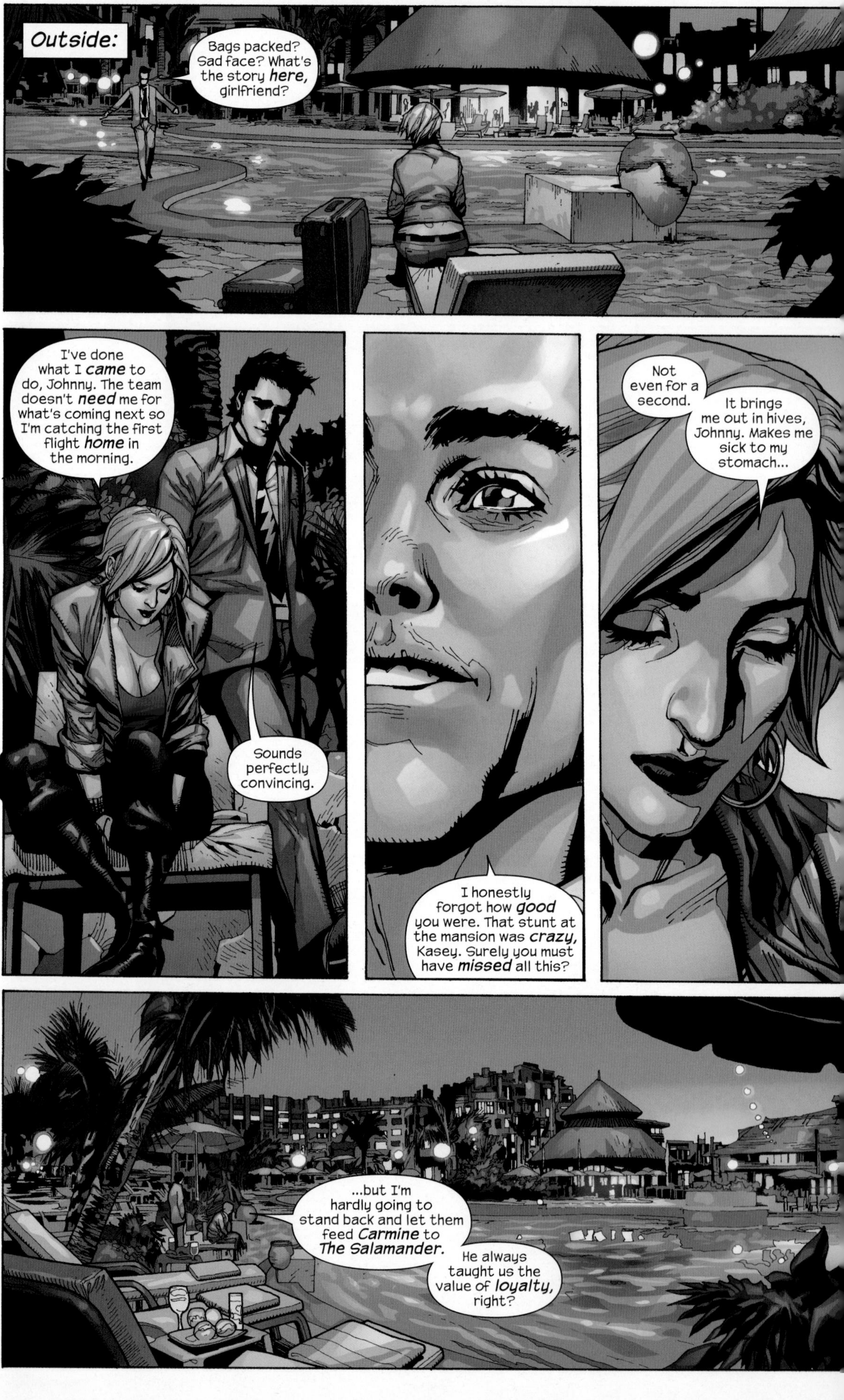
Outside:
Bags packed? Sad face? What's the story here, girlfriend?
I've done what I came to do, Johnny. The team doesn't need me for what's coming next so I'm catching the first flight home in the morning.
Sounds perfectly convincing.
I honestly forgot how good you were. That stunt at the mansion was crazy, Kasey. Surely you must have missed all this?
Not even for a second.
It brings me out in hives, Johnny. Makes me sick to my stomach...
...but I'm hardly going to stand back and let them feed Carmine to The Salamander.
He always taught us the value of loyalty, right?

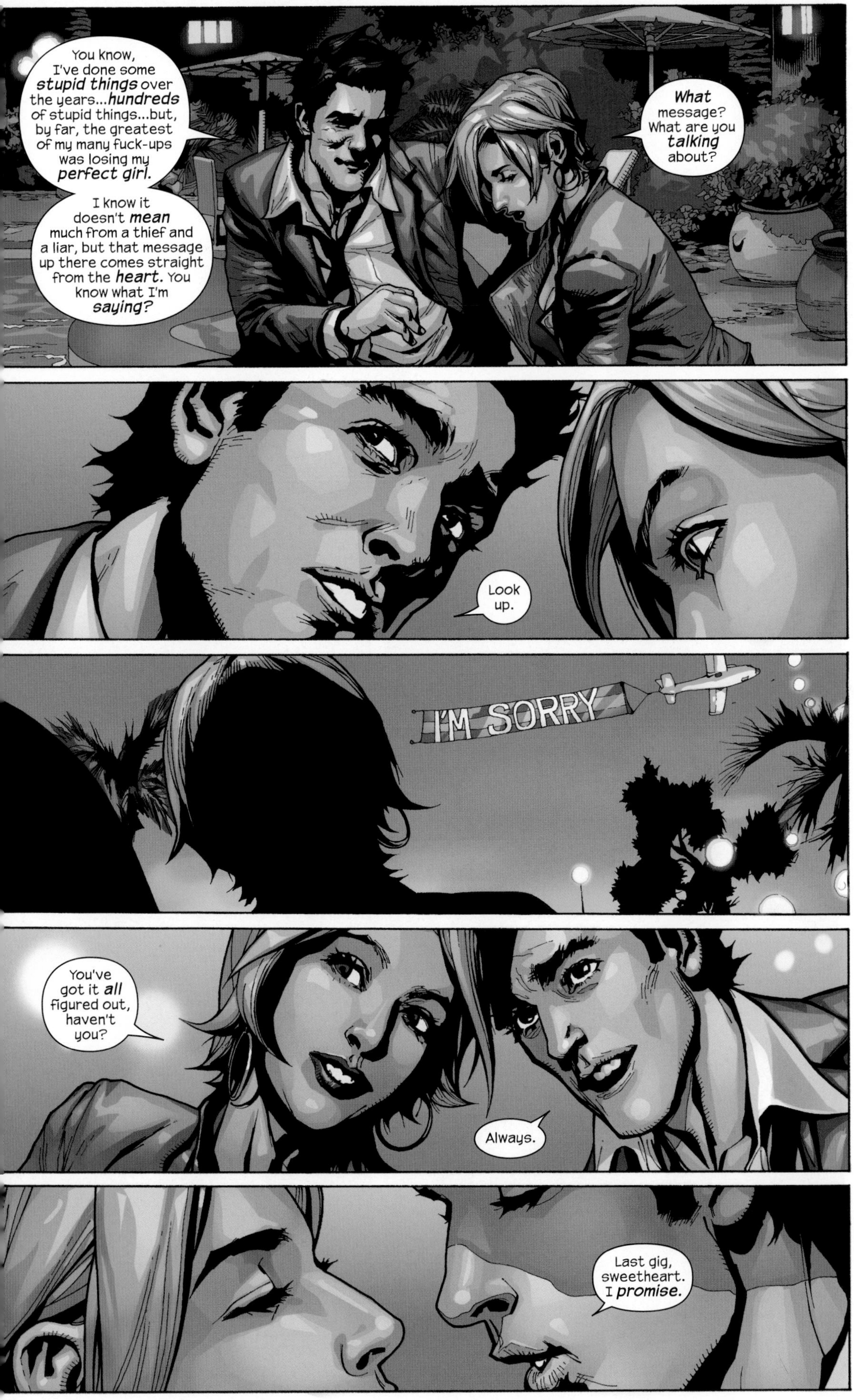
You know, I've done some *stupid things* over the years...*hundreds* of stupid things...but, by far, the greatest of my many fuck-ups was losing my *perfect girl.*
I know it doesn't *mean* much from a thief and a liar, but that message up there comes straight from the *heart.* You know what I'm *saying?*
*What* message? What are you *talking* about?
Look up.
I'M SORRY
You've got it *all* figured out, haven't you?
Always.
Last gig, sweetheart. I *promise.*

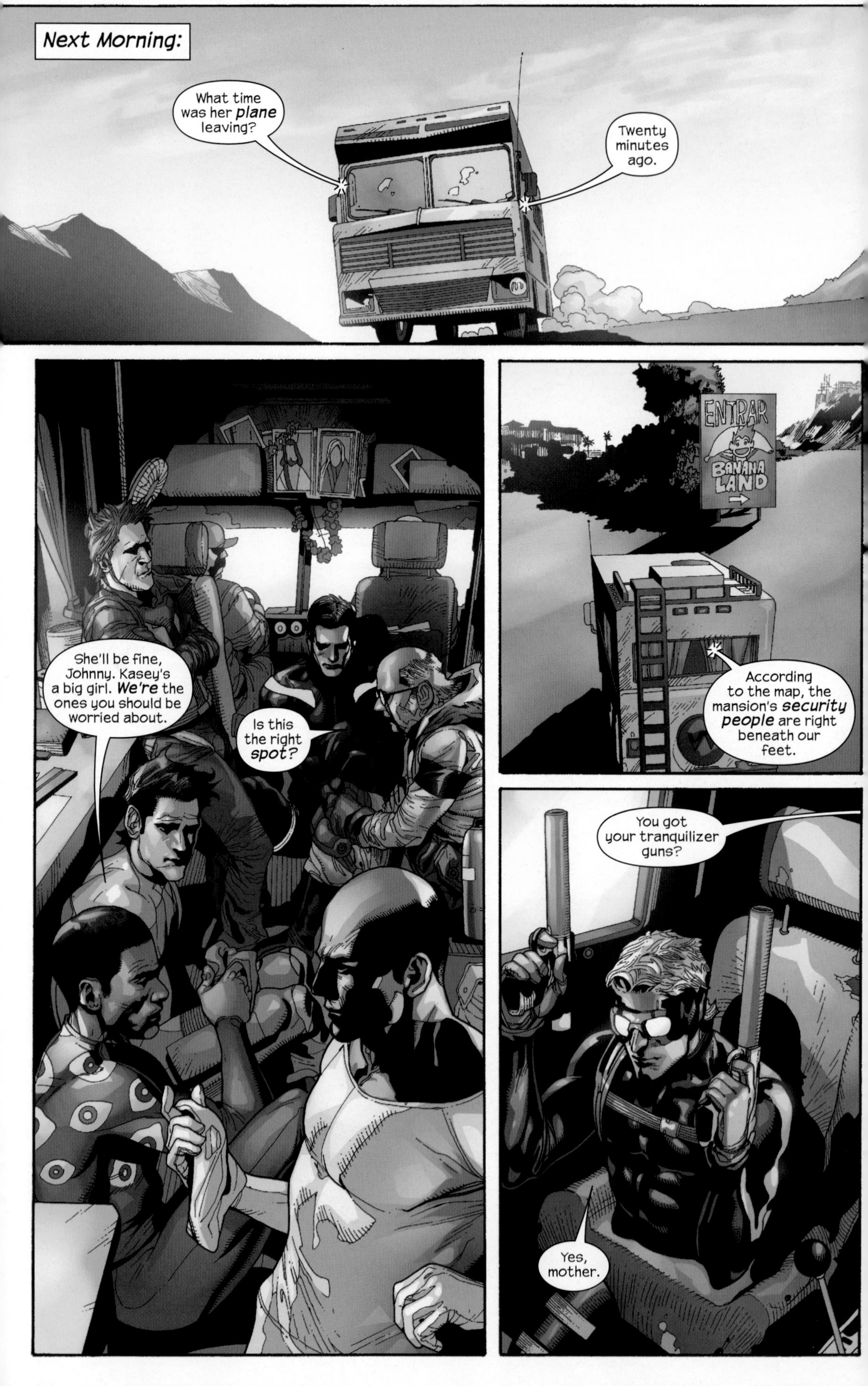
Next Morning:
What time was her plane leaving?
Twenty minutes ago.
She'll be fine, Johnny. Kasey's a big girl. We're the ones you should be worried about.
Is this the right spot?
ENTRAR
BANANA LAND
According to the map, the mansion's security people are right beneath our feet.
You got your tranquilizer guns?
Yes, mother.

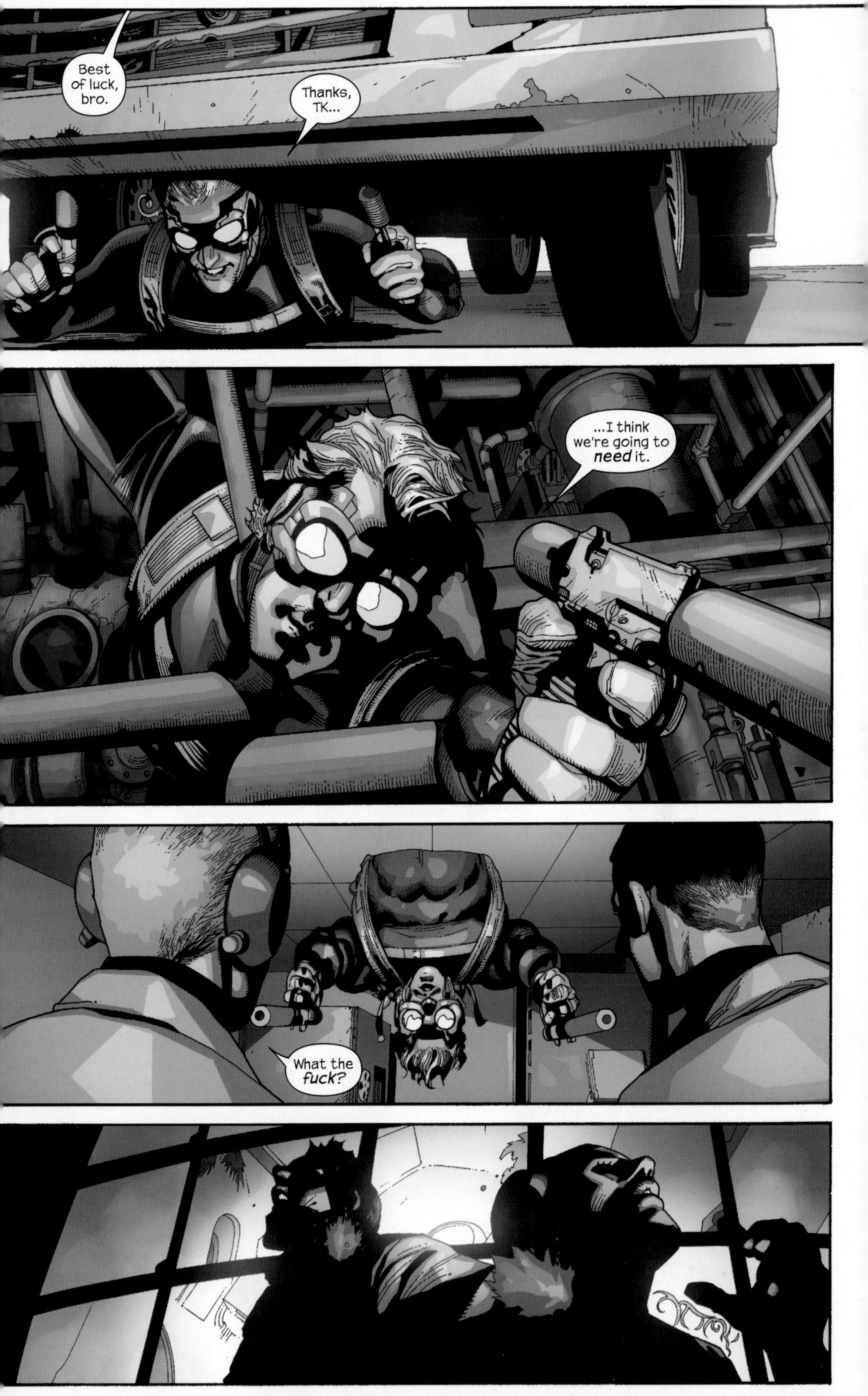

Best of luck, bro.
Thanks, TK...
...I think we're going to *need* it.
What the *fuck?*

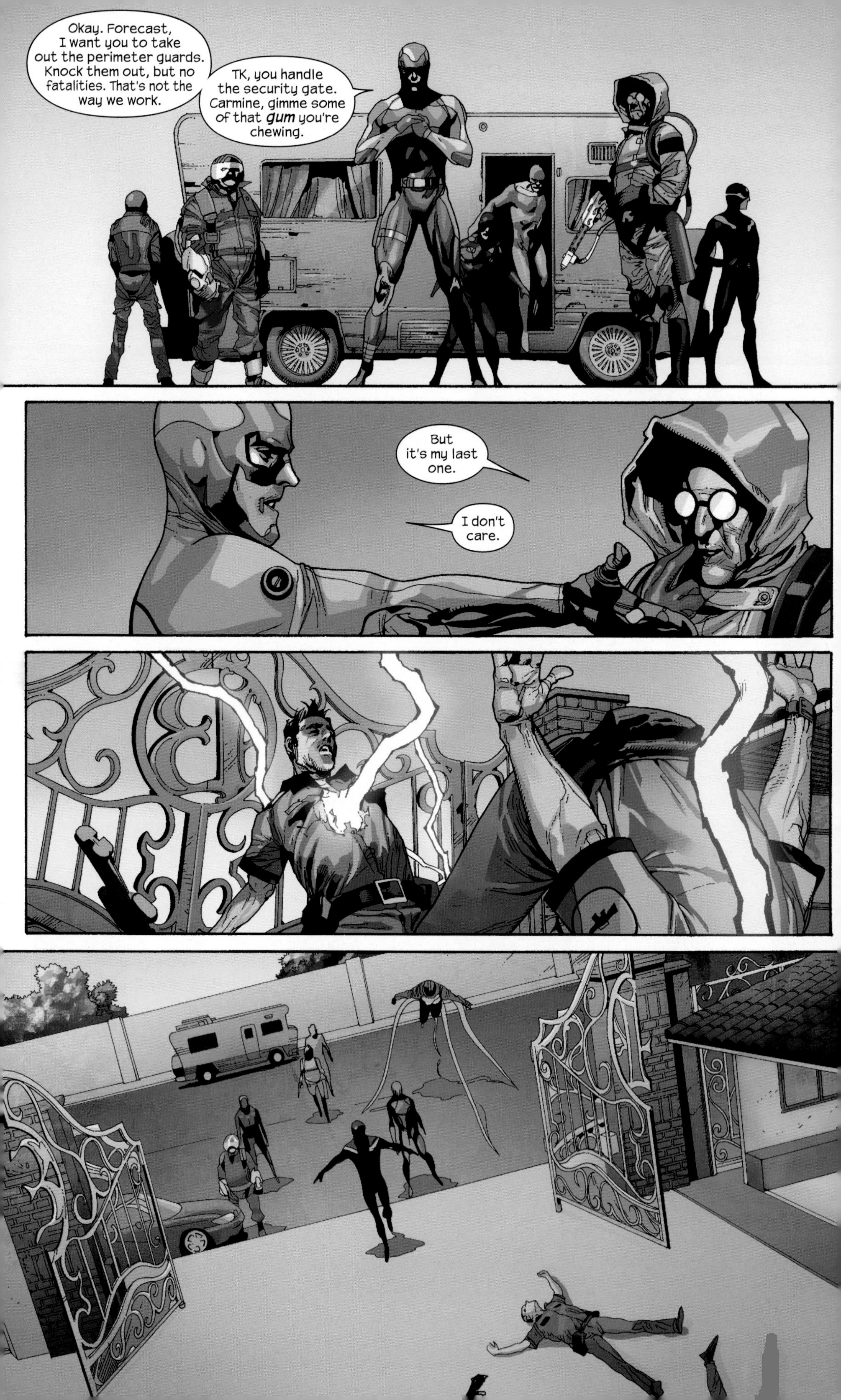
Okay. Forecast, I want you to take out the perimeter guards. Knock them out, but no fatalities. That's not the way we work.
TK, you handle the security gate. Carmine, gimme some of that *gum* you're chewing.
But it's my last one.
I don't care.

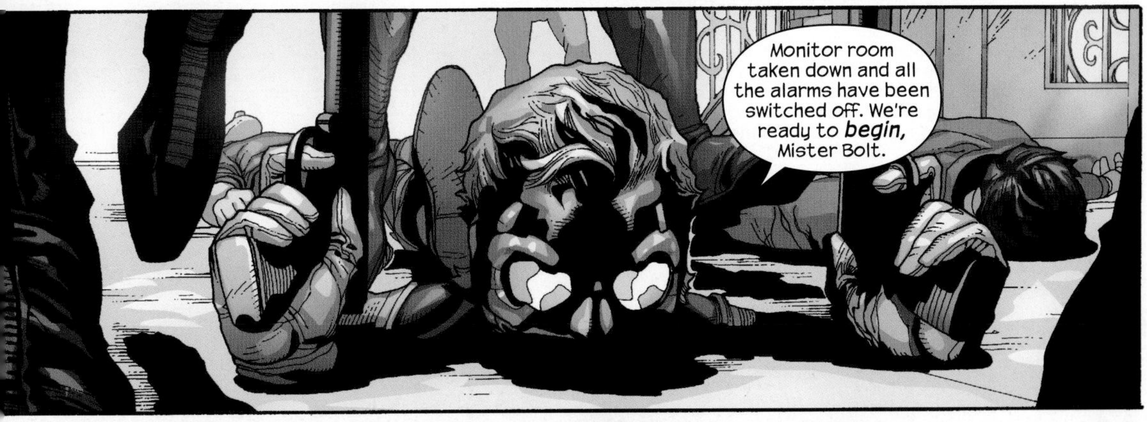
Monitor room taken down and all the alarms have been switched off. We're ready to **begin,** Mister Bolt.

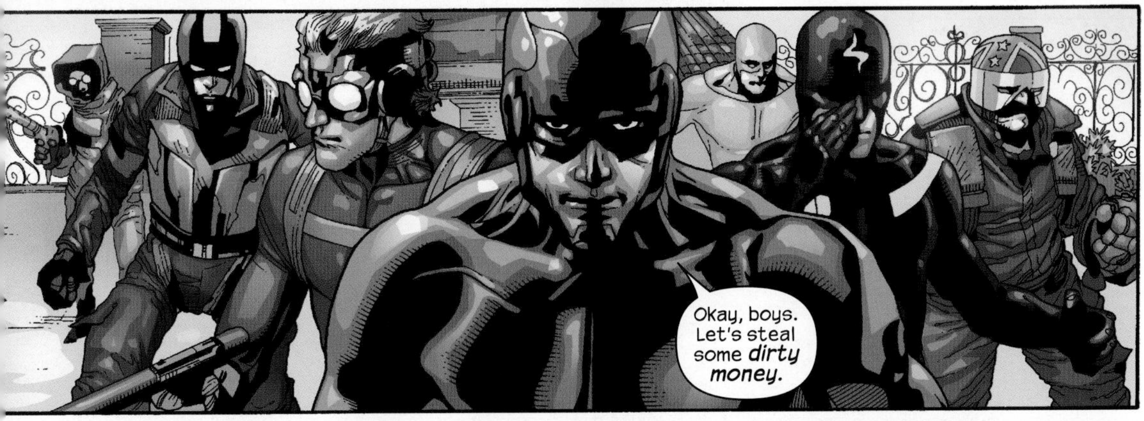
Okay, boys. Let's steal some ***dirty money.***

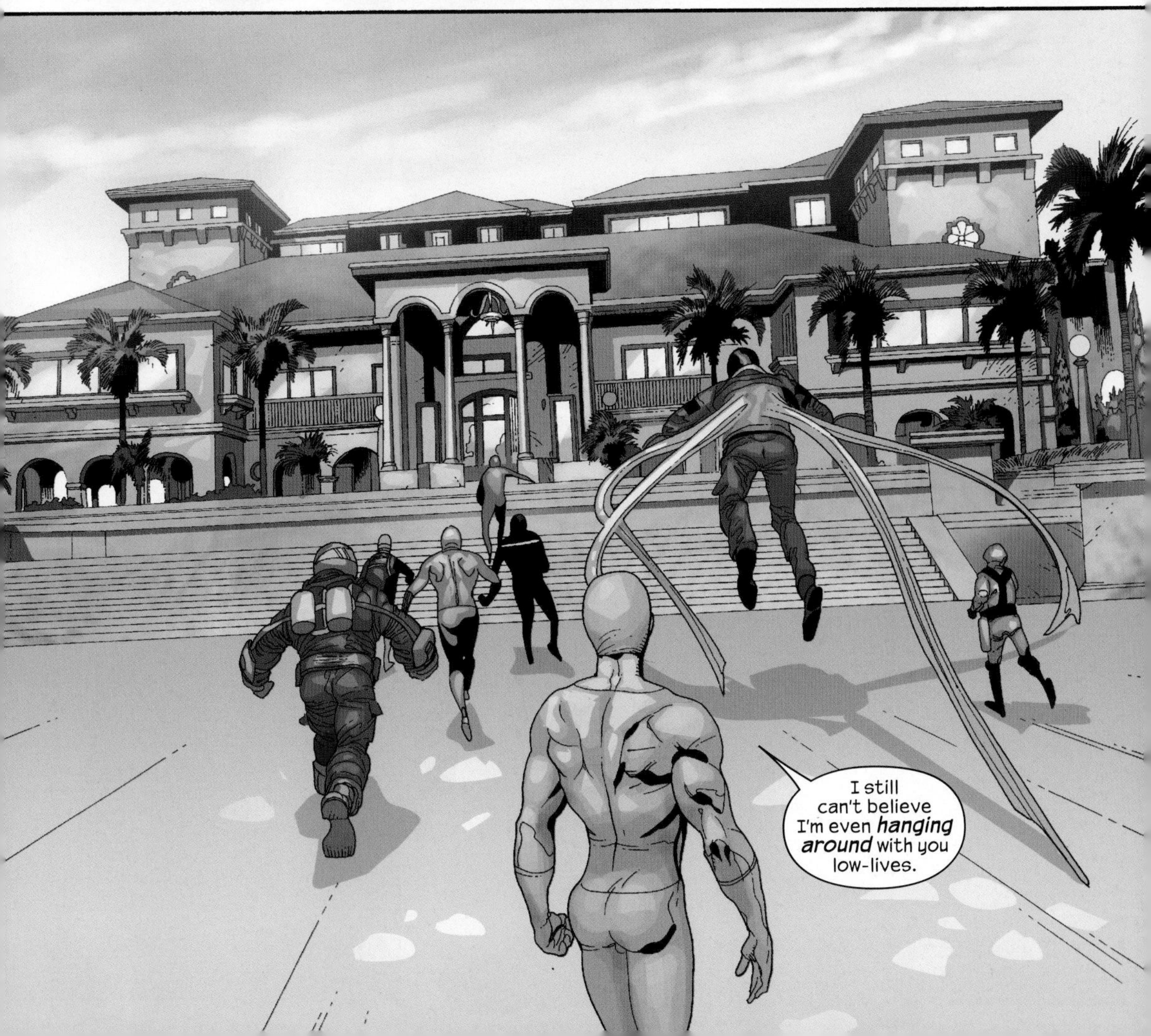
I still can't believe I'm even ***hanging around*** with you low-lives.

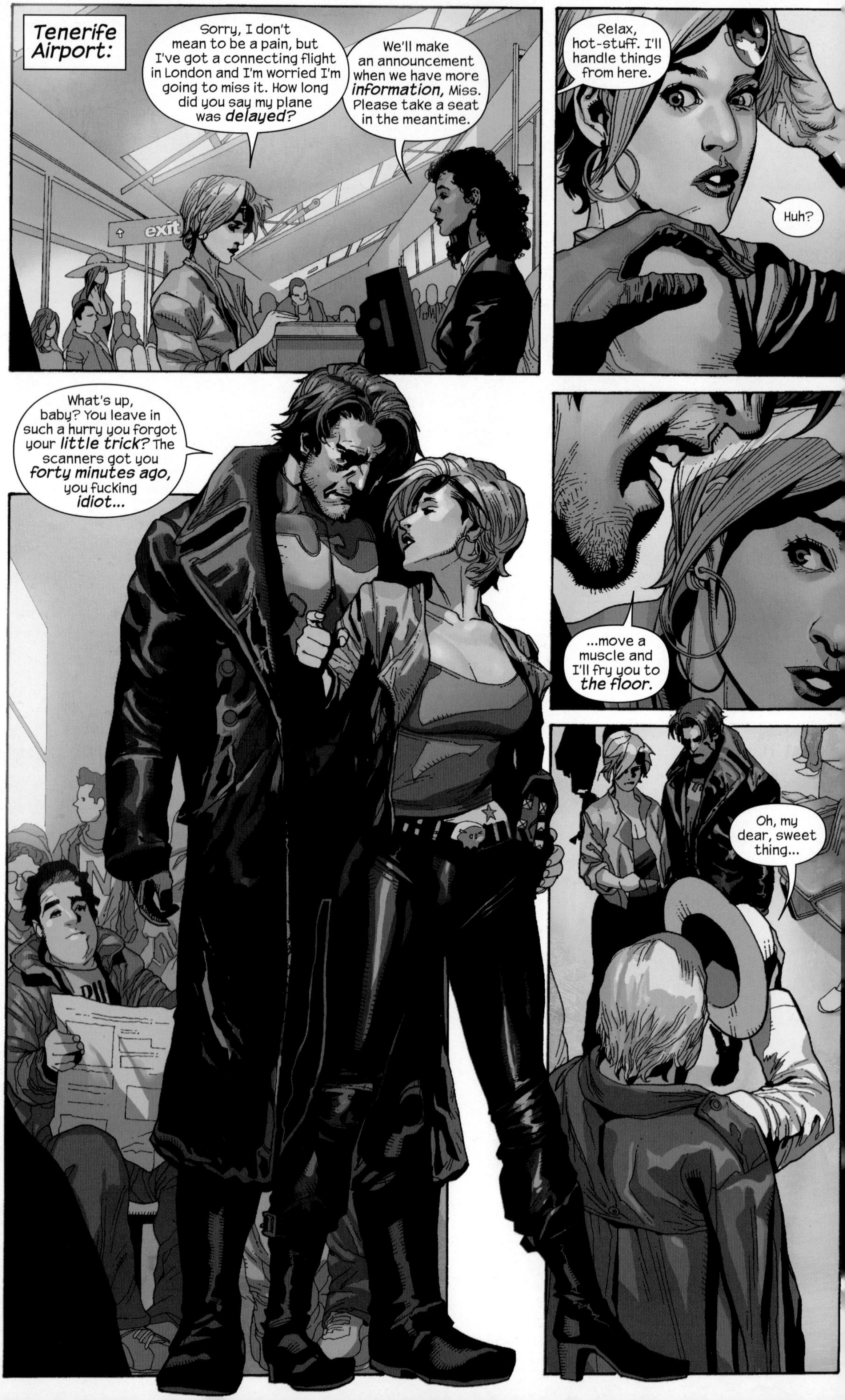
Tenerife Airport:
Sorry, I don't mean to be a pain, but I've got a connecting flight in London and I'm worried I'm going to miss it. How long did you say my plane was delayed?
We'll make an announcement when we have more information, Miss. Please take a seat in the meantime.
Relax, hot-stuff. I'll handle things from here.
Huh?
exit
What's up, baby? You leave in such a hurry you forgot your little trick? The scanners got you forty minutes ago, you fucking idiot...
...move a muscle and I'll fry you to the floor.
Oh, my dear, sweet thing...

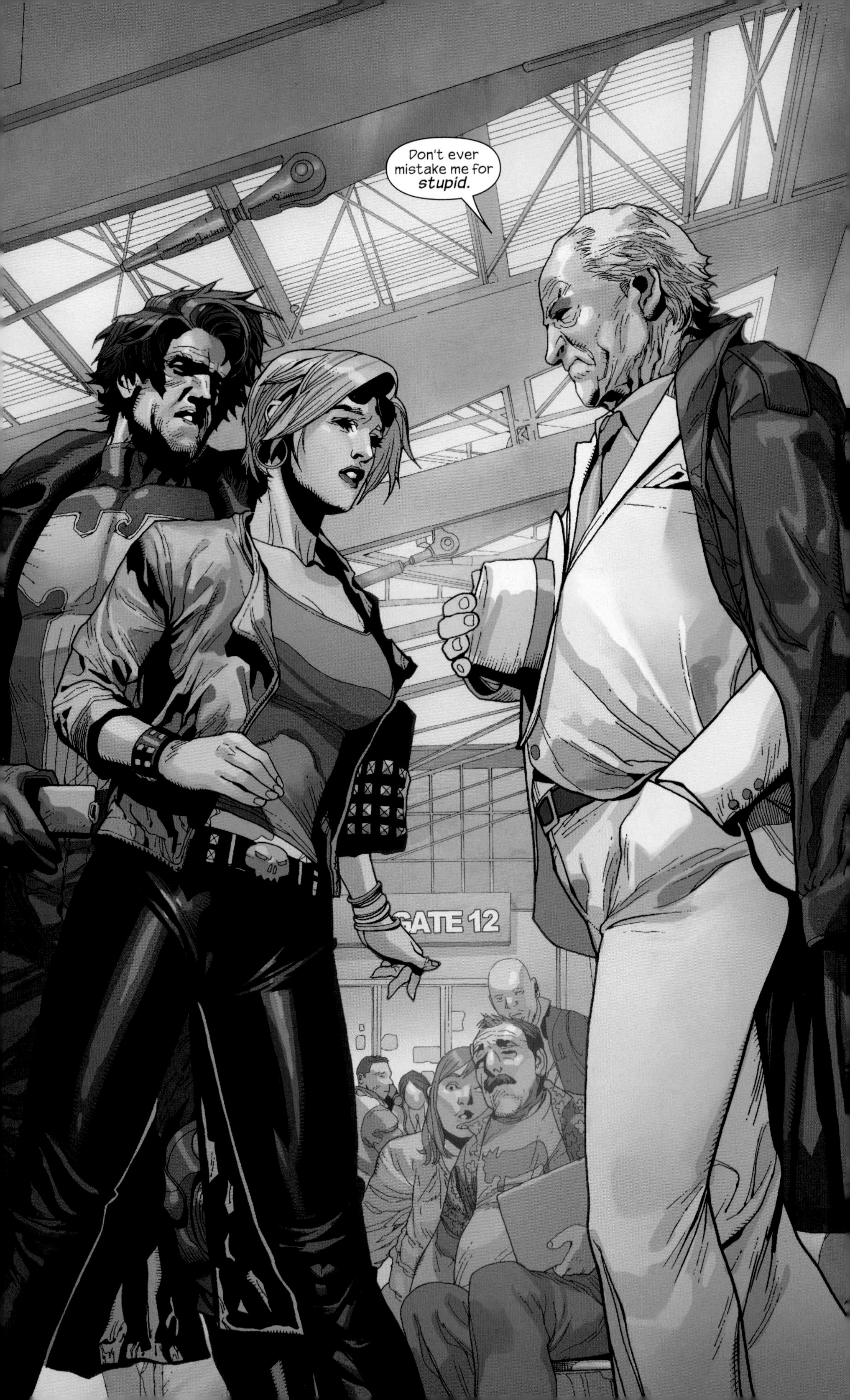
Don't ever mistake me for *stupid*.
GATE 12

# FOUR

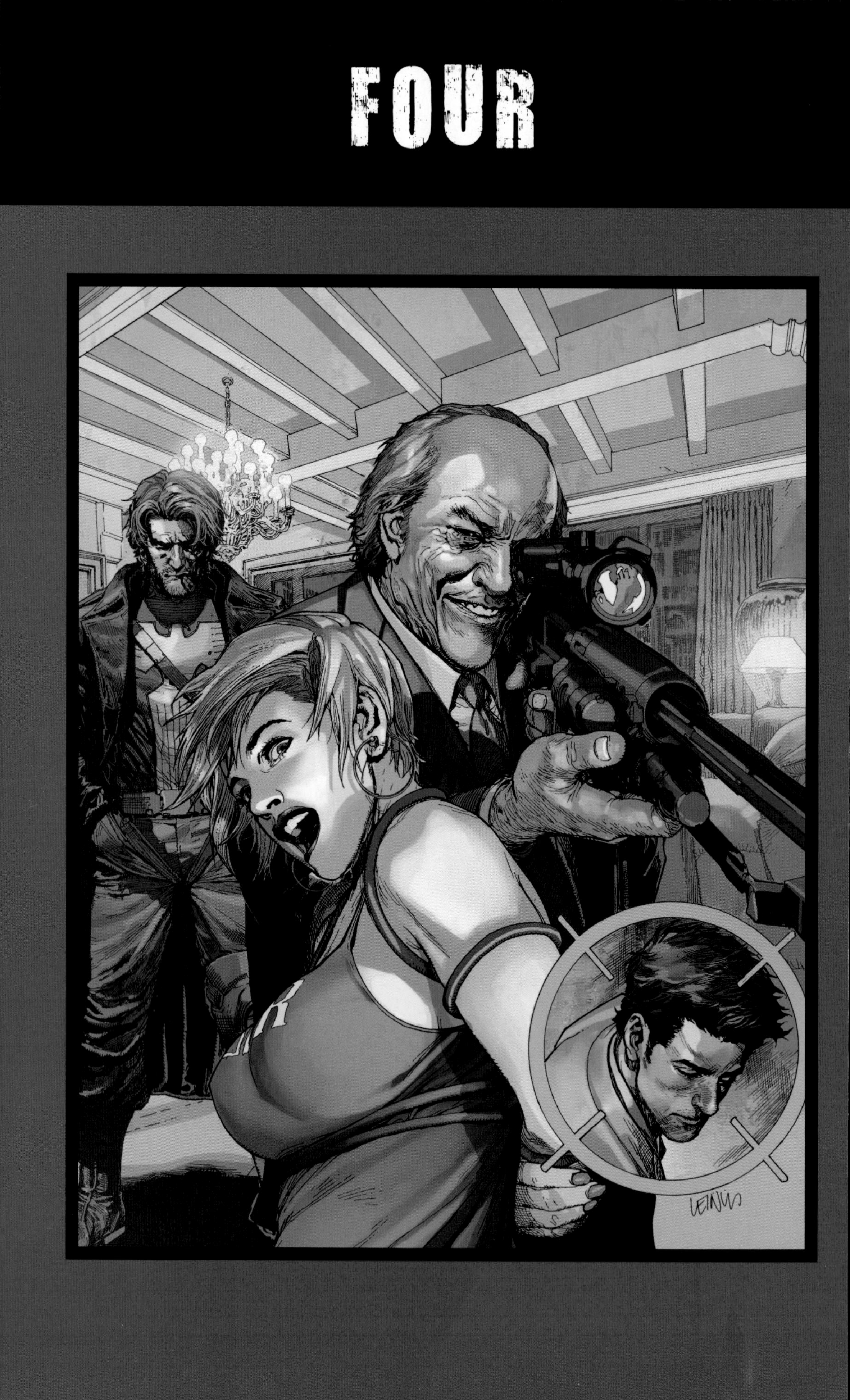

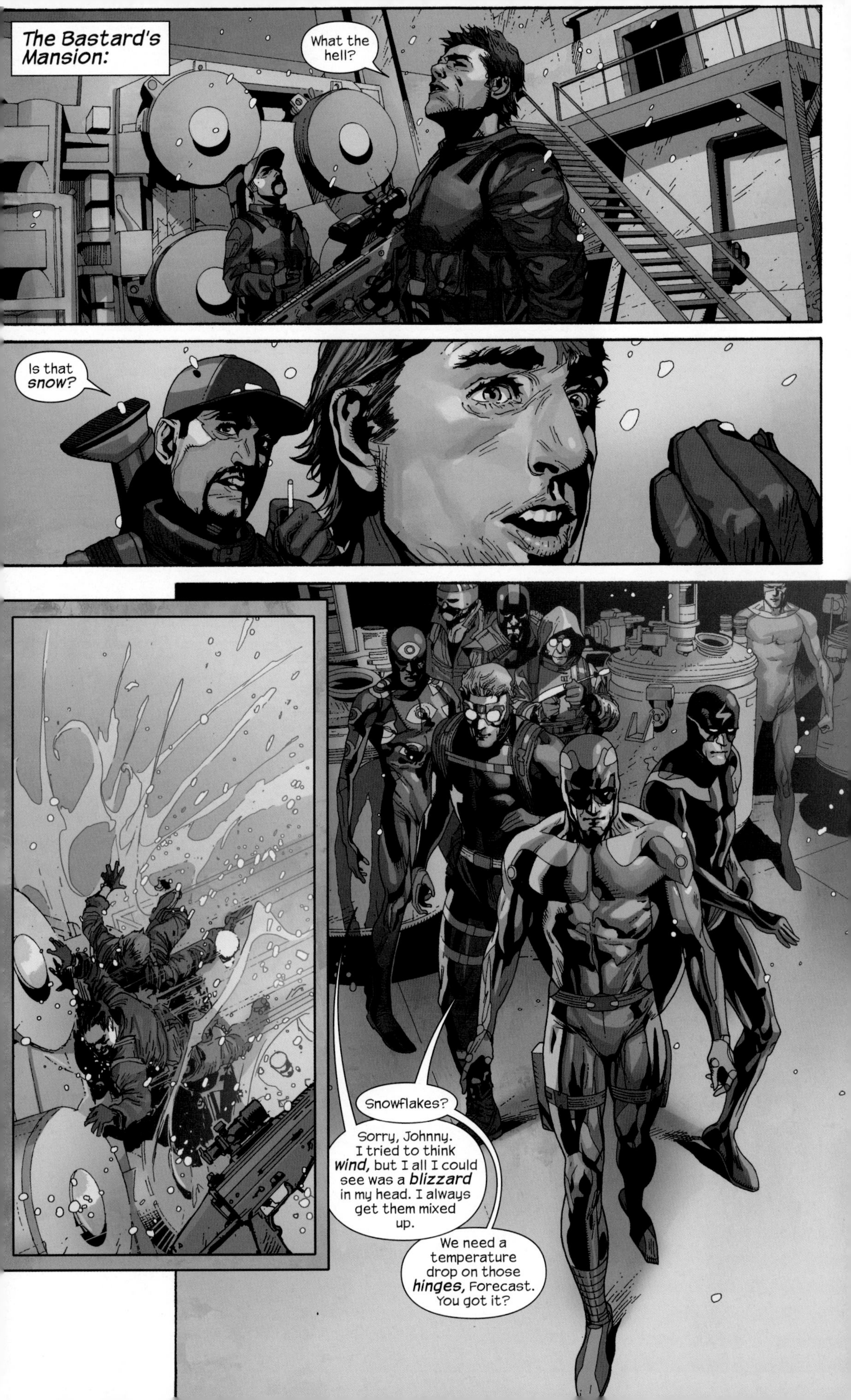
The Bastard's Mansion:
What the hell?
Is that snow?
Snowflakes?
Sorry, Johnny. I tried to think wind, but I all I could see was a blizzard in my head. I always get them mixed up.
We need a temperature drop on those hinges, Forecast. You got it?

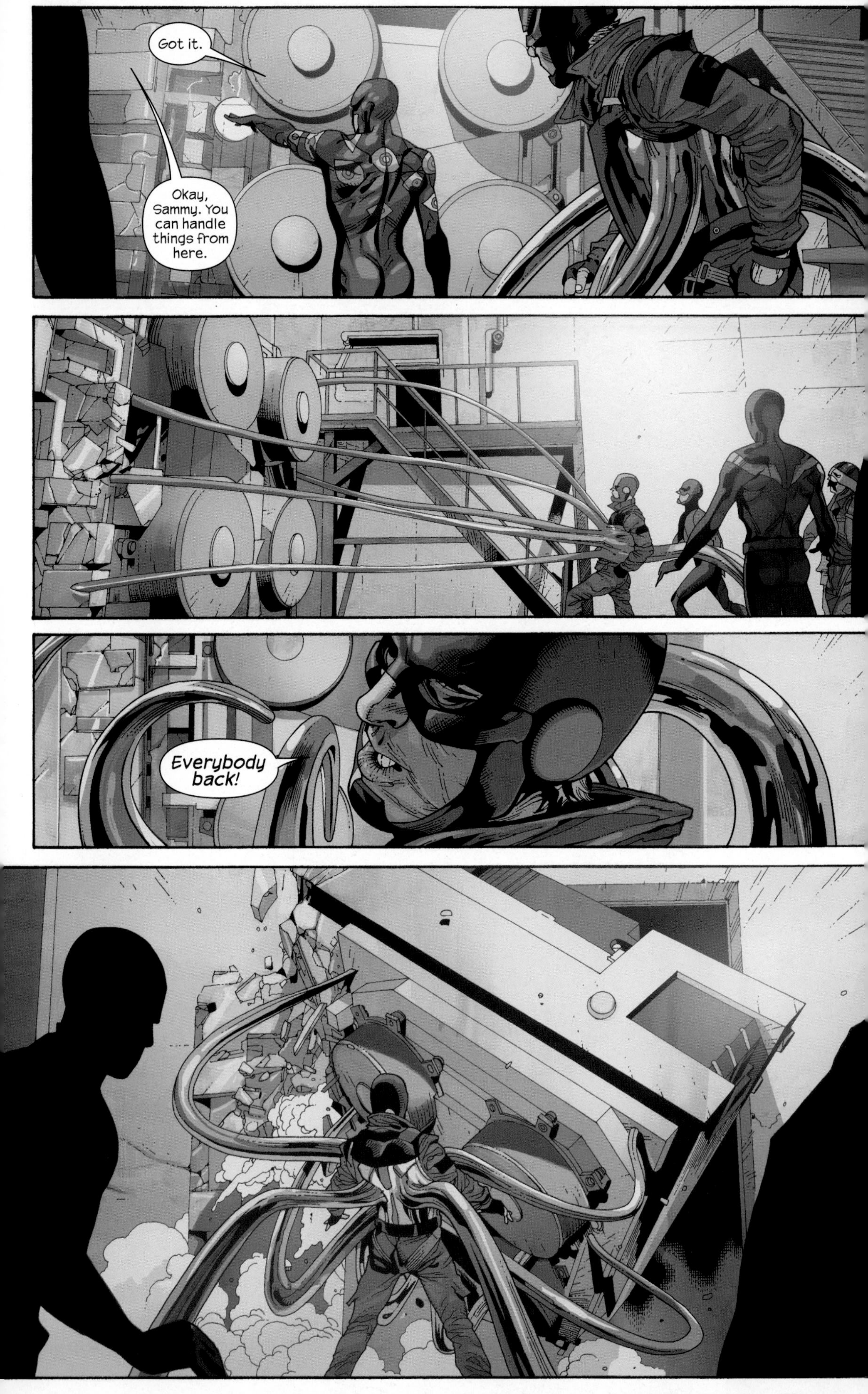
Got it.
Okay, Sammy. You can handle things from here.
Everybody back!

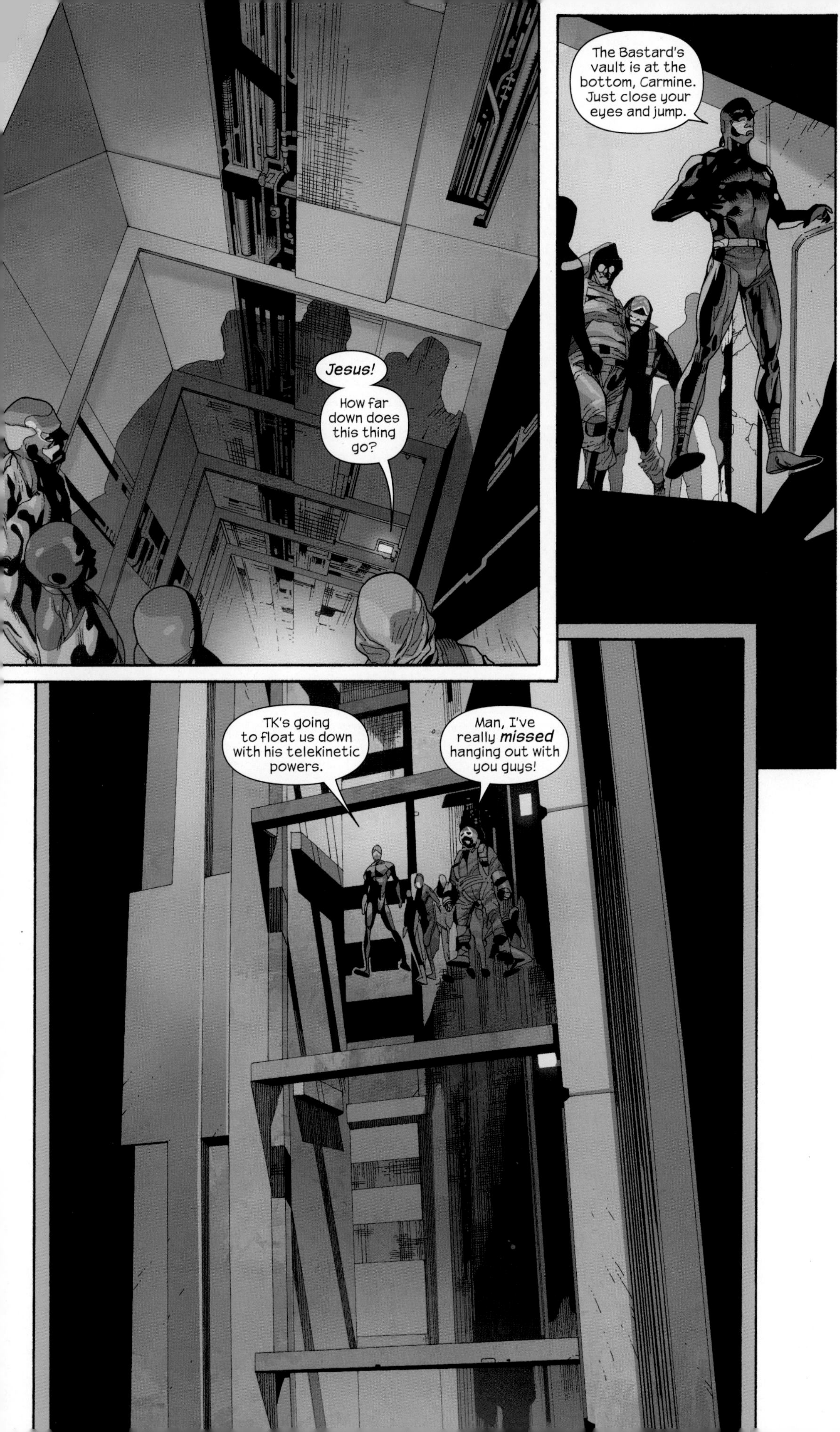
Jesus!
How far down does this thing go?
The Bastard's vault is at the bottom, Carmine. Just close your eyes and jump.
TK's going to float us down with his telekinetic powers.
Man, I've really *missed* hanging out with you guys!

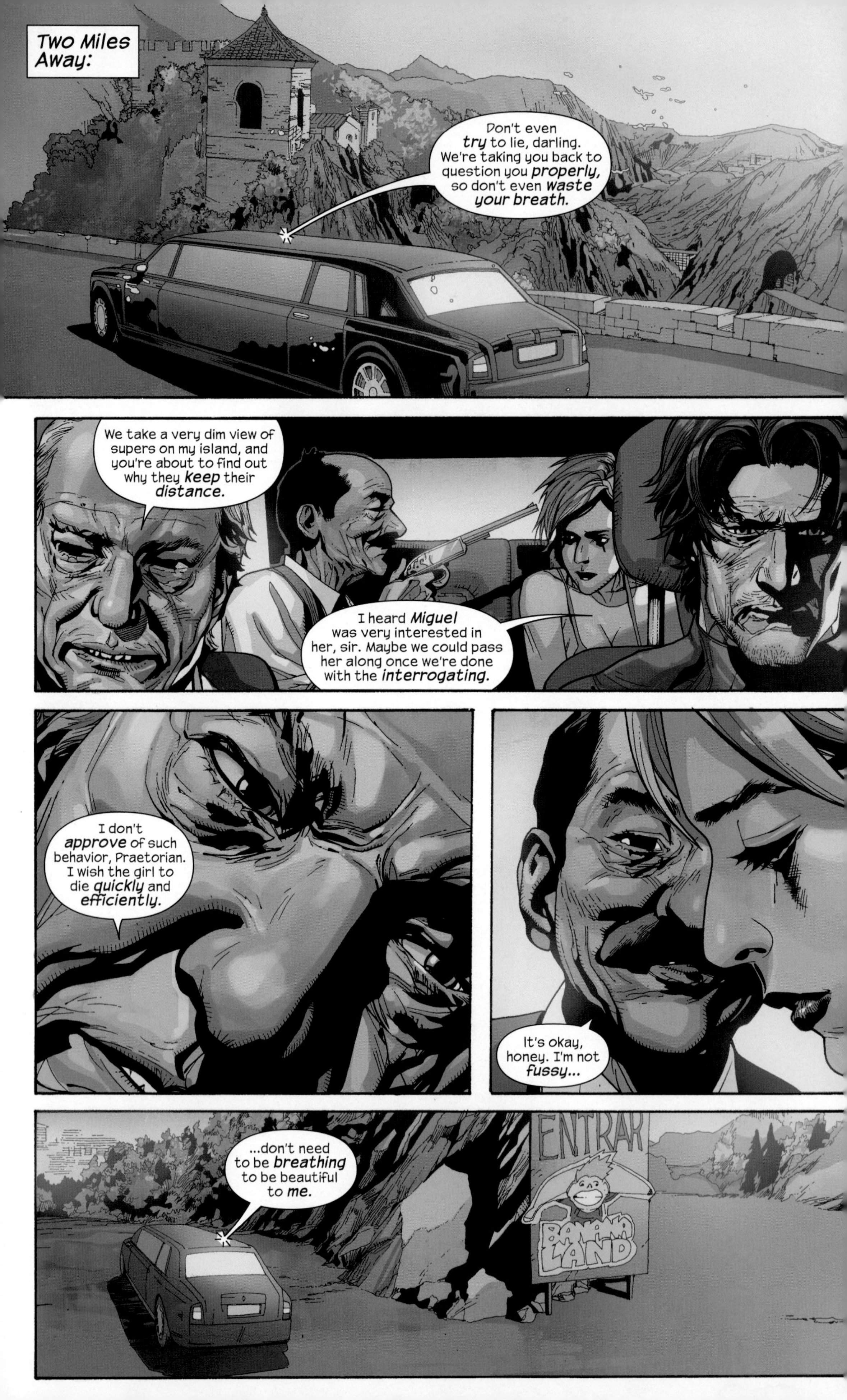
Two Miles Away:
Don't even try to lie, darling. We're taking you back to question you properly, so don't even waste your breath.
We take a very dim view of supers on my island, and you're about to find out why they keep their distance.
I heard Miguel was very interested in her, sir. Maybe we could pass her along once we're done with the interrogating.
I don't approve of such behavior, Praetorian. I wish the girl to die quickly and efficiently.
It's okay, honey. I'm not fussy...
...don't need to be breathing to be beautiful to me.
ENTRAR
BANANA LAND

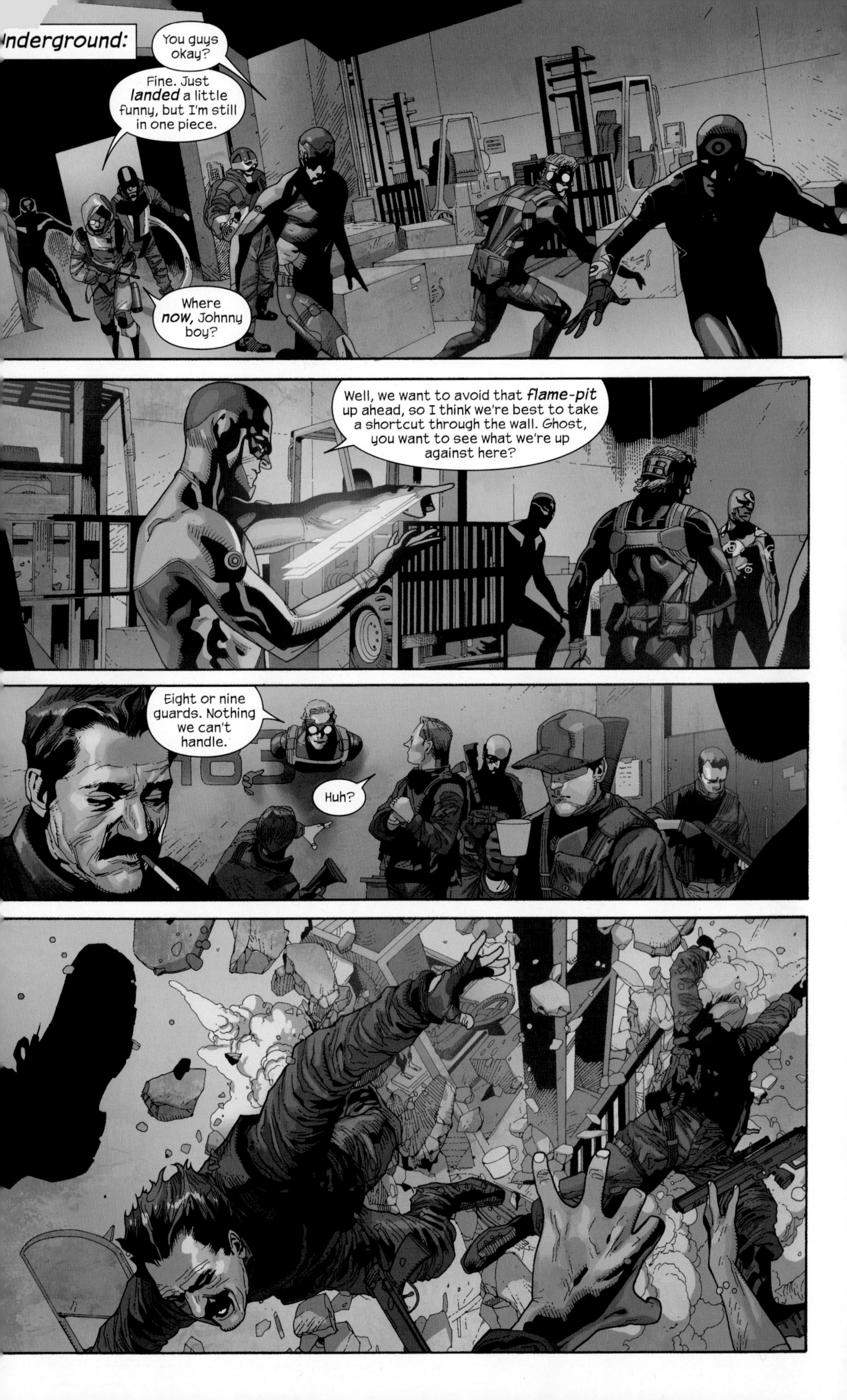
nderground:
You guys okay?
Fine. Just landed a little funny, but I'm still in one piece.
Where now, Johnny boy?
Well, we want to avoid that flame-pit up ahead, so I think we're best to take a shortcut through the wall. Ghost, you want to see what we're up against here?
Eight or nine guards. Nothing we can't handle.
Huh?

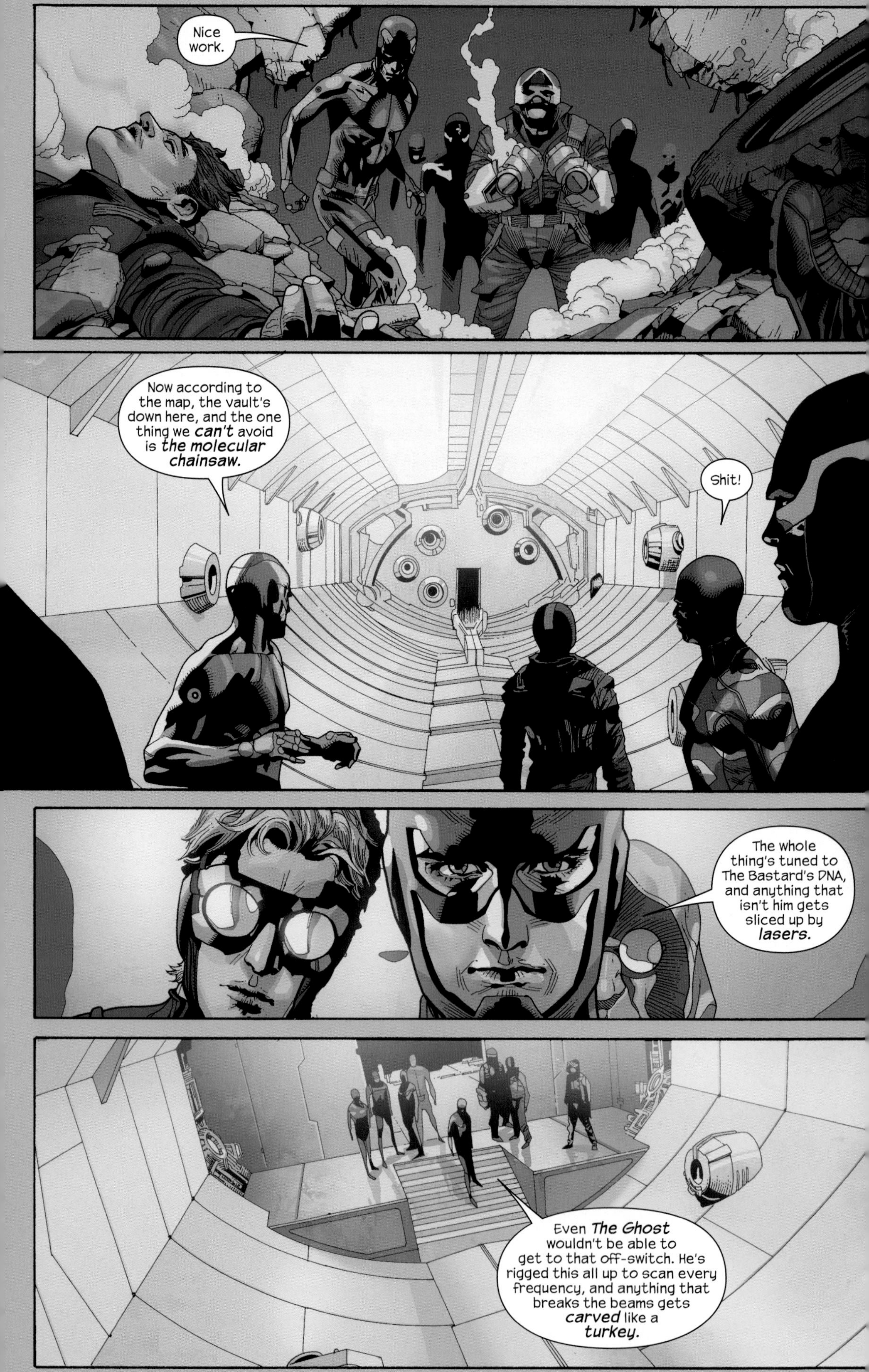
Nice work.
Now according to the map, the vault's down here, and the one thing we *can't* avoid is *the molecular chainsaw.*
Shit!
The whole thing's tuned to The Bastard's DNA, and anything that isn't him gets sliced up by *lasers.*
Even *The Ghost* wouldn't be able to get to that off-switch. He's rigged this all up to scan every frequency, and anything that breaks the beams gets *carved* like a *turkey.*

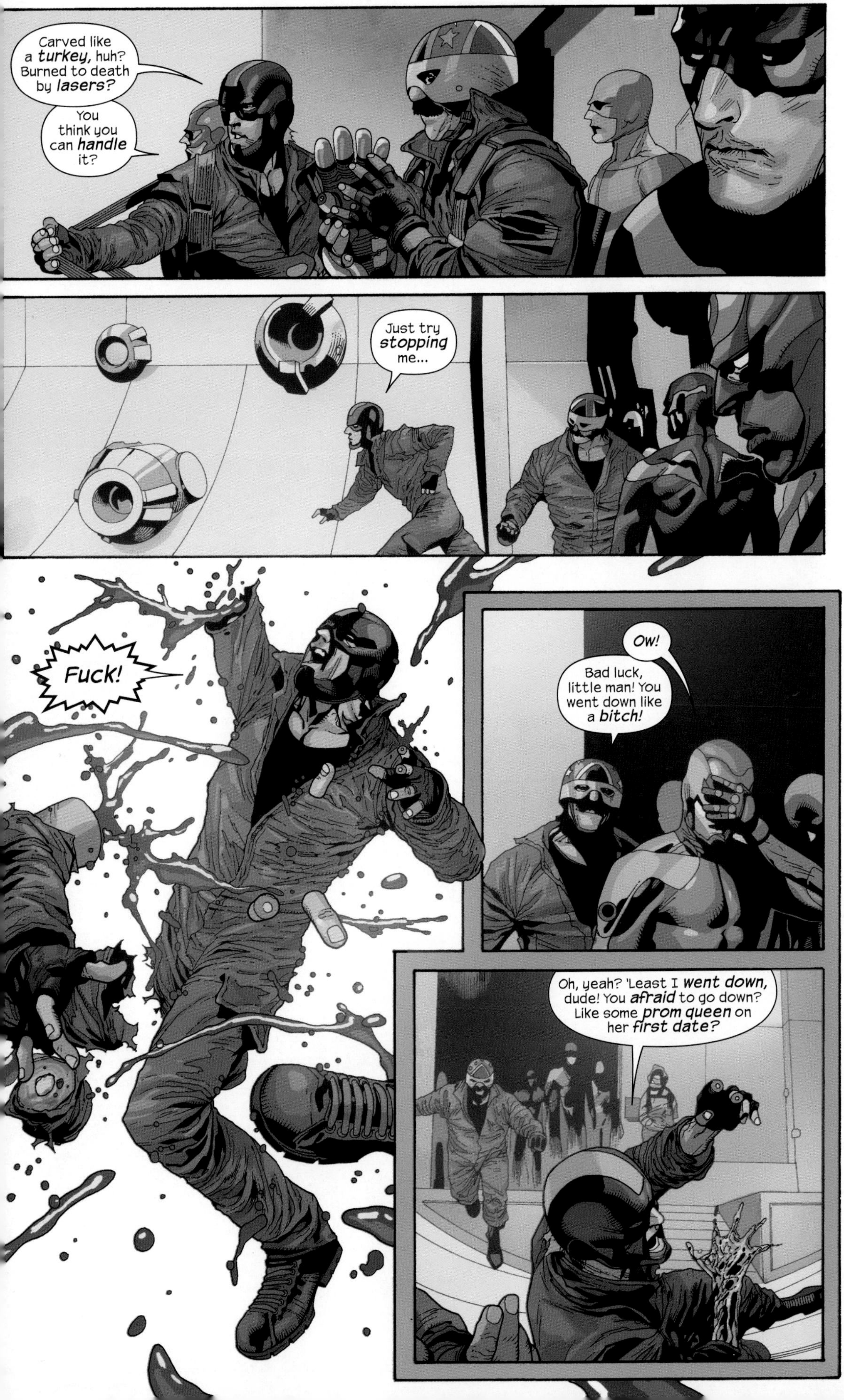
Carved like a turkey, huh? Burned to death by lasers?
You think you can handle it?
Just try stopping me...
Fuck!
Ow!
Bad luck, little man! You went down like a bitch!
Oh, yeah? 'Least I went down, dude! You afraid to go down? Like some prom queen on her first date?

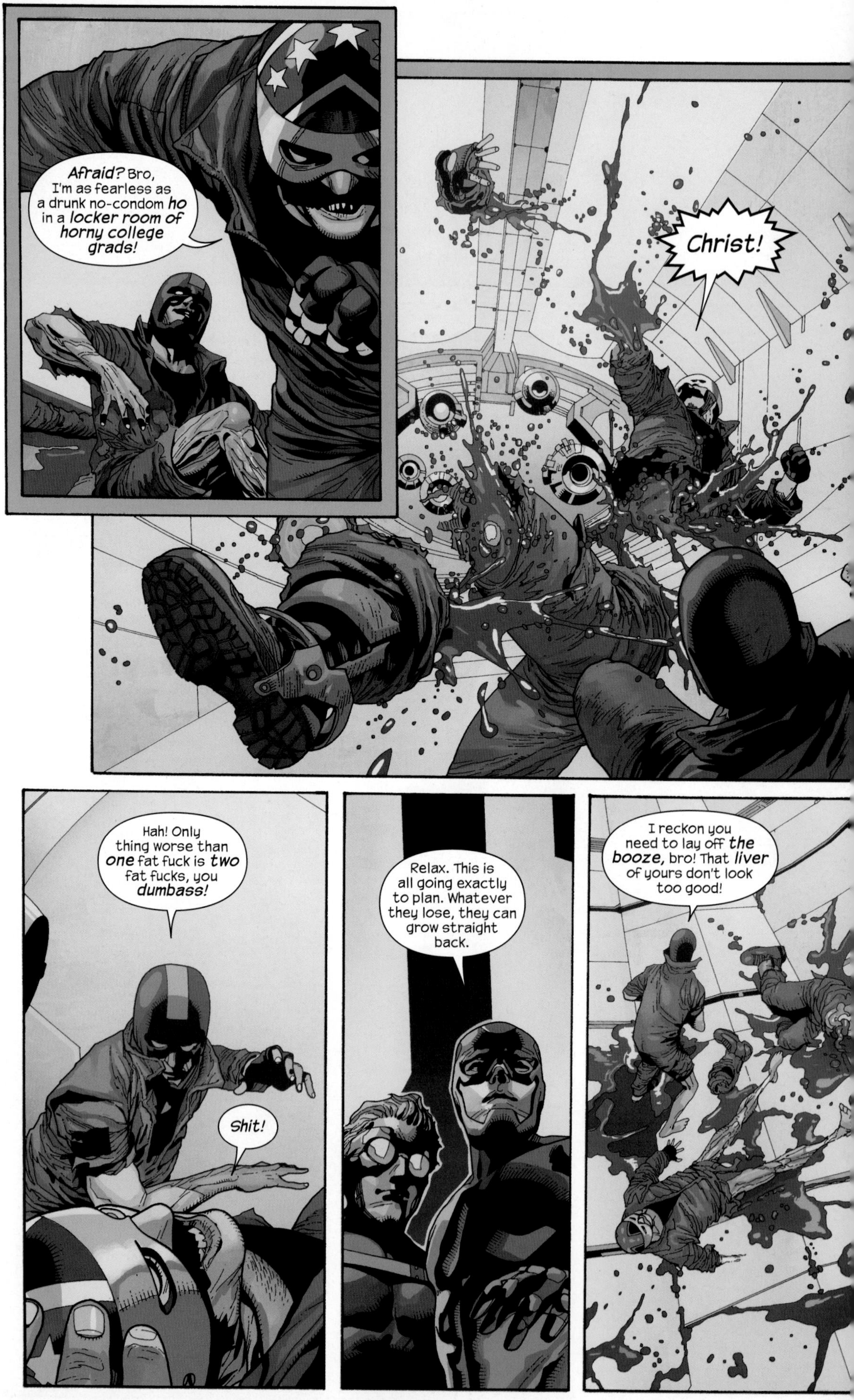
Afraid? Bro, I'm as fearless as a drunk no-condom ho in a locker room of horny college grads!
Christ!
Hah! Only thing worse than one fat fuck is two fat fucks, you dumbass!
Shit!
Relax. This is all going exactly to plan. Whatever they lose, they can grow straight back.
I reckon you need to lay off the booze, bro! That liver of yours don't look too good!

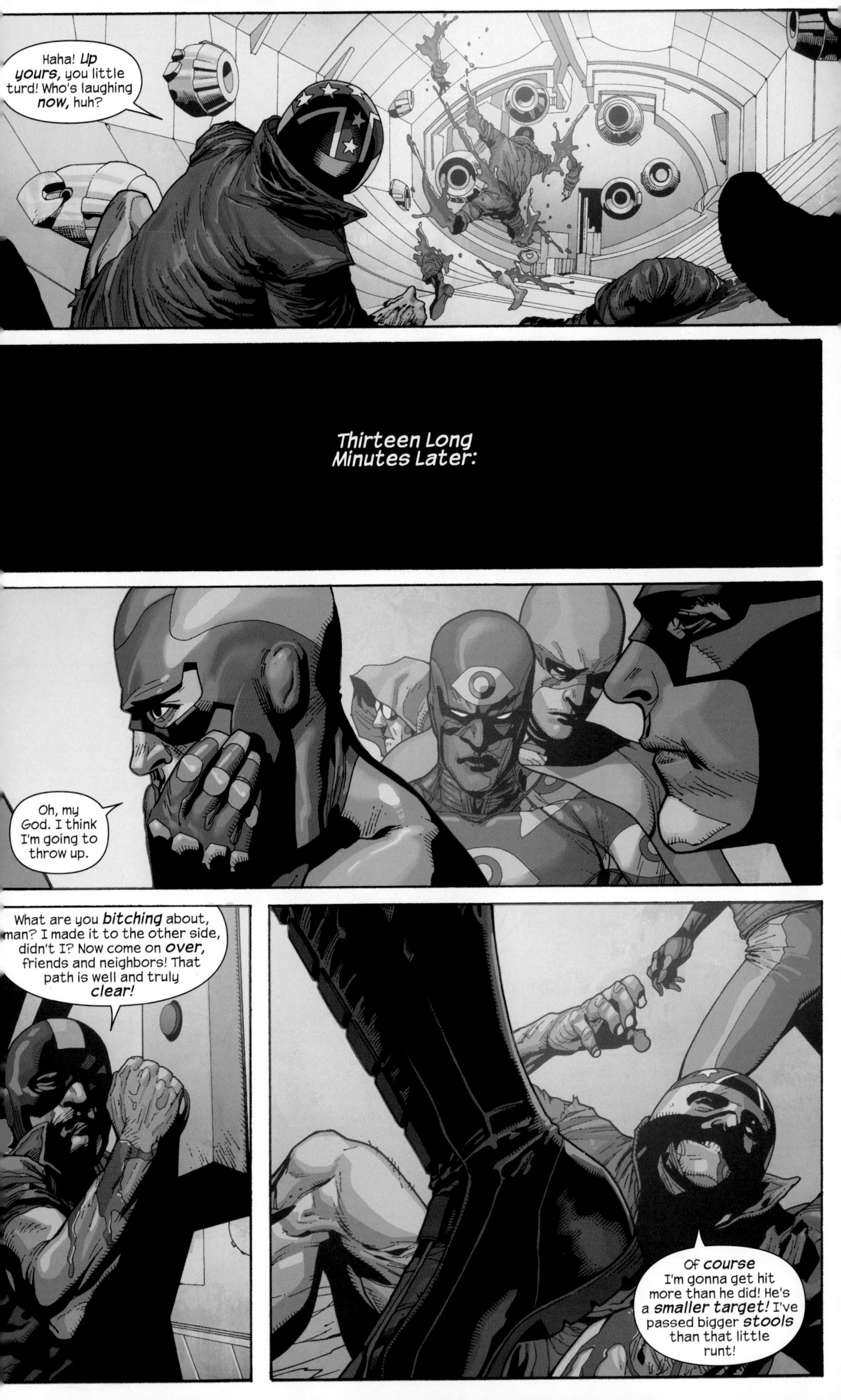

Haha! Up yours, you little turd! Who's laughing now, huh?
Thirteen Long Minutes Later:
Oh, my God. I think I'm going to throw up.
What are you bitching about, man? I made it to the other side, didn't I? Now come on over, friends and neighbors! That path is well and truly clear!
Of course I'm gonna get hit more than he did! He's a smaller target! I've passed bigger stools than that little runt!

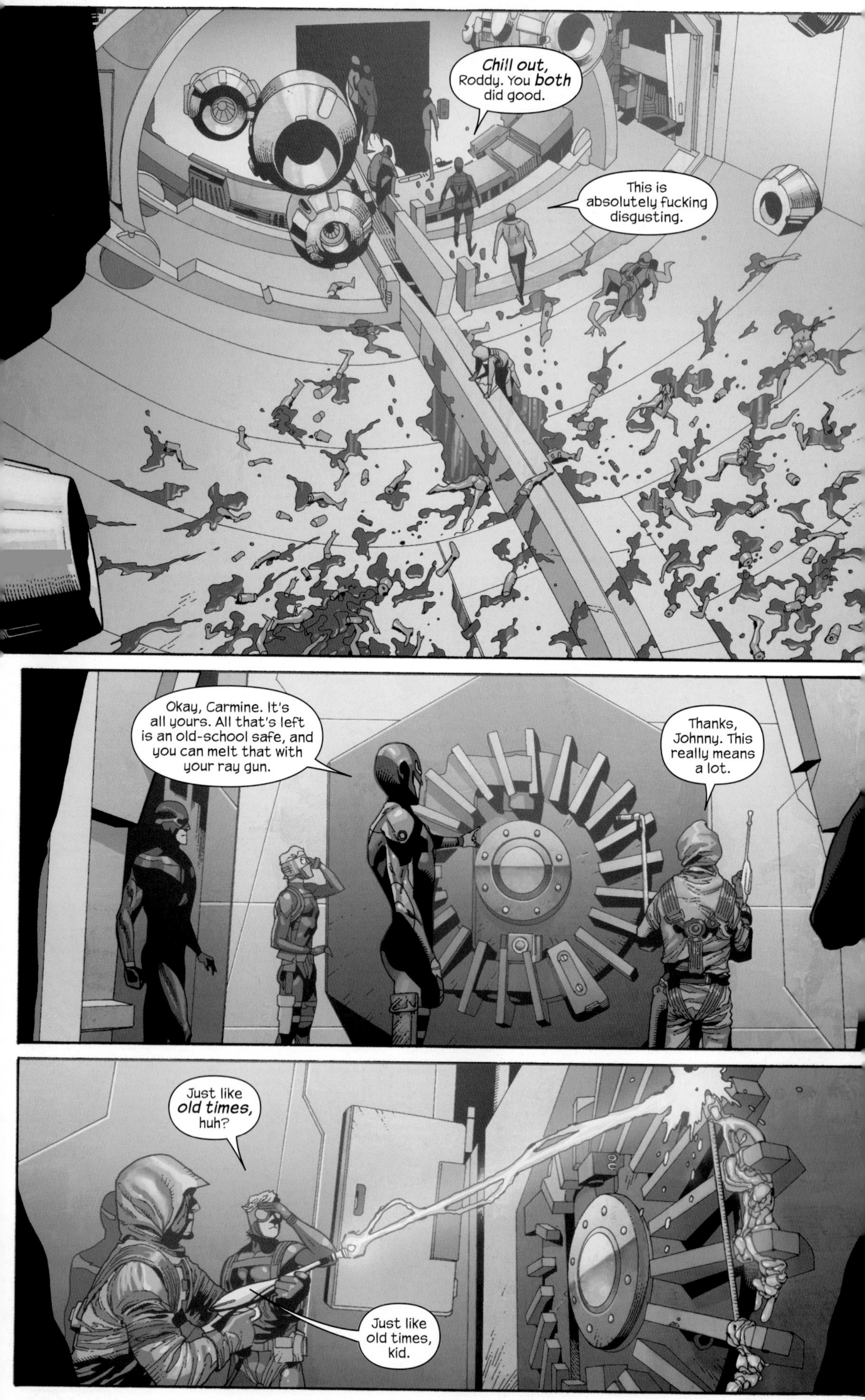

*Chill out,* Roddy. You **both** did good.
This is absolutely fucking disgusting.
Okay, Carmine. It's all yours. All that's left is an old-school safe, and you can melt that with your ray gun.
Thanks, Johnny. This really means a lot.
Just like ***old times,*** huh?
Just like old times, kid.

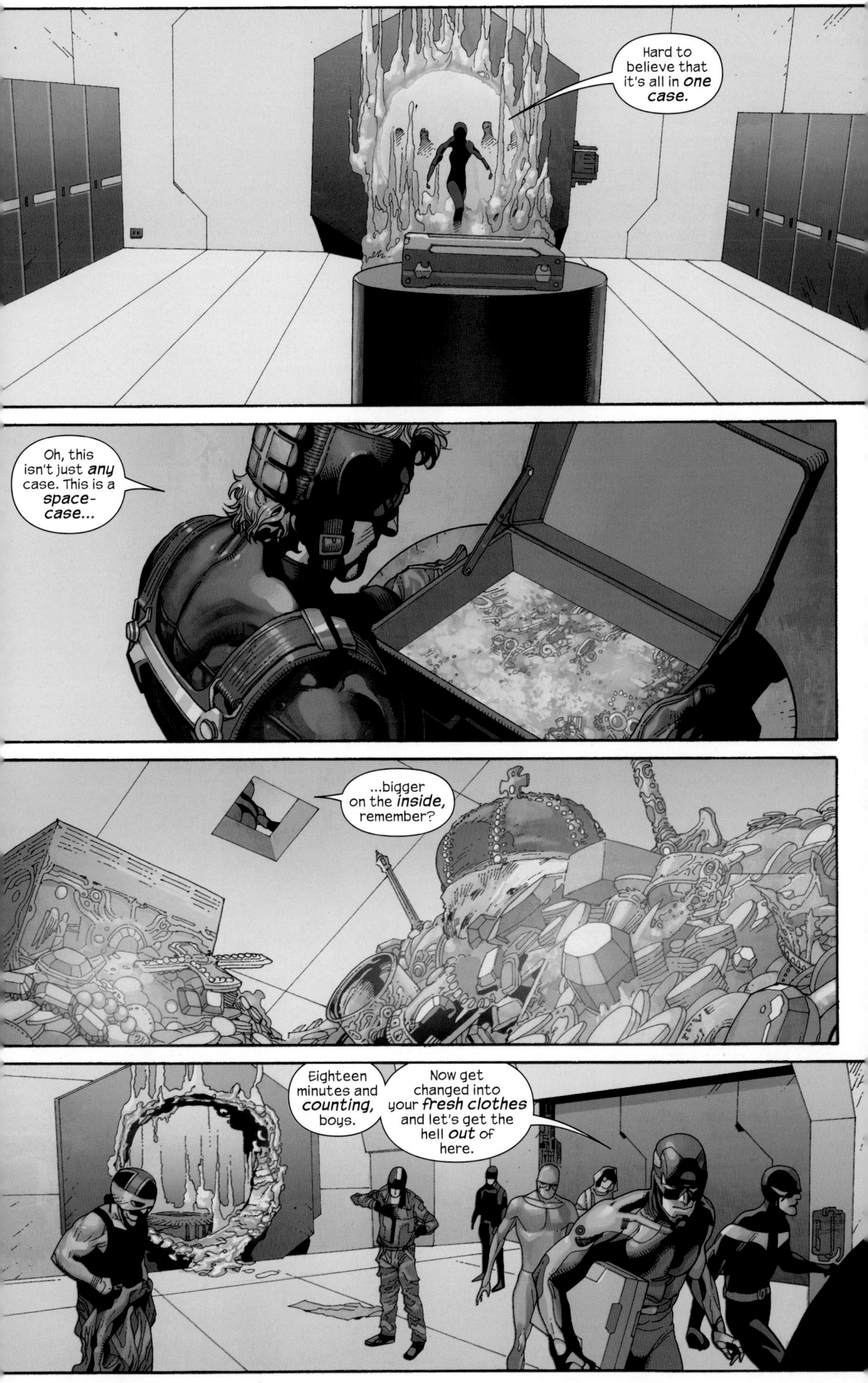
Hard to believe that it's all in *one case.*
Oh, this isn't just *any* case. This is a *space-case...*
...bigger on the *inside,* remember?
Eighteen minutes and *counting,* boys.
Now get changed into your *fresh clothes* and let's get the hell *out* of here.

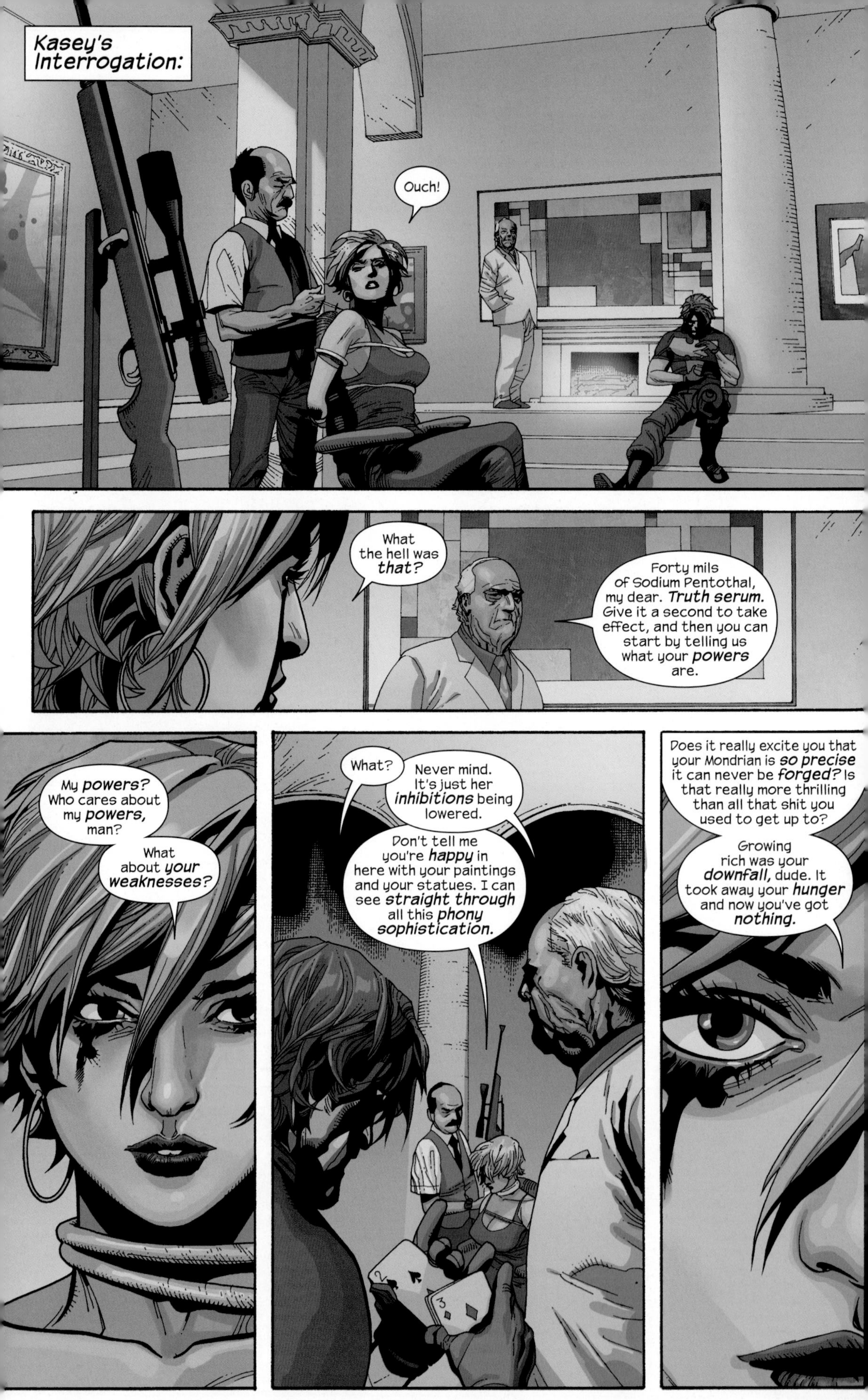

Kasey's Interrogation:
Ouch!
What the hell was that?
Forty mils of Sodium Pentothal, my dear. Truth serum. Give it a second to take effect, and then you can start by telling us what your powers are.
My powers? Who cares about my powers, man?
What about your weaknesses?
What?
Never mind. It's just her inhibitions being lowered.
Don't tell me you're happy in here with your paintings and your statues. I can see straight through all this phony sophistication.
Does it really excite you that your Mondrian is so precise it can never be forged? Is that really more thrilling than all that shit you used to get up to?
Growing rich was your downfall, dude. It took away your hunger and now you've got nothing.

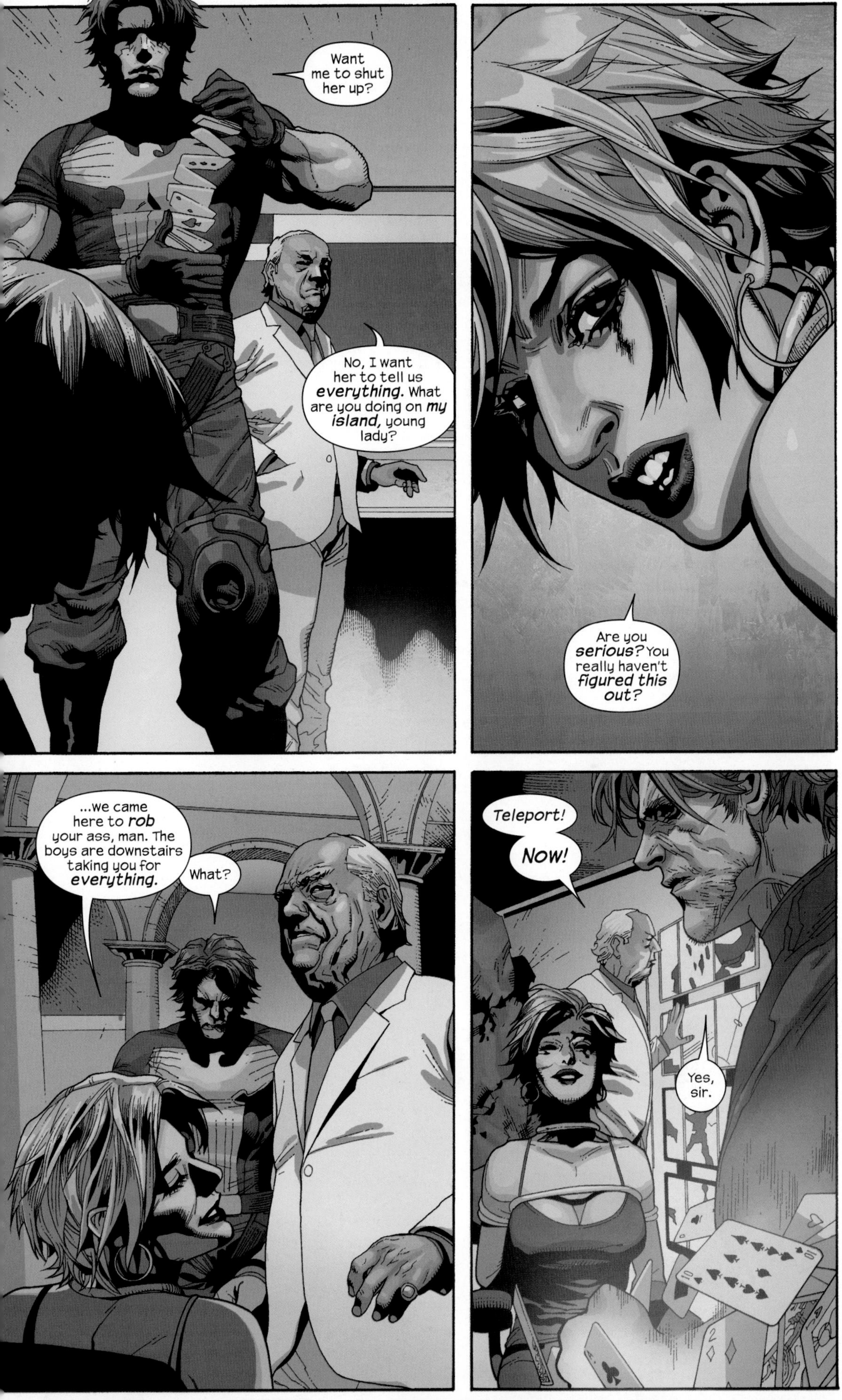
Want me to shut her up?
No, I want her to tell us *everything.* What are you doing on *my island,* young lady?
Are you *serious?* You really haven't *figured this out?*
...we came here to *rob* your ass, man. The boys are downstairs taking you for *everything.*
What?
*Teleport!*
*Now!*
Yes, sir.

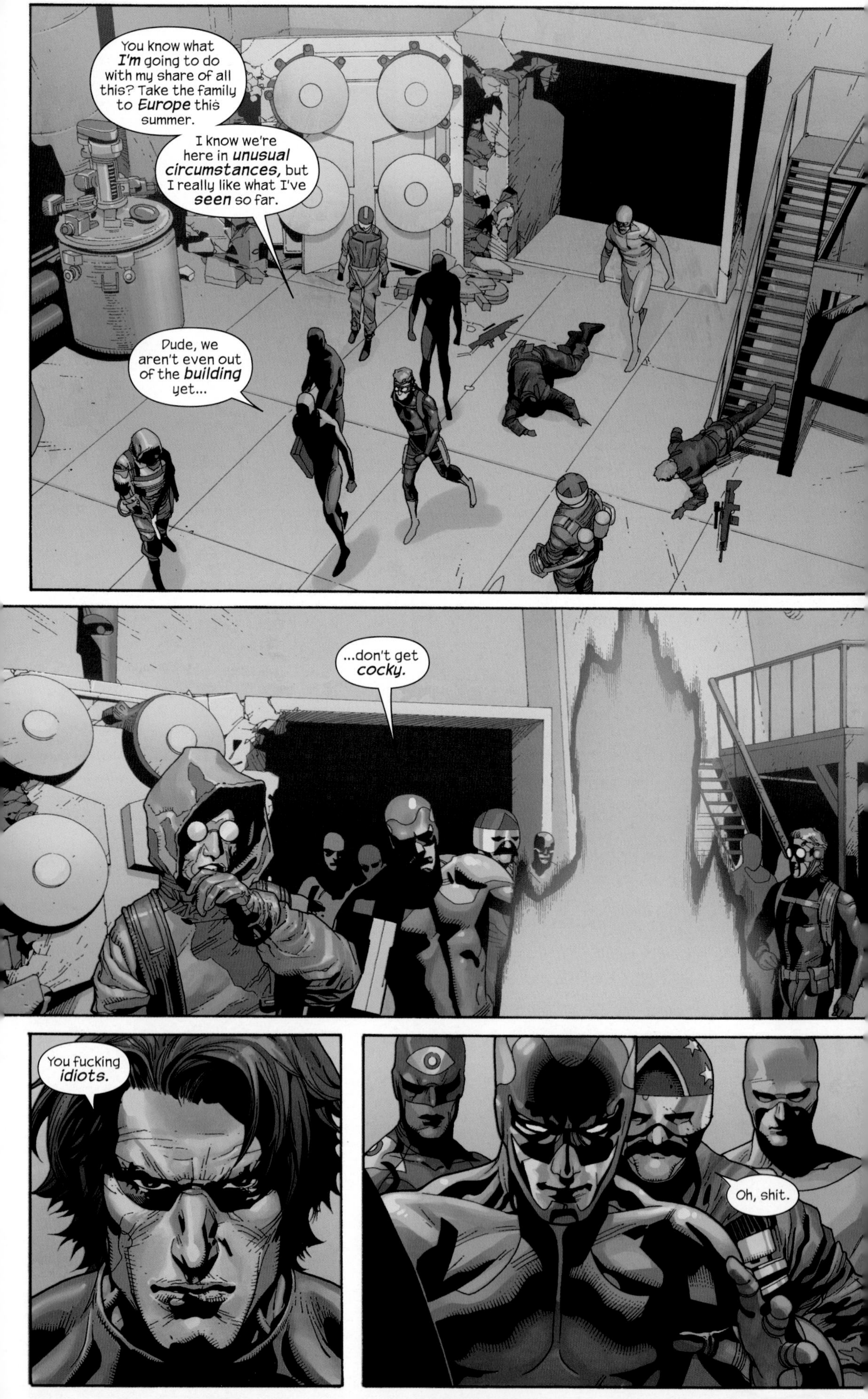

You know what *I'm* going to do with my share of all this? Take the family to *Europe* this summer.
I know we're here in *unusual circumstances,* but I really like what I've *seen* so far.
Dude, we aren't even out of the *building* yet...
...don't get *cocky.*
You fucking *idiots.*
Oh, shit.

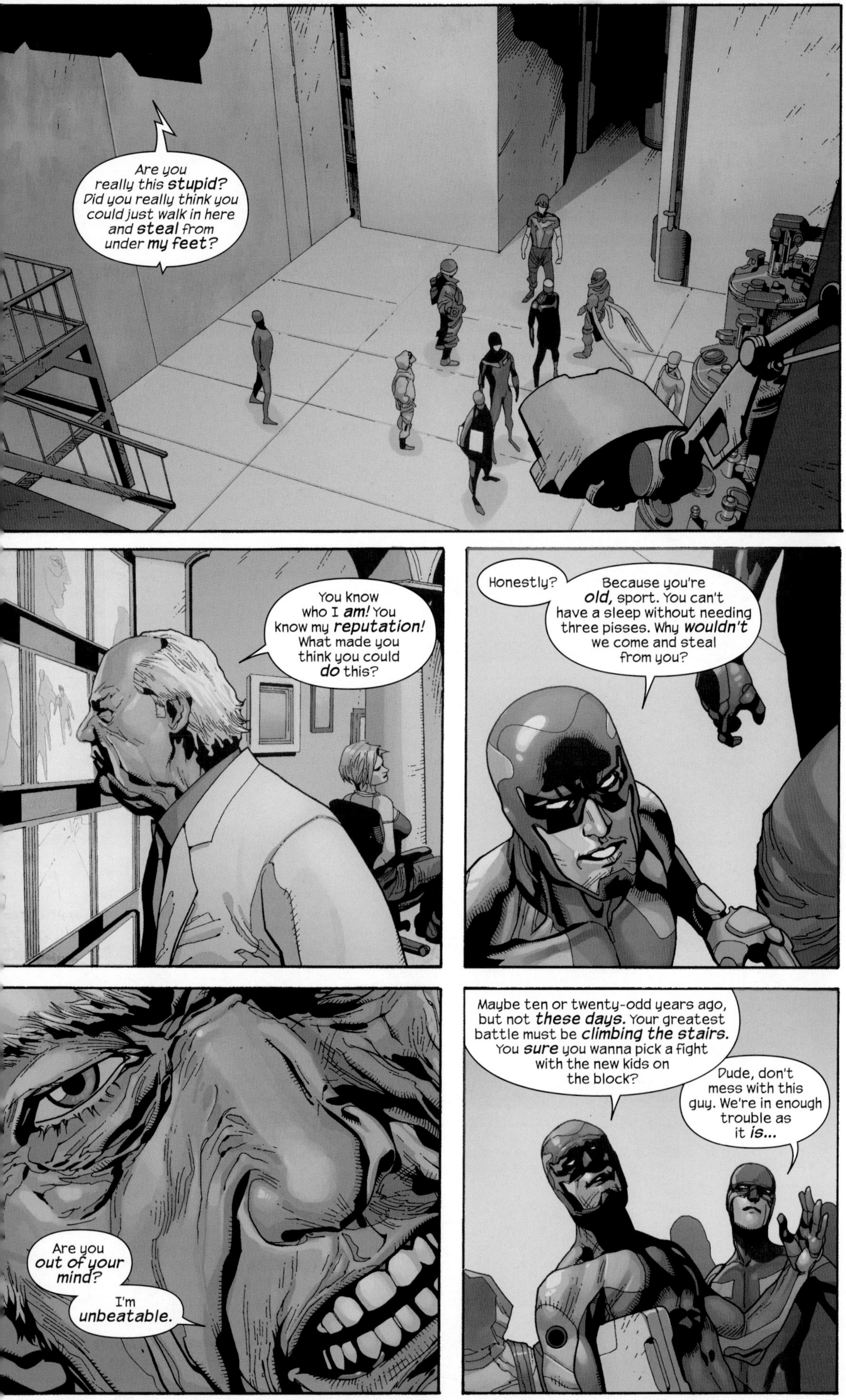
Are you really this stupid? Did you really think you could just walk in here and steal from under my feet?
You know who I am! You know my reputation! What made you think you could do this?
Honestly?
Because you're old, sport. You can't have a sleep without needing three pisses. Why wouldn't we come and steal from you?
Are you out of your mind?
I'm unbeatable.
Maybe ten or twenty-odd years ago, but not these days. Your greatest battle must be climbing the stairs. You sure you wanna pick a fight with the new kids on the block?
Dude, don't mess with this guy. We're in enough trouble as it is...

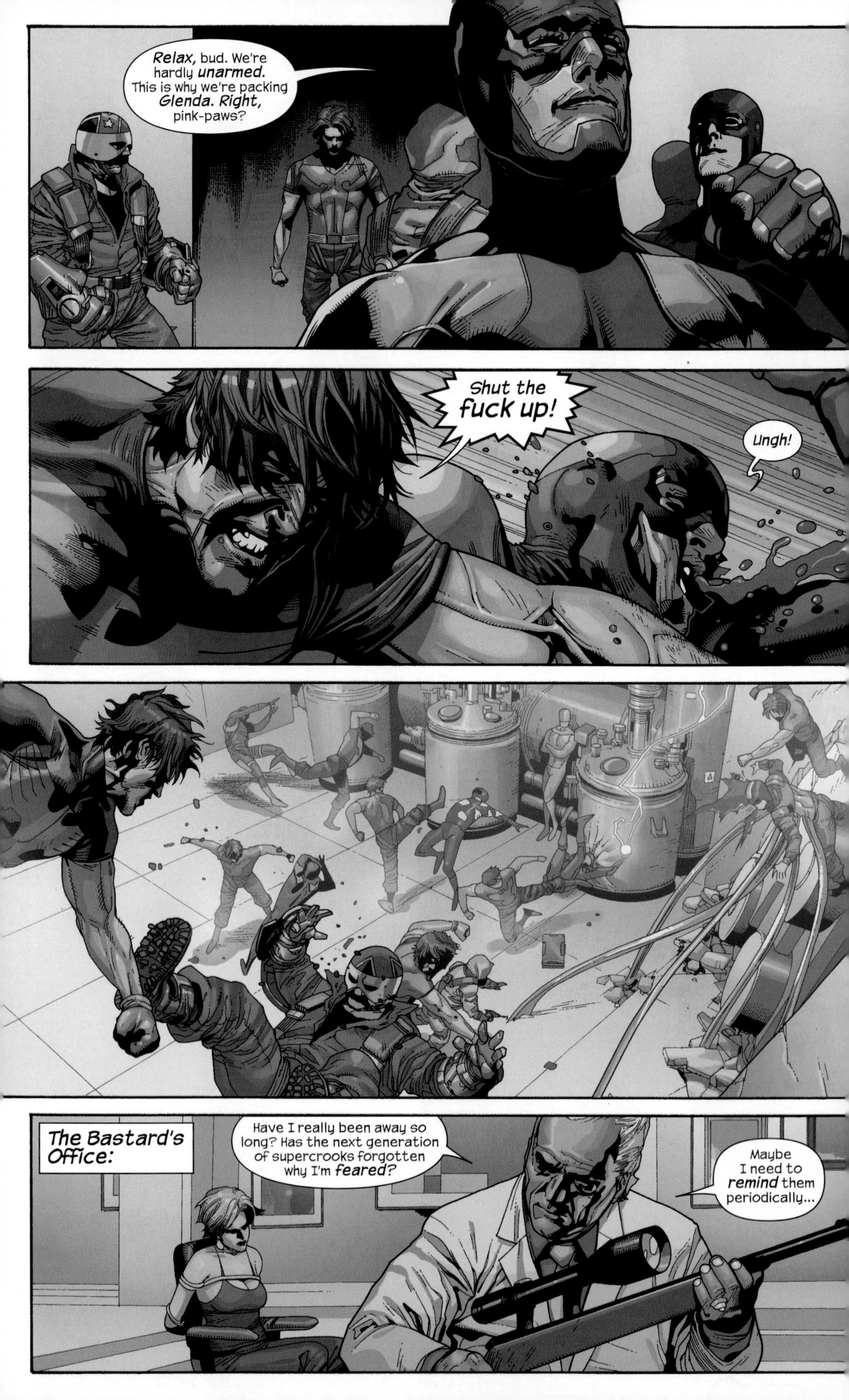
Relax, bud. We're hardly unarmed. This is why we're packing Glenda. Right, pink-paws?
Shut the fuck up!
Ungh!
The Bastard's Office:
Have I really been away so long? Has the next generation of supercrooks forgotten why I'm feared?
Maybe I need to remind them periodically...

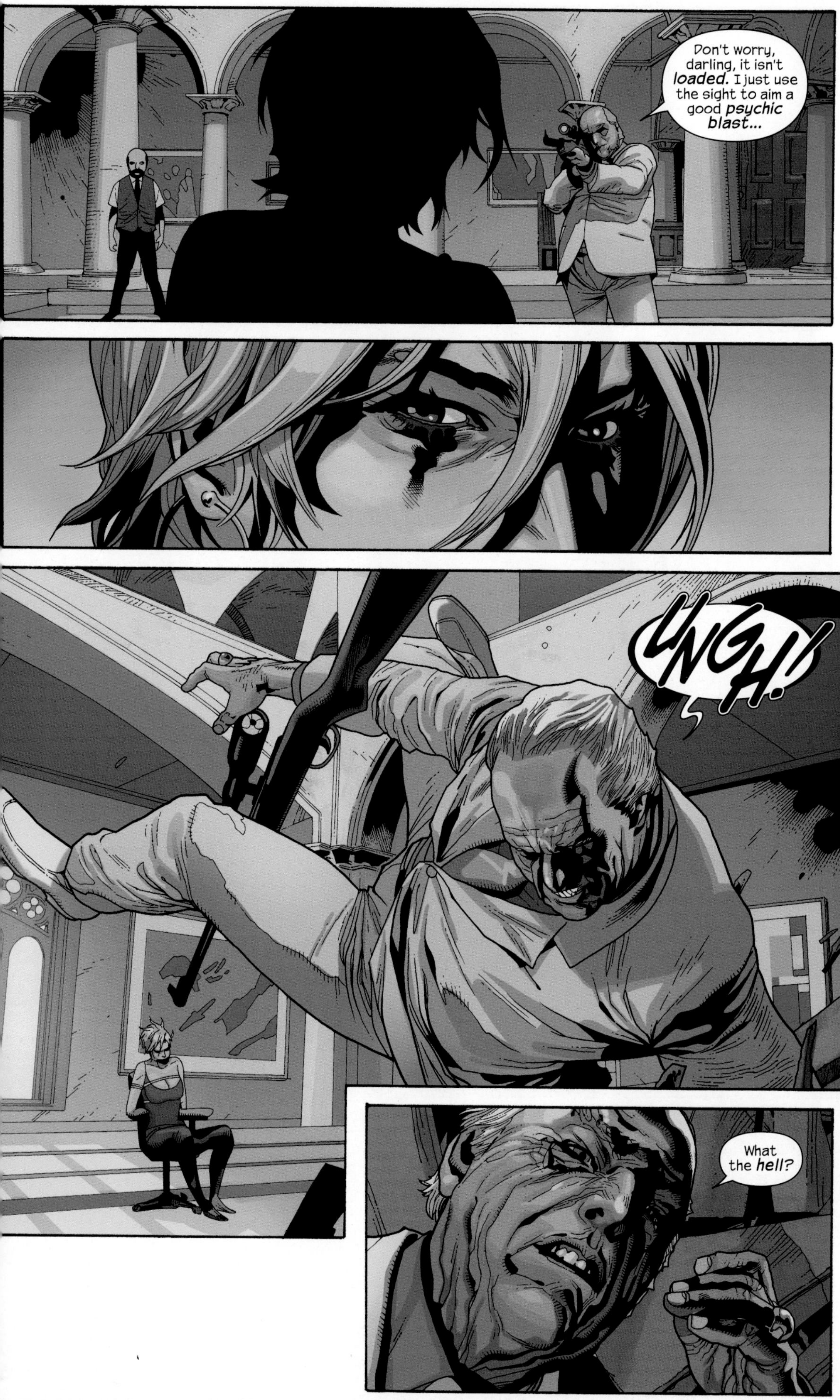
Don't worry, darling, it isn't loaded. I just use the sight to aim a good psychic blast...
UNGH!
What the hell?

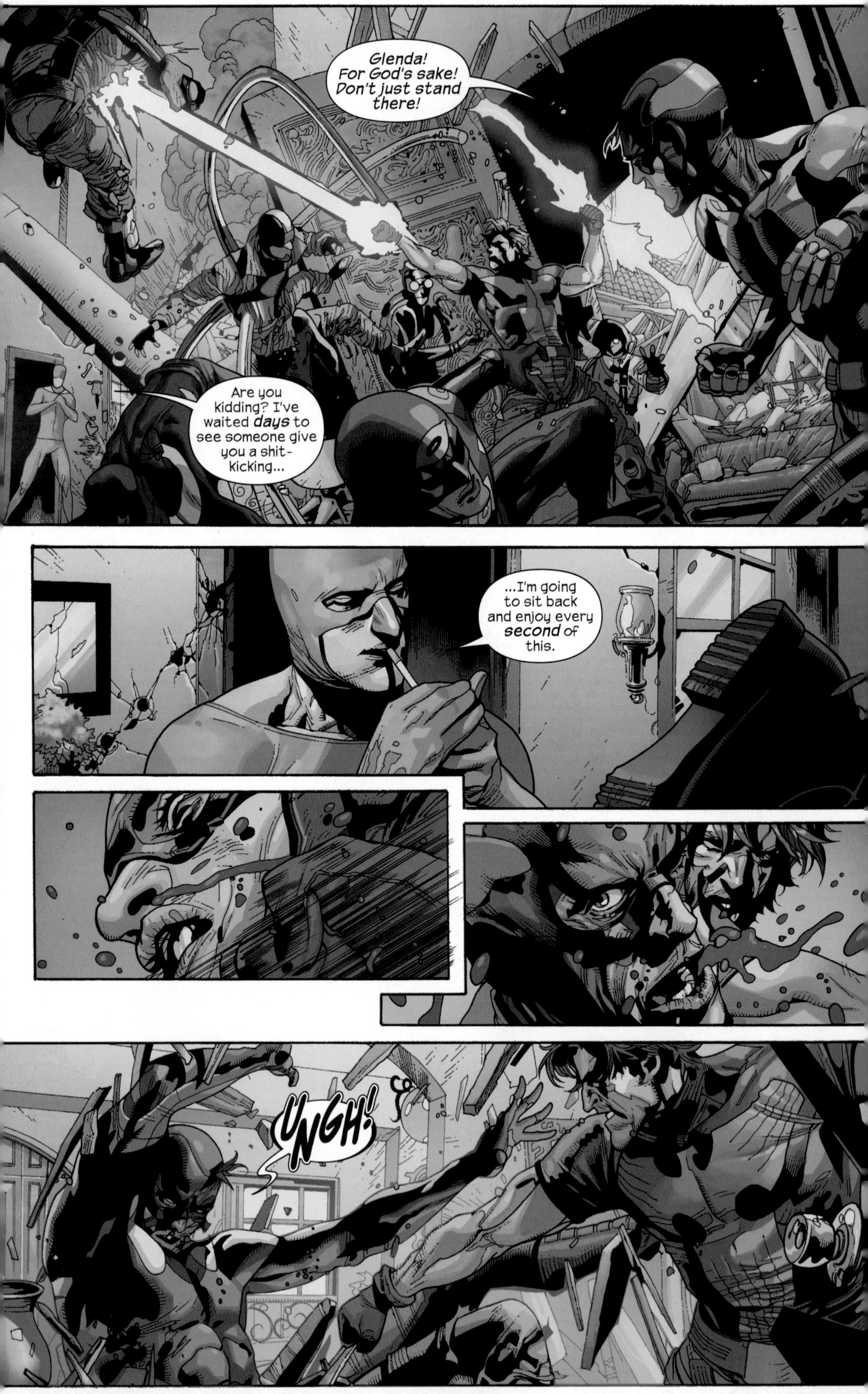
Glenda! For God's sake! Don't just stand there!
Are you kidding? I've waited days to see someone give you a shit-kicking...
...I'm going to sit back and enjoy every second of this.
UNGH!

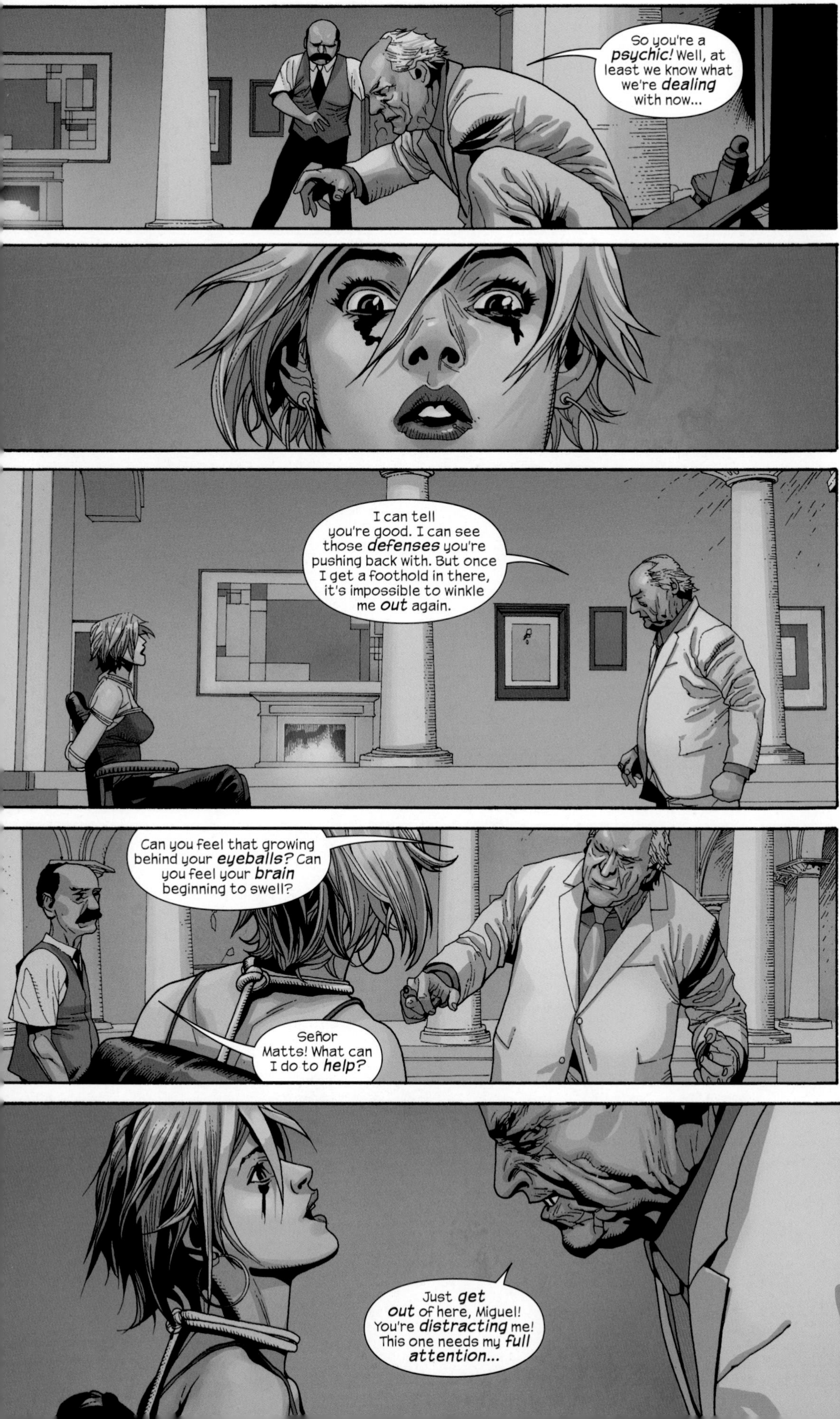
So you're a psychic! Well, at least we know what we're dealing with now...
I can tell you're good. I can see those defenses you're pushing back with. But once I get a foothold in there, it's impossible to winkle me out again.
Can you feel that growing behind your eyeballs? Can you feel your brain beginning to swell?
Señor Matts! What can I do to help?
Just get out of here, Miguel! You're distracting me! This one needs my full attention...

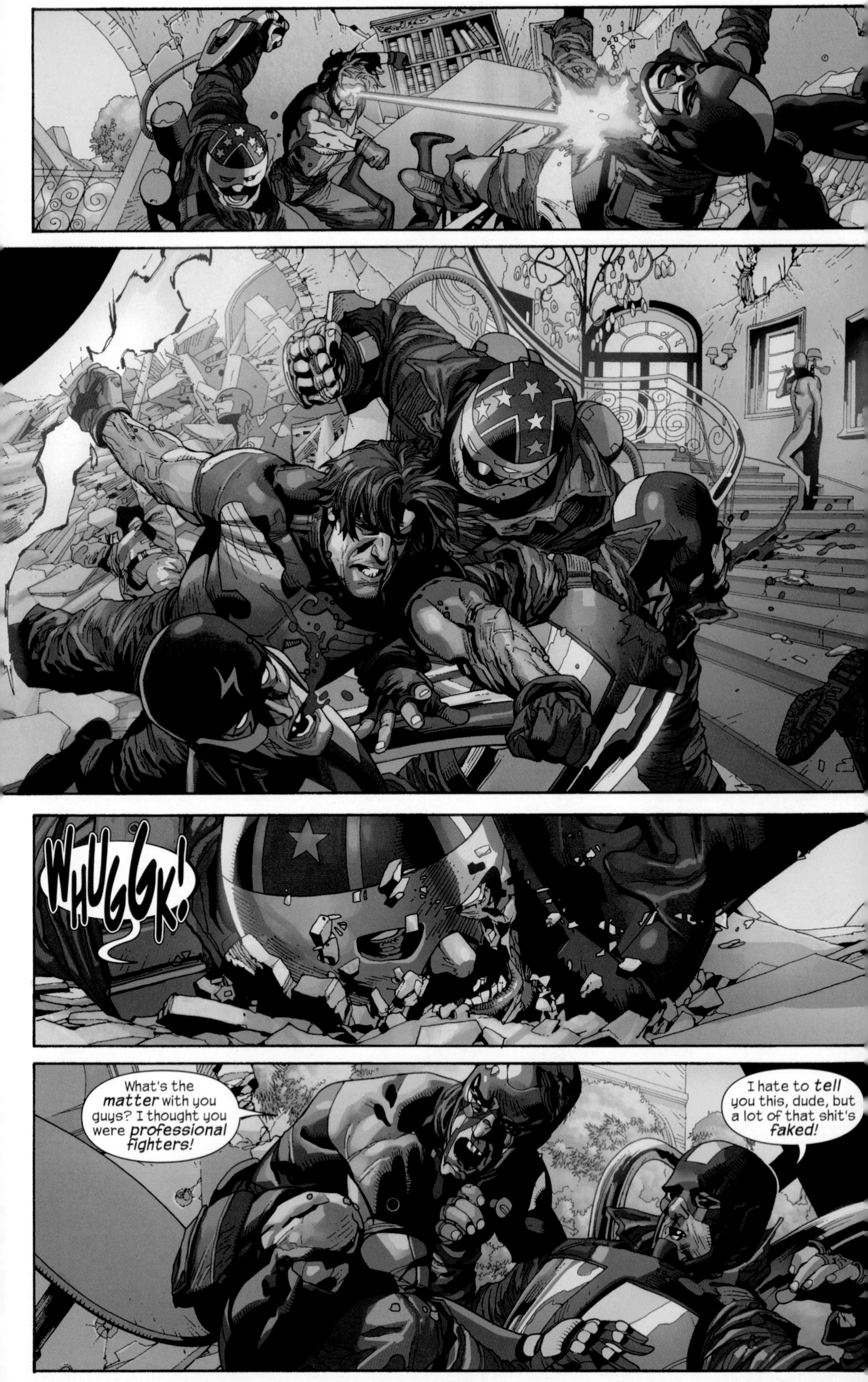
WHUGGK!
What's the matter with you guys? I thought you were professional fighters!
I hate to tell you this, dude, but a lot of that shit's faked!

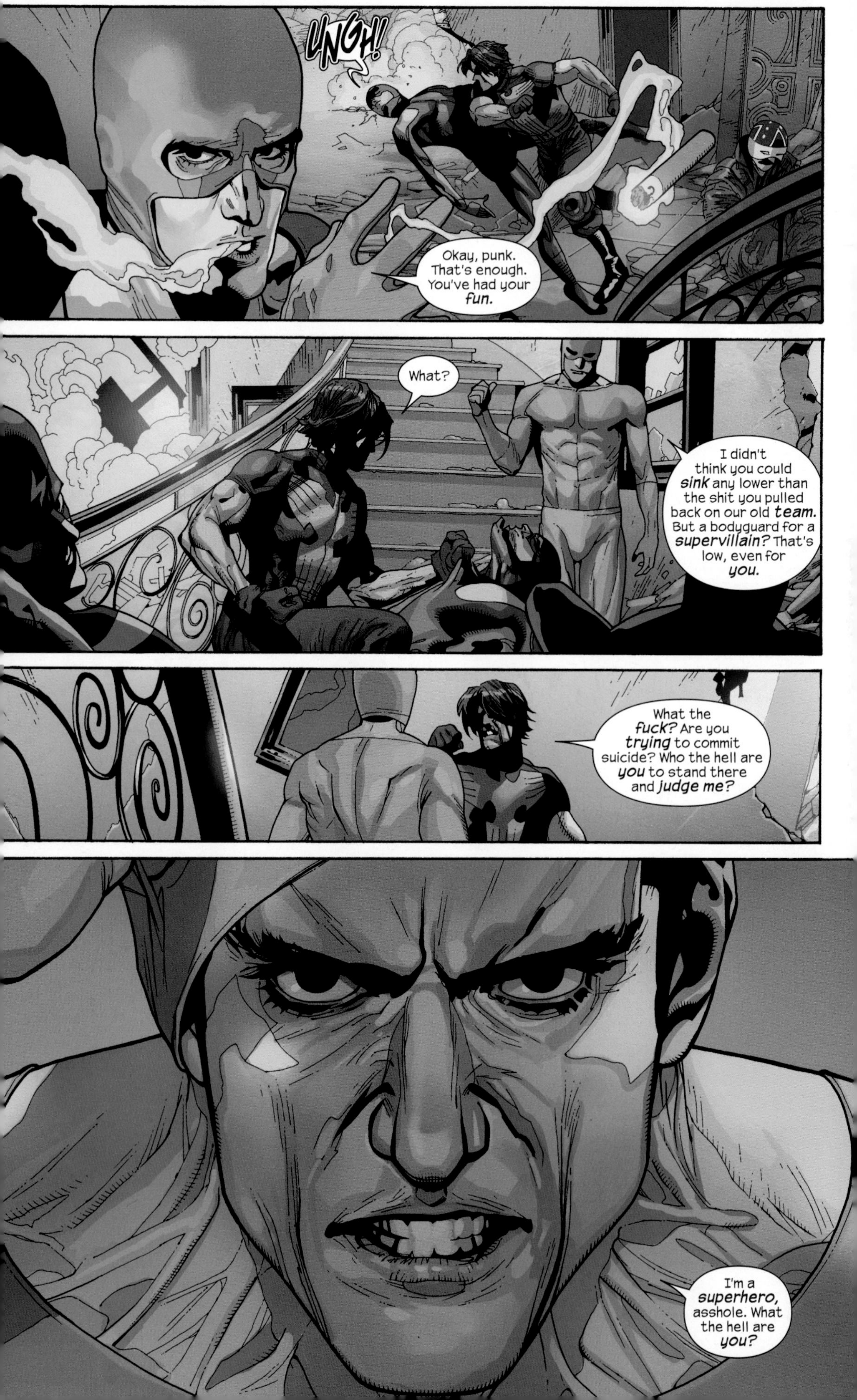
UNGH!
Okay, punk. That's enough. You've had your fun.
What?
I didn't think you could sink any lower than the shit you pulled back on our old team. But a bodyguard for a supervillain? That's low, even for you.
What the fuck? Are you trying to commit suicide? Who the hell are you to stand there and judge me?
I'm a superhero, asshole. What the hell are you?

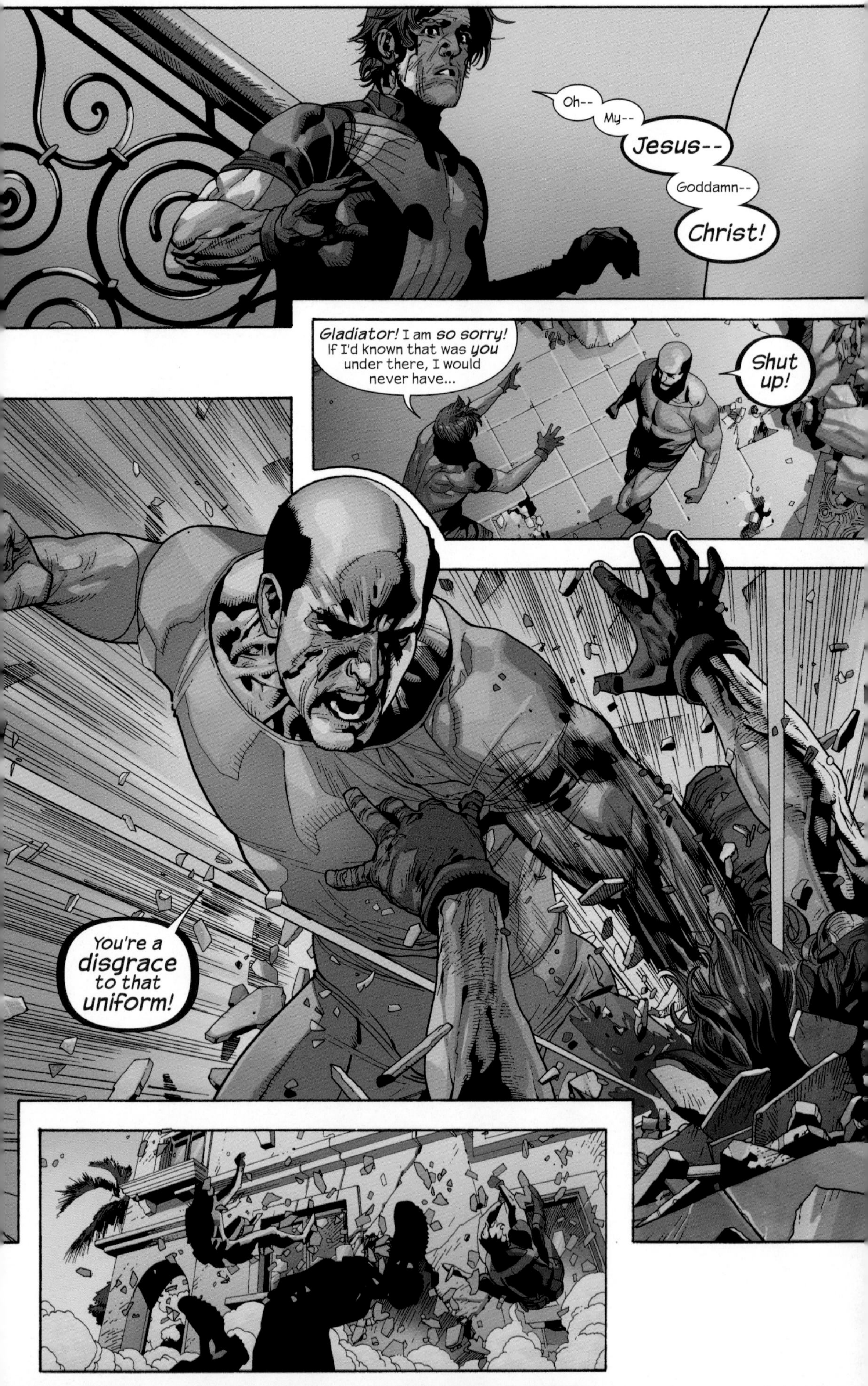
Oh--
My--
Jesus--
Goddamn--
Christ!
Gladiator! I am so sorry! If I'd known that was you under there, I would never have...
Shut up!
You're a disgrace to that uniform!

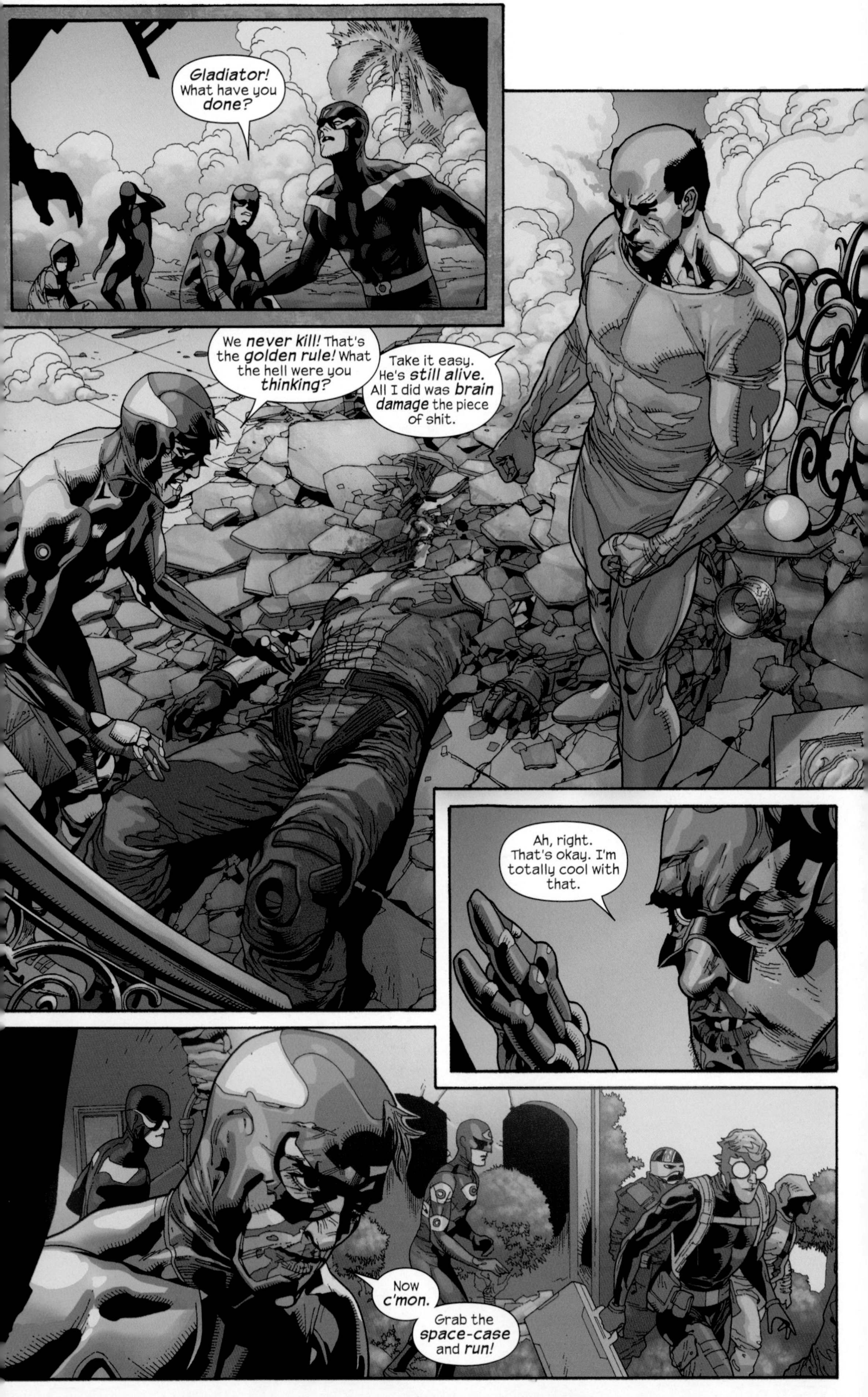
Gladiator! What have you done?
We never kill! That's the golden rule! What the hell were you thinking?
Take it easy. He's still alive. All I did was brain damage the piece of shit.
Ah, right. That's okay. I'm totally cool with that.
Now c'mon.
Grab the space-case and run!

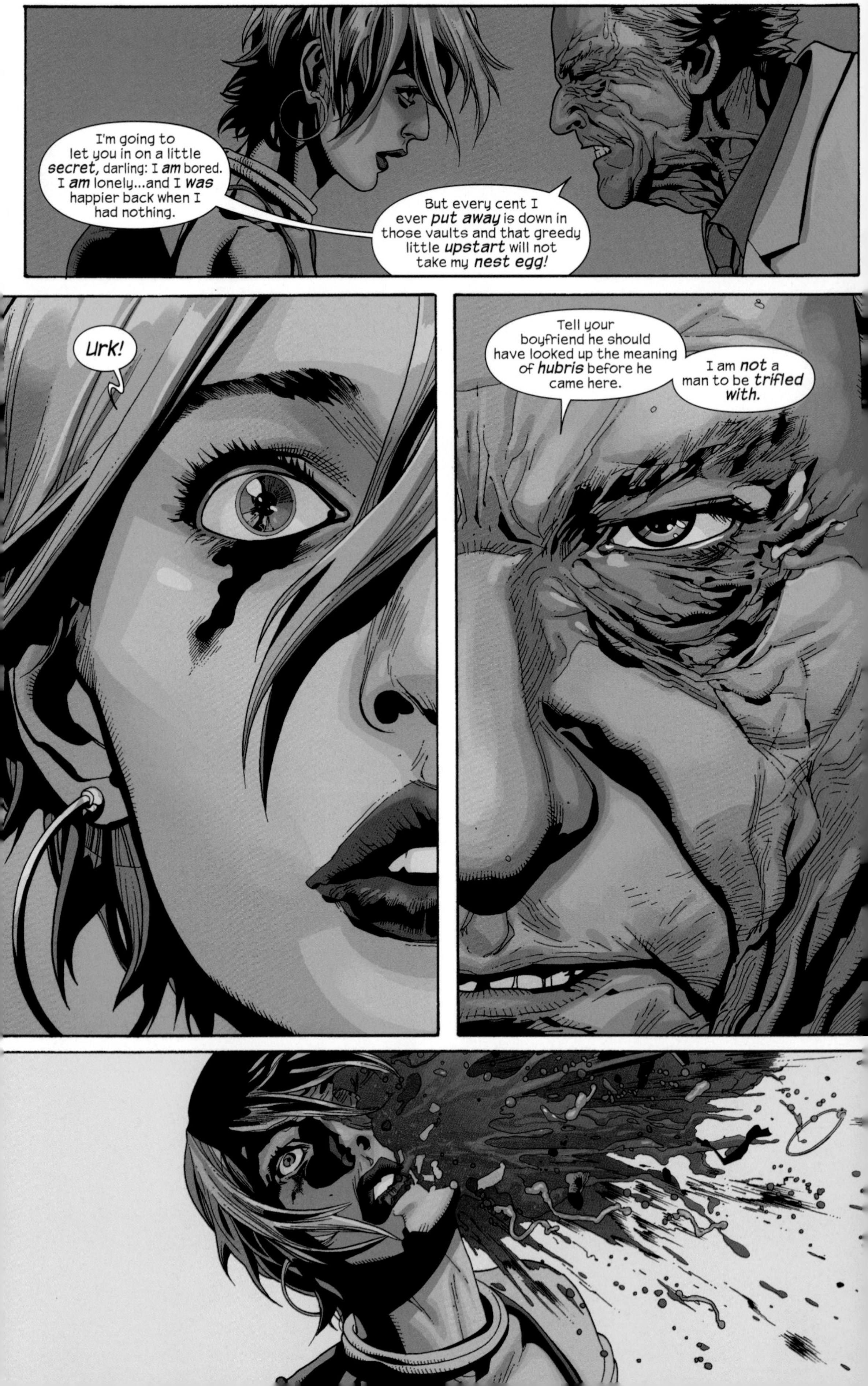
I'm going to let you in on a little secret, darling: I am bored. I am lonely...and I was happier back when I had nothing.
But every cent I ever put away is down in those vaults and that greedy little upstart will not take my nest egg!
Urk!
Tell your boyfriend he should have looked up the meaning of hubris before he came here.
I am not a man to be trifled with.

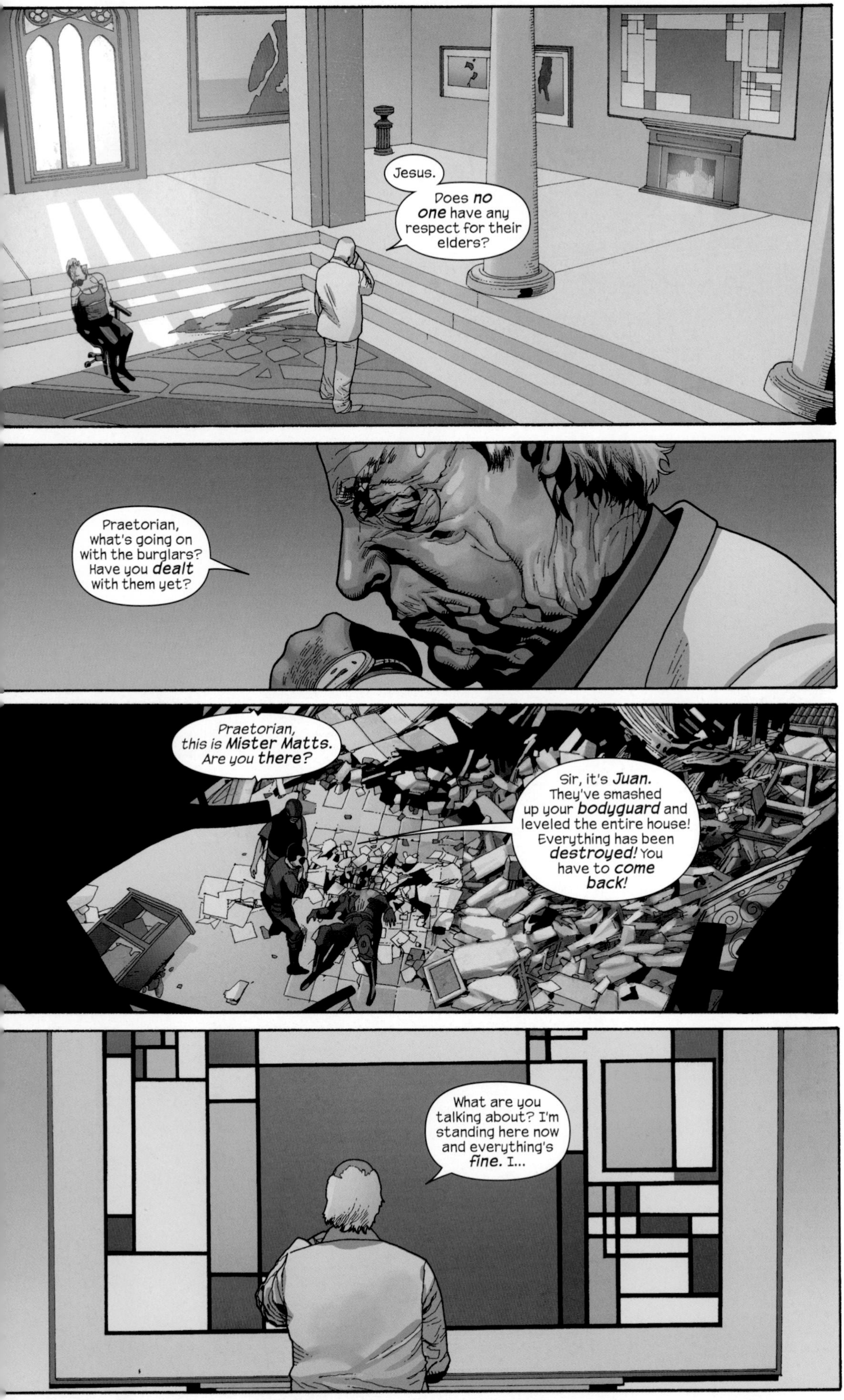
Jesus.
Does no one have any respect for their elders?
Praetorian, what's going on with the burglars? Have you dealt with them yet?
Praetorian, this is Mister Matts. Are you there?
Sir, it's Juan. They've smashed up your bodyguard and leveled the entire house! Everything has been destroyed! You have to come back!
What are you talking about? I'm standing here now and everything's fine. I...

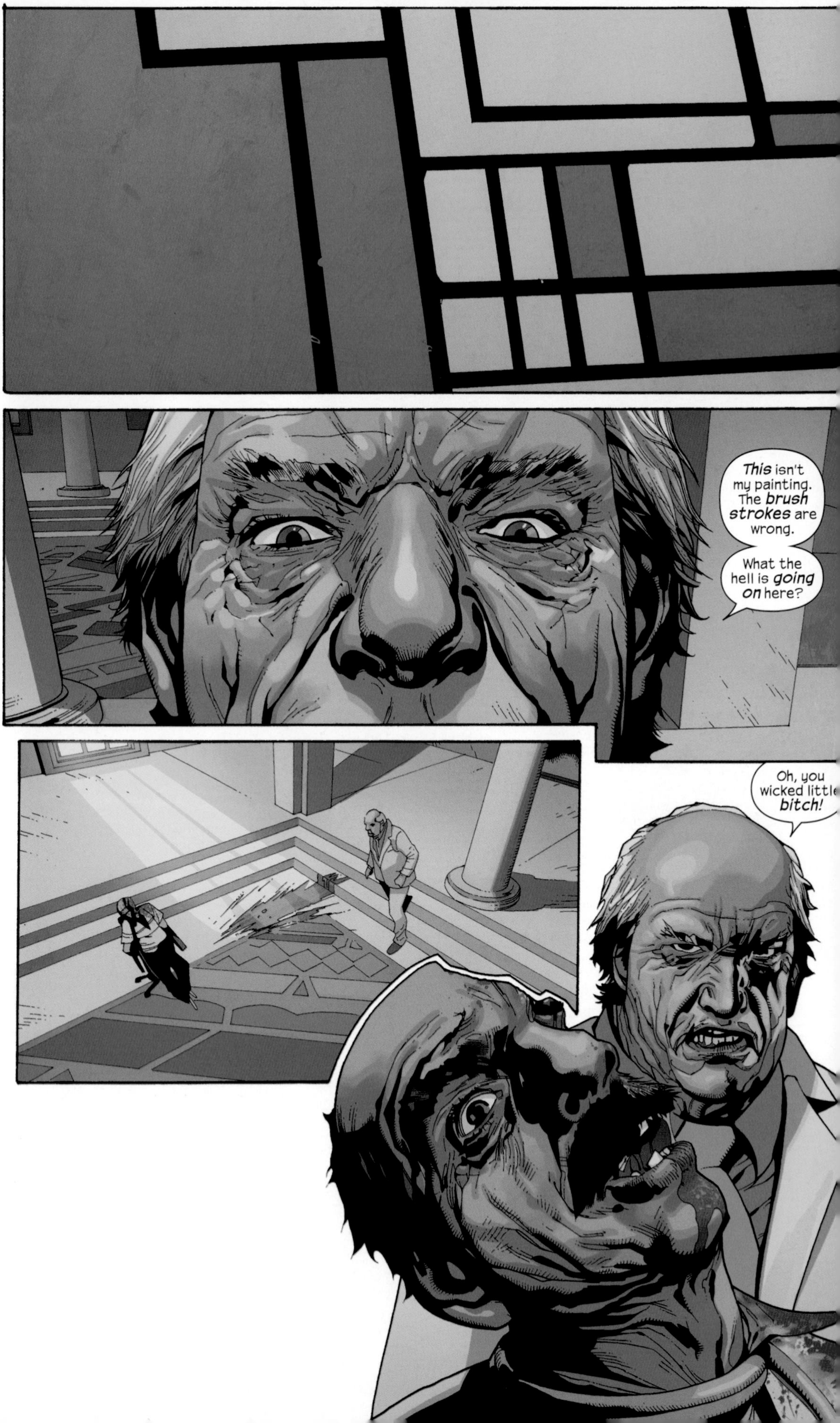

This isn't my painting. The brush strokes are wrong.
What the hell is going on here?
Oh, you wicked little bitch!

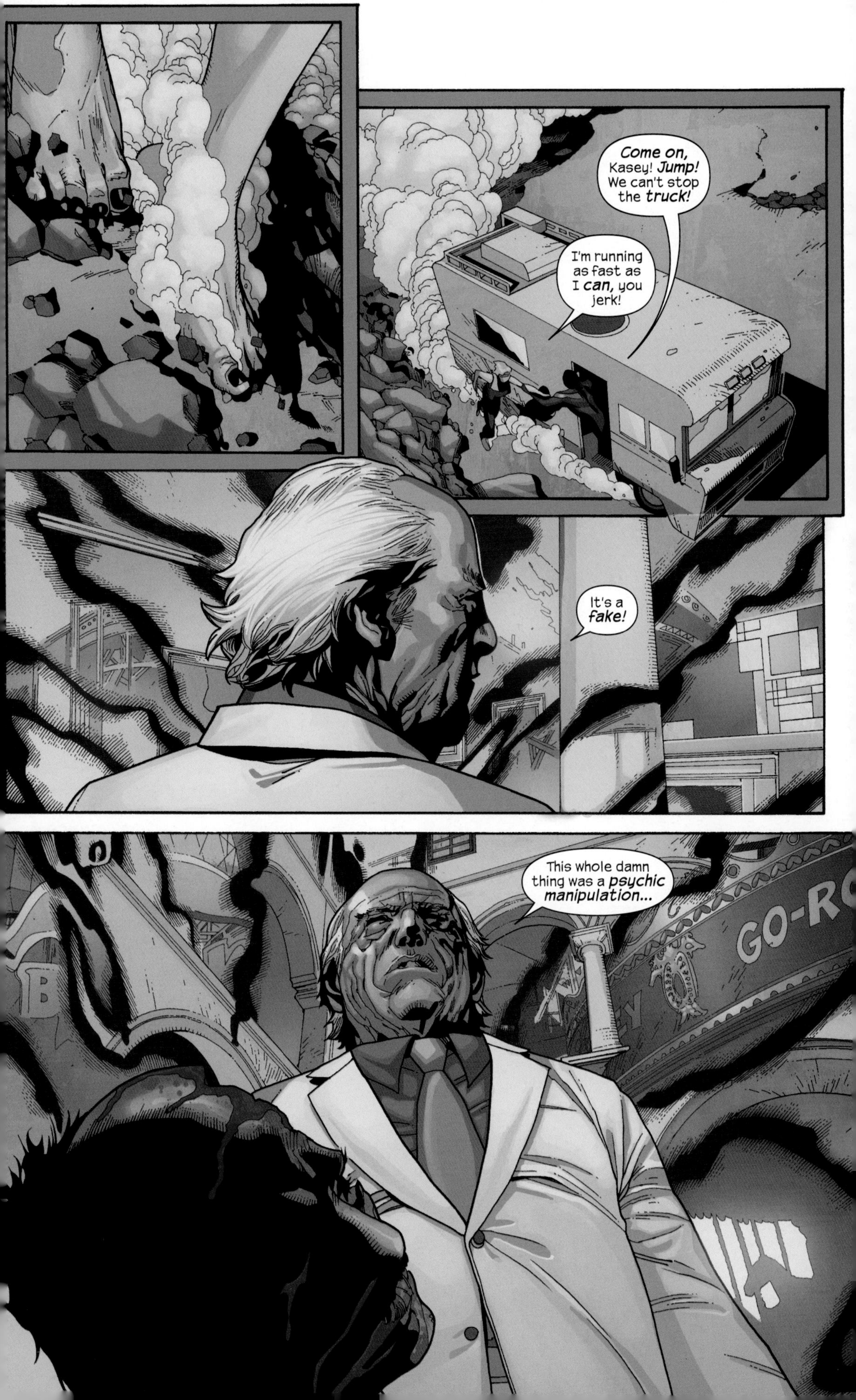

Come on, Kasey! Jump! We can't stop the truck!
I'm running as fast as I can, you jerk!
It's a fake!
This whole damn thing was a psychic manipulation...
GO-RO

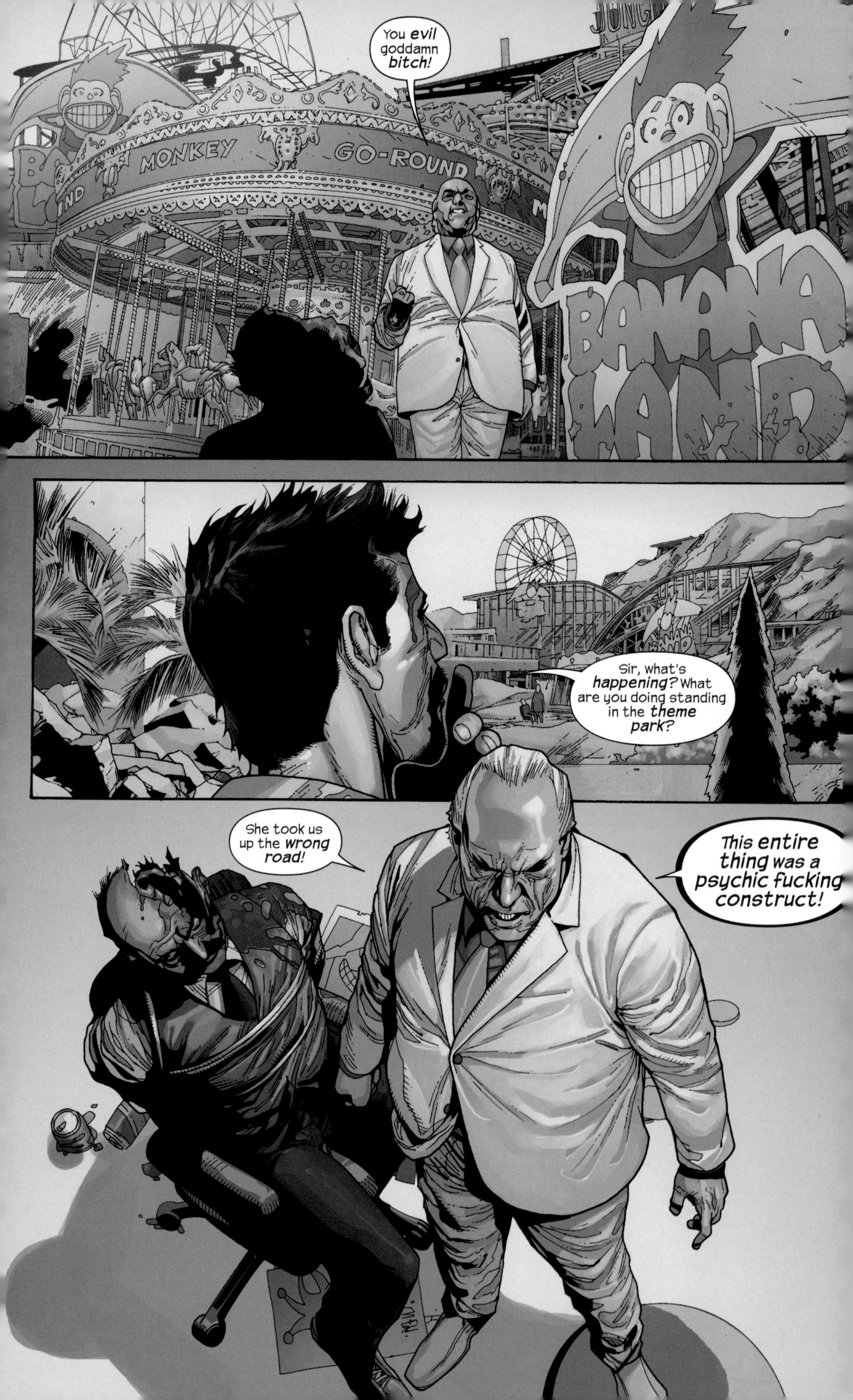

You evil goddamn bitch!
MONKEY GO-ROUND
BANANA LAND
Sir, what's happening? What are you doing standing in the theme park?
She took us up the wrong road!
This entire thing was a psychic fucking construct!

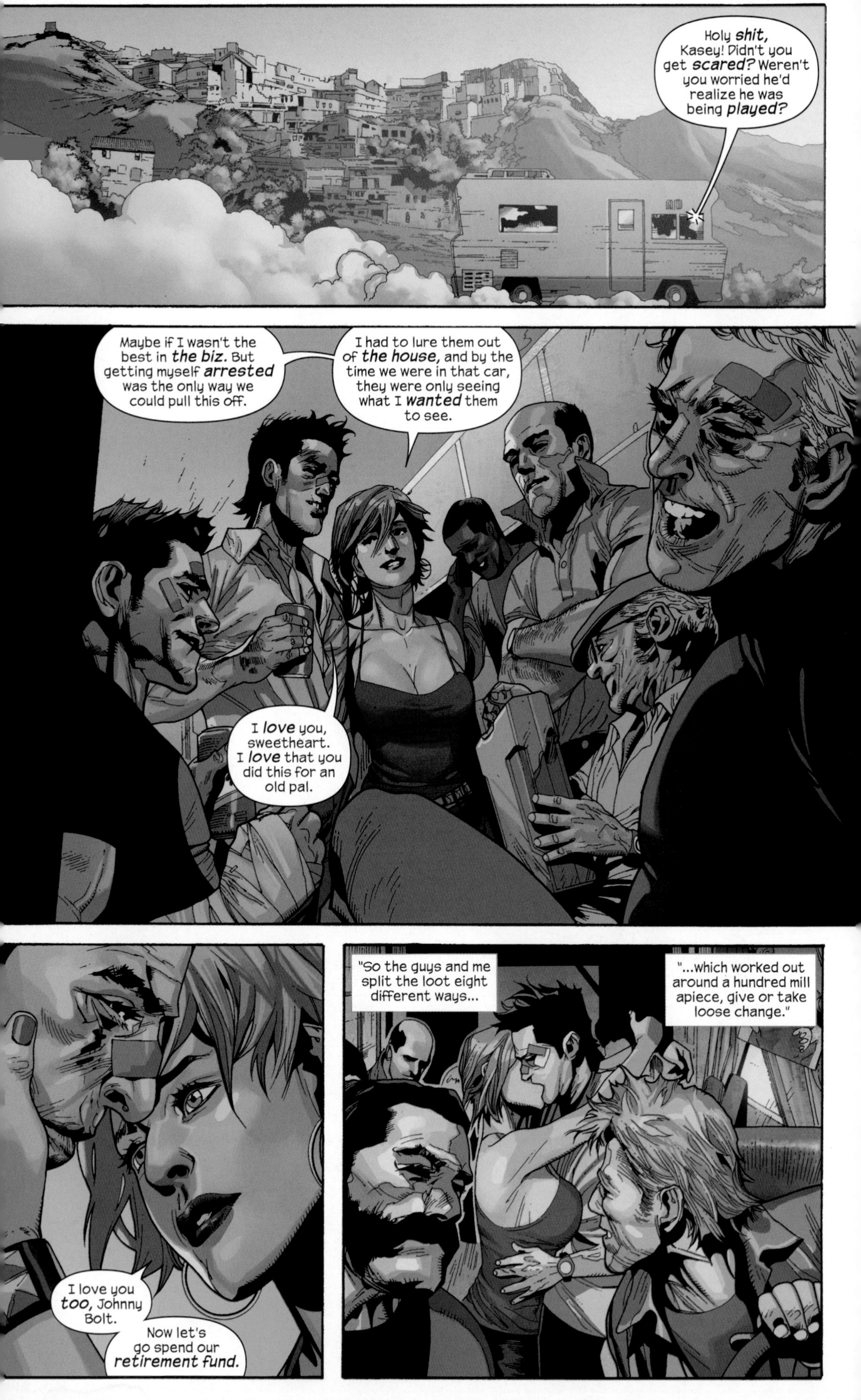
Holy shit, Kasey! Didn't you get scared? Weren't you worried he'd realize he was being played?
Maybe if I wasn't the best in the biz. But getting myself arrested was the only way we could pull this off.
I had to lure them out of the house, and by the time we were in that car, they were only seeing what I wanted them to see.
I love you, sweetheart. I love that you did this for an old pal.
I love you too, Johnny Bolt.
Now let's go spend our retirement fund.
"So the guys and me split the loot eight different ways...
"...which worked out around a hundred mill apiece, give or take loose change."

Manila,
One Year Later:

...Johnny told us all to *lie low* for a while, but you know what Supercrooks are like. Money burns holes in our friggin' *pockets*...

"TK McCabe took his family on that European vacation...

"...in a big, fancy cruiseship he paid for in *cash*.

"Forecast bought a *space shuttle*...

"The Ghost heard about their *financial woes* and managed to snap up most of *Greece*.

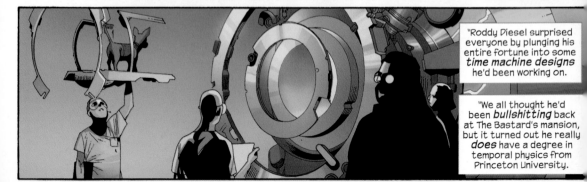

"Roddy Diesel surprised everyone by plunging his entire fortune into some *time machine designs* he'd been working on.

"We all thought he'd been *bullshitting* back at The Bastard's mansion, but it turned out he really *does* have a degree in temporal physics from Princeton University.

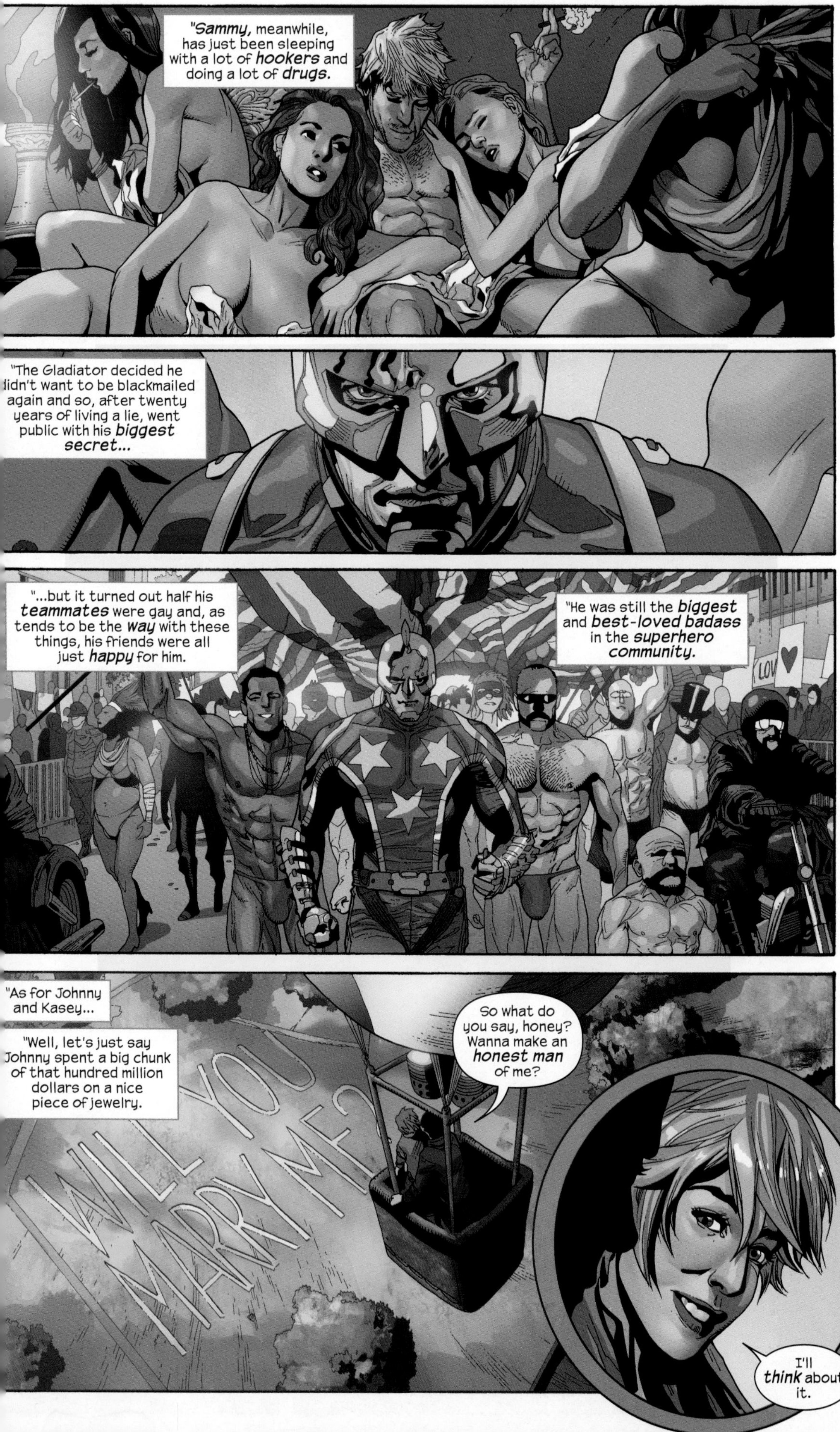
"Sammy, meanwhile, has just been sleeping with a lot of hookers and doing a lot of drugs.
"The Gladiator decided he idn't want to be blackmailed again and so, after twenty years of living a lie, went public with his biggest secret...
"...but it turned out half his teammates were gay and, as tends to be the way with these things, his friends were all just happy for him.
"He was still the biggest and best-loved badass in the superhero community.
"As for Johnny and Kasey...
"Well, let's just say Johnny spent a big chunk of that hundred million dollars on a nice piece of jewelry.
WILL YOU MARRY ME?
So what do you say, honey? Wanna make an honest man of me?
I'll think about it.

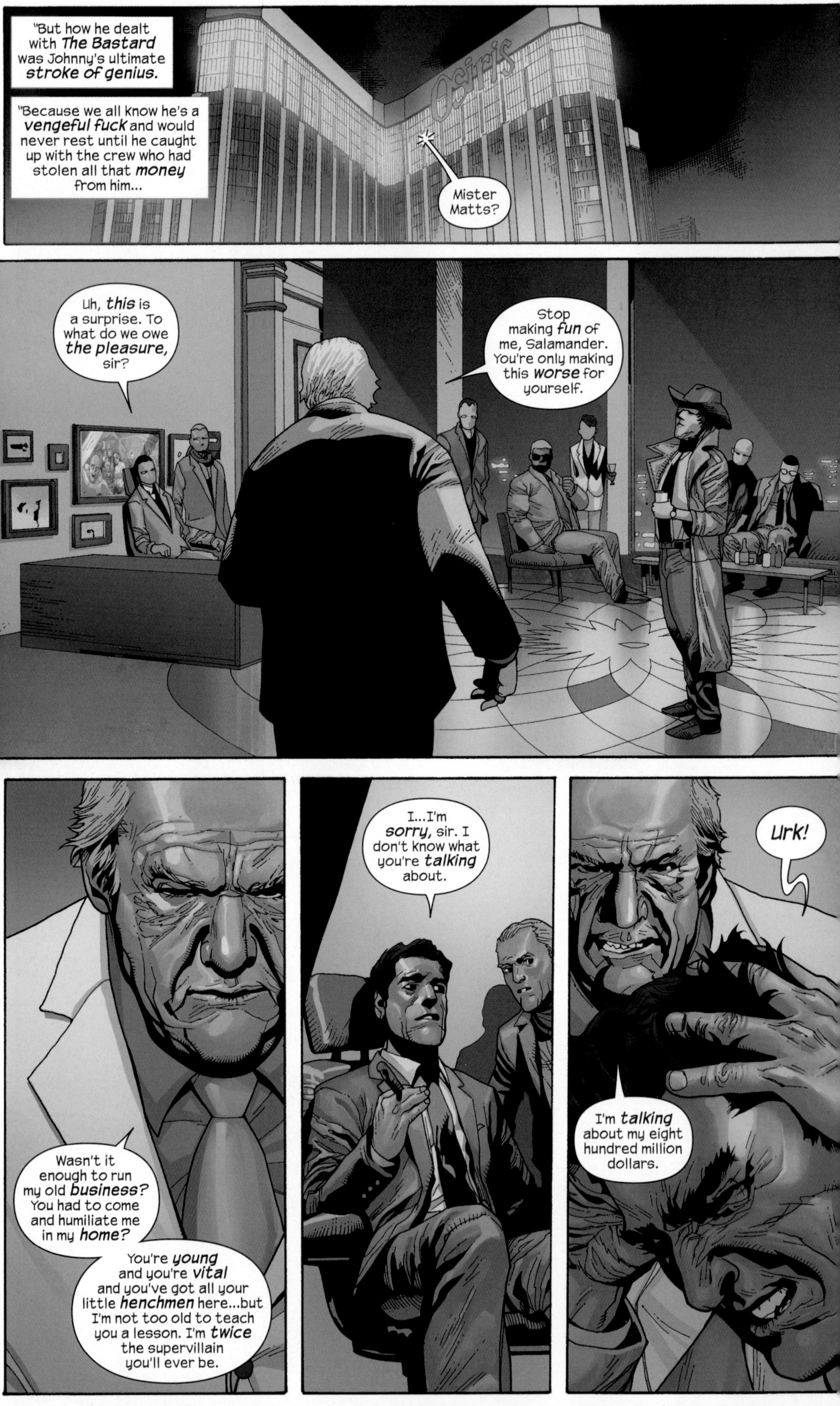
"But how he dealt with *The Bastard* was Johnny's ultimate *stroke of genius.*
"Because we all know he's a *vengeful fuck* and would never rest until he caught up with the crew who had stolen all that *money* from him...
Osiris
Mister Matts?
Uh, *this* is a surprise. To what do we owe *the pleasure,* sir?
Stop making *fun* of me, Salamander. You're only making this *worse* for yourself.
Wasn't it enough to run my old *business?* You had to come and humiliate me in my *home?*
You're *young* and you're *vital* and you've got all your little *henchmen* here...but I'm not too old to teach you a lesson. I'm *twice* the supervillain you'll ever be.
I...I'm *sorry,* sir. I don't know what you're *talking* about.
*Urk!*
I'm *talking* about my eight hundred million dollars.

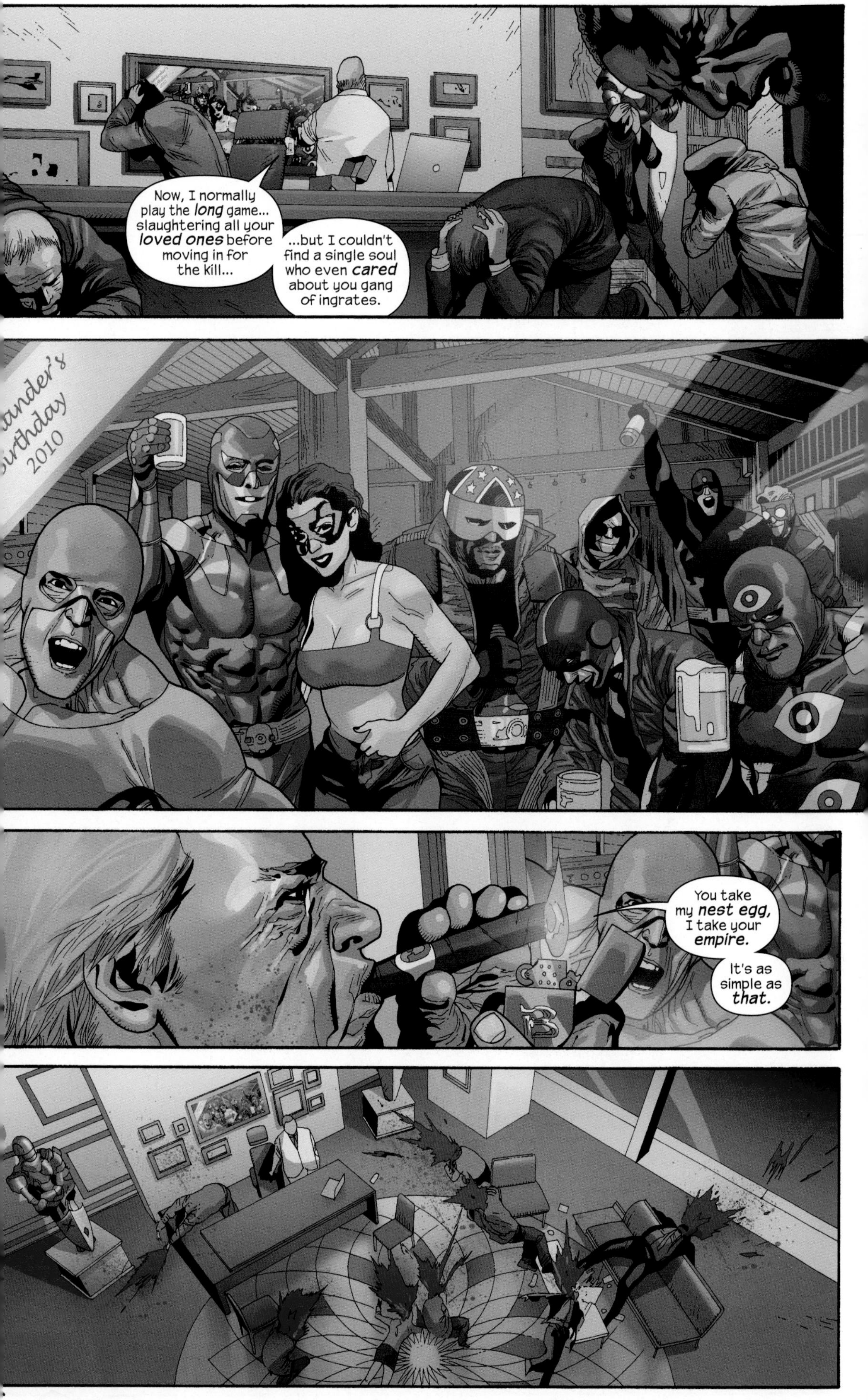

Now, I normally play the *long* game... slaughtering all your ***loved ones*** before moving in for the kill...
...but I couldn't find a single soul who even ***cared*** about you gang of ingrates.
You take my ***nest egg,*** I take your ***empire.***
It's as simple as ***that.***

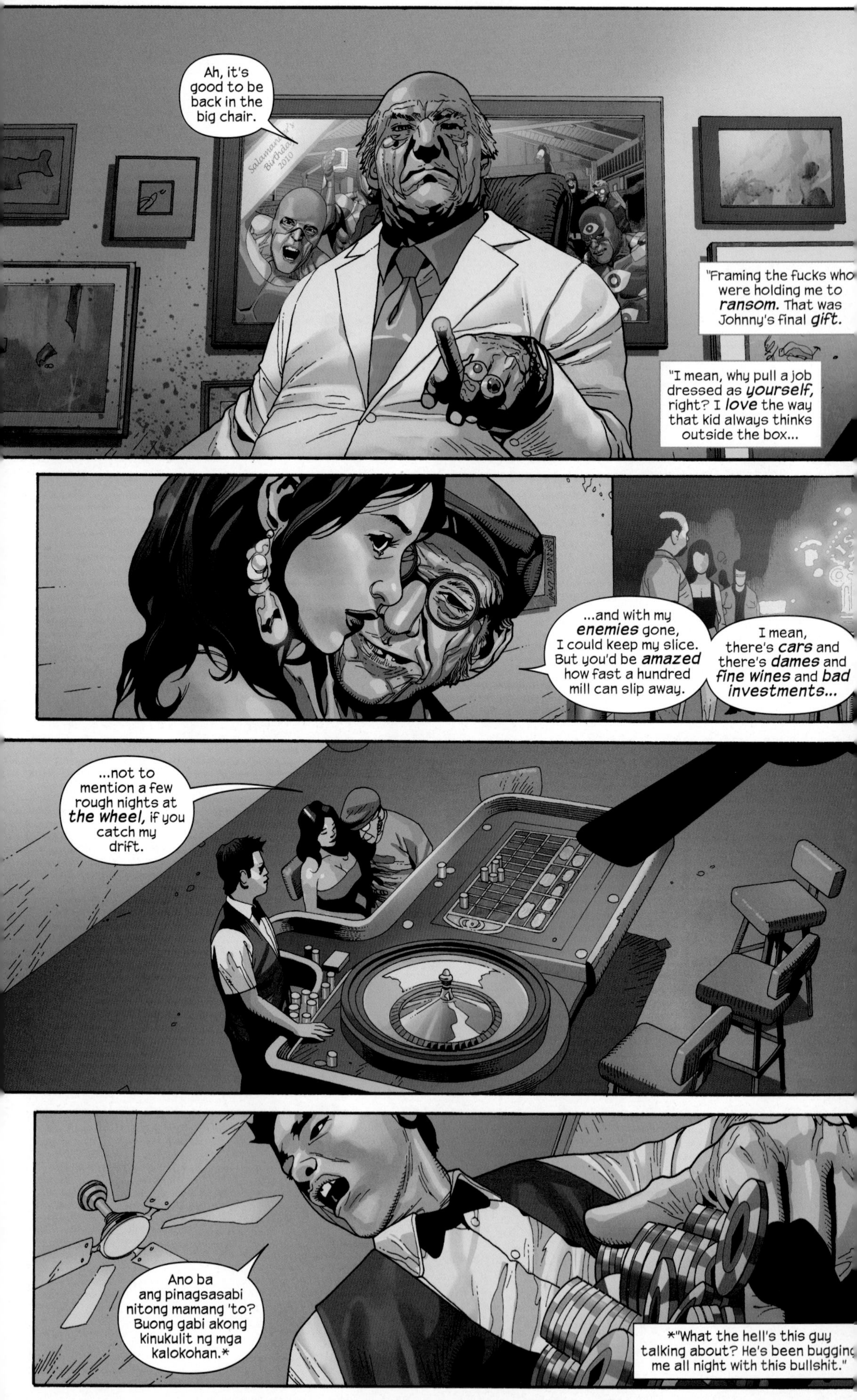

Ah, it's good to be back in the big chair.
"Framing the fucks who were holding me to ransom. That was Johnny's final gift.
"I mean, why pull a job dressed as yourself, right? I love the way that kid always thinks outside the box...
...and with my enemies gone, I could keep my slice. But you'd be amazed how fast a hundred mill can slip away.
I mean, there's cars and there's dames and fine wines and bad investments...
...not to mention a few rough nights at the wheel, if you catch my drift.
Ano ba ang pinagsasabi nitong mamang 'to? Buong gabi akong kinukulit ng mga kalokohan.*
*"What the hell's this guy talking about? He's been bugging me all night with this bullshit."

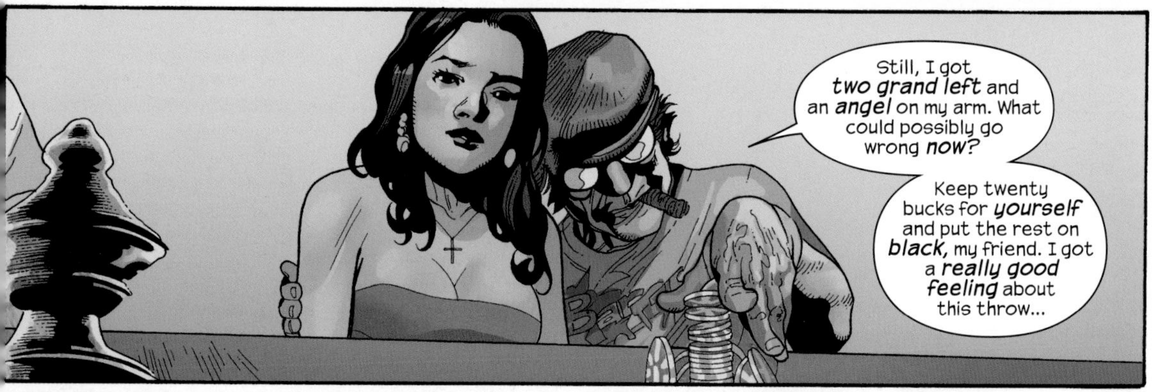
Still, I got *two grand left* and an *angel* on my arm. What could possibly go wrong *now?*
Keep twenty bucks for *yourself* and put the rest on *black,* my friend. I got a *really good feeling* about this throw...

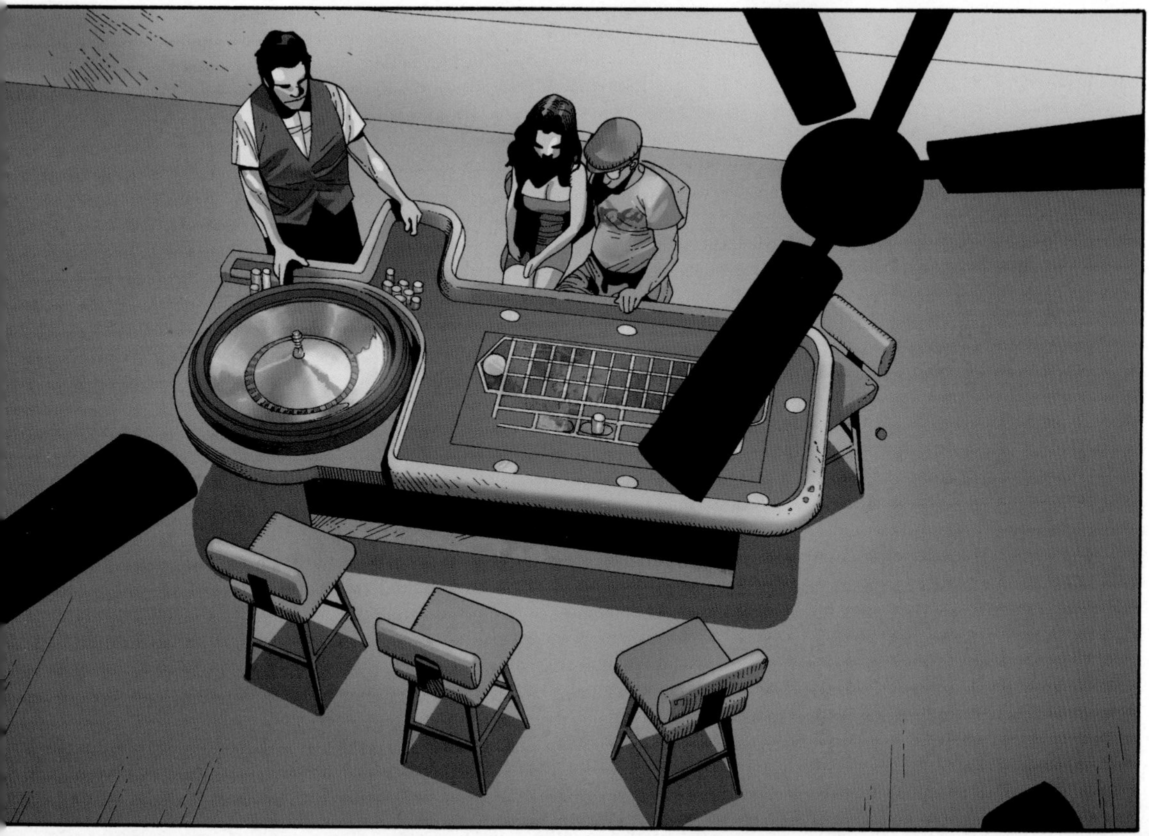

**MARK MILLAR** has written some of Marvel's biggest hits in recent years including *The Ultimates*, *Ultimate X-Men*, *Spider-Man*, *Wolverine: Old Man Logan* and *Civil War*, the industry's biggest-selling series of the past decade. His Millarworld line boasts a roster of creator-owned books such as *Wanted*, turned into a blockbuster movie starring Angelina Jolie; *Kick-Ass*, which starred Nicolas Cage; and *Nemesis*, which Fox is developing with director Joe Carnahan. Both movies currently have sequels in the works and Millar is now focusing on new projects such as *Hit-Girl*, *The Secret Service*, *Nemesis Returns* and *Jupiter's Children*. In his native UK, he's the editor of CLiNT magazine, an advisor on film to the Scottish government, and managing director of film and television company Millarworld Productions.

**LEINIL YU**'s first interest in comics was sparked by a copy of *How to Draw Comics the Marvel Way* when he was 11. It was later reinforced by positive responses from talent scouts from Wildstorm/Homage and Dark Horse, and by having fan art published in *Wizard* magazine. The major break was Whilce Portacio's tutelage where the training landed him his first mainstream comics gig: *Wolverine* in 1997. After a successful run, he later took on the *Uncanny X-Men*, *X-Men*, *Highroads*, *Superman: Birthright*, *Silent Dragon*, *Ultimate Wolverine vs. Hulk*, *New Avengers*, Marvel's 2008 epic *Secret Invasion*, and film/game concept art. He is now happily working with his all-time favorite writer, Mark Millar.

**GERRY ALANGUILAN** is an architect by profession, but chooses to create comics instead. He has inked for Marvel and DC for the last 16 years on titles like *New X-Men*, *Fantastic Four*, *Incredible Hulk*, *X-Force*, *Superman*, *Batman* and more recently *Ultimate Avengers*. He has also been creating his own stories since 1992. He has written and drawn stories for various Philippine publications and his own Komikero Publishing titles like *Wasted*, *Johnny Balbona*, *Crest Hut Butt Shop*, *Humanis Rex!*, *Timawa* and *Elmer*. *Elmer* has been released internationally by SLG and Editions çà et là in English and French, which won the Prix Asie ACBD for Best Asian Comic Book in 2011, and was nominated for Best New Album in the 2011 Will Eisner Industry Awards.

**SUNNY GHO** is the one of first Indonesian artists to break into the US comics industry. His unique strokes and color palette have won him many fans, readers and publishers alike. While busy coloring some of the industry's top titles such as *Superior* and *Incredible Hulk*, Sunny spent the rest of his time managing his Jakarta-based illustration company, Imaginary Friends Studios, and also founded the online comic publisher MAKKO.

**CLAYTON COWLES** is a son of two artists who talk about him a lot. He graduated from the Joe Kubert School of Cartoon and Graphic Art in 2009, and has been working for Chris Eliopoulos's Virtual Calligraphy lettering studio ever since. He has served as letterer on numerous high-selling and critically acclaimed Marvel comics, including *Fantastic Four*, *Journey Into Mystery*, *Defenders*, *Red Skull*, *Heralds*, *Ultimate Comics*: *Ultimates*, the *Season One* line of books, and countless others. When not lettering, Clayton makes artwork that he sometimes sells to people. He lives in upstate New York with his cat.

**NACHO VIGALONDO** became an Oscar nominee filmmaker in 2005 thanks to a black and white musical about terrorism called *7:35 in the morning*. This gave him the chance to direct the worldwide acclaimed sci-fi feature films *Timecrimes* (soon to be remade by Dreamworks) and *Extraterrestrial* (Distributed by Focus Features). His most immediate plan is jumping from Spain to Hollywood before the euro collapses, that's the reason he is currently shooting his first English language film *Windows*, a real time giallo with lots of split screens, and will direct, inmediatly after, the film adaptation of *Supercrooks*, whose script, written hand-in-hand with Mark Millar, doubles the number of twists of the comic-book!

**NICOLE BOOSE** began in the comics industry in the '90s, working as an editor at Harris Comics (*Vampirella*). She later joined the staff at Marvel, where she edited titles including *Cable & Deadpool*, *Iron Man* and *Stephen King's The Dark Tower*, and headed multiple projects in Marvel's custom publishing program. She recently relocated from New York City to Cleveland, Ohio, and now works as a freelancer. She lives with her husband and daughter.

# VARIANT BY DAVE GIBBONS

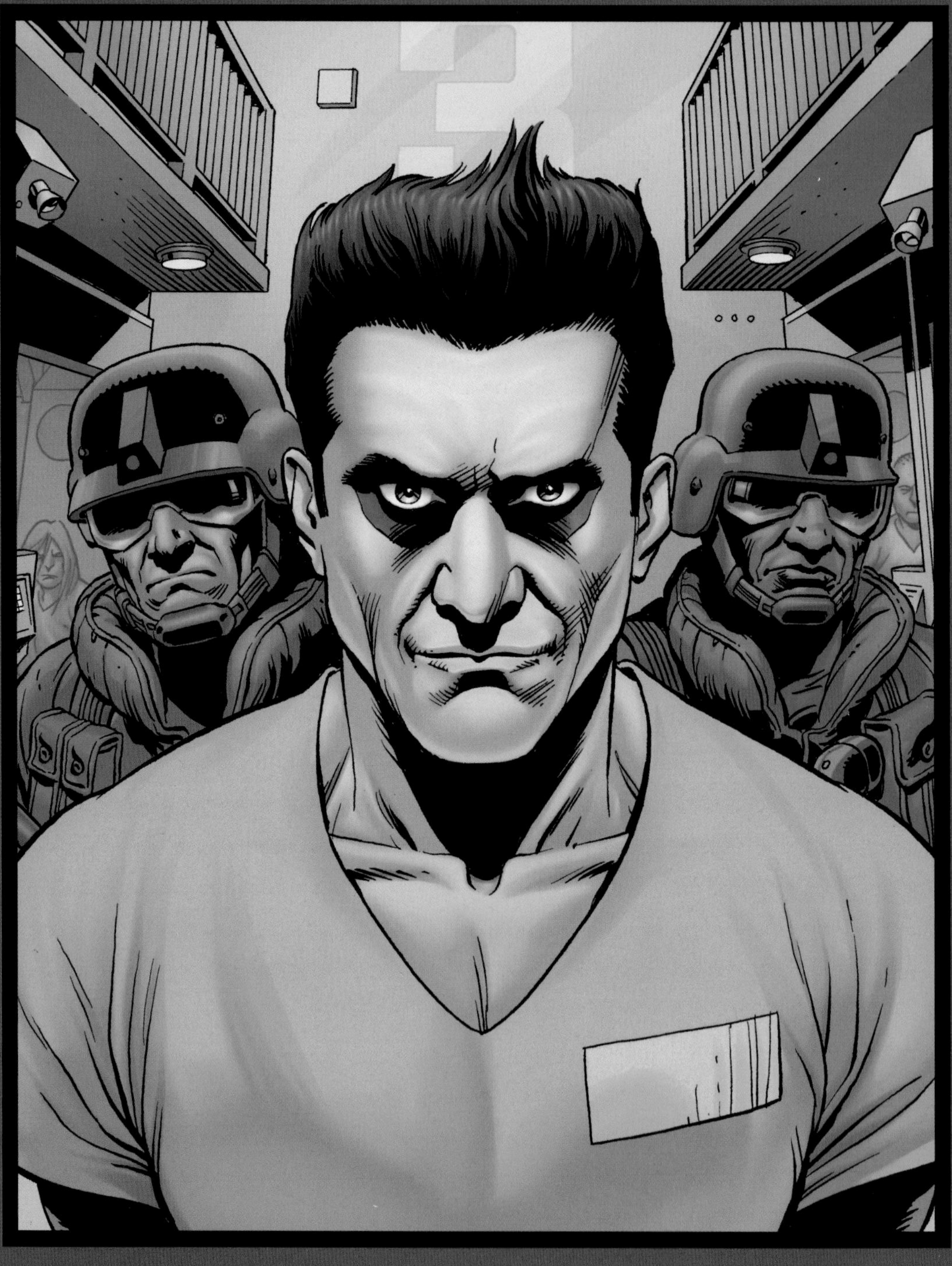

# TWO
## VARIANT BY BRYAN HITCH

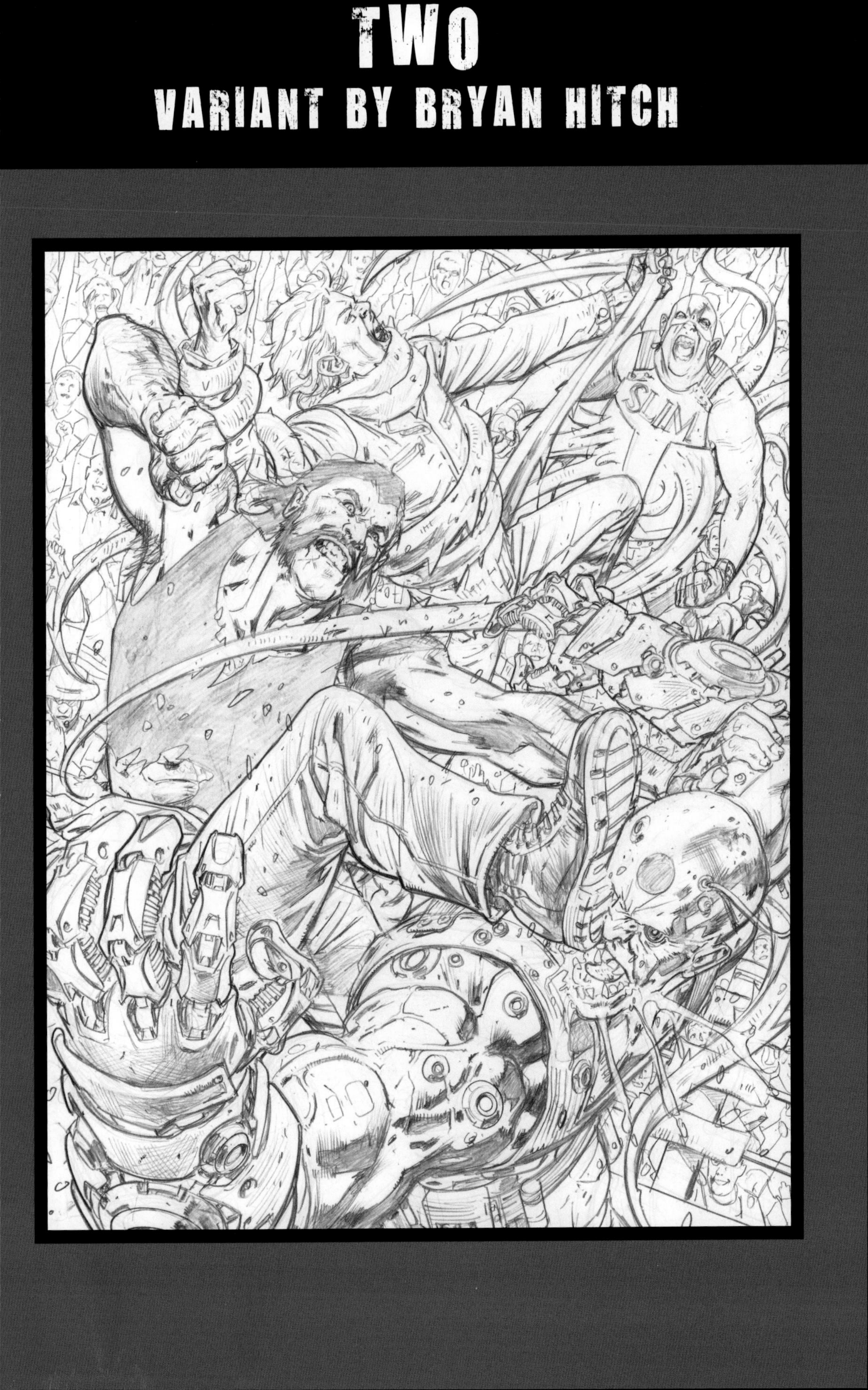
SLIM

# CHARACTER SKETCHES

## BY LEINIL YU

Artist Leinil Yu's characters aren't just works of art — they're the result of extensive planning and experimentation. Here, Leinil shares some of his preliminary work as he began to shape the characters who became the heart and soul of SUPERCROOKS.

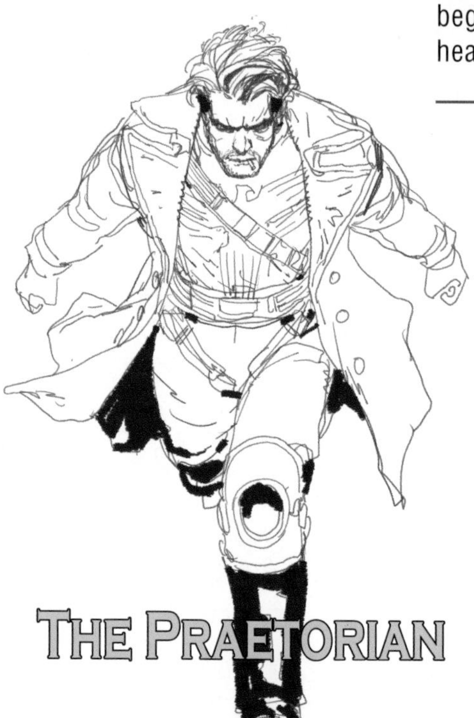

THE PRAETORIAN

JOHNNY BOLT

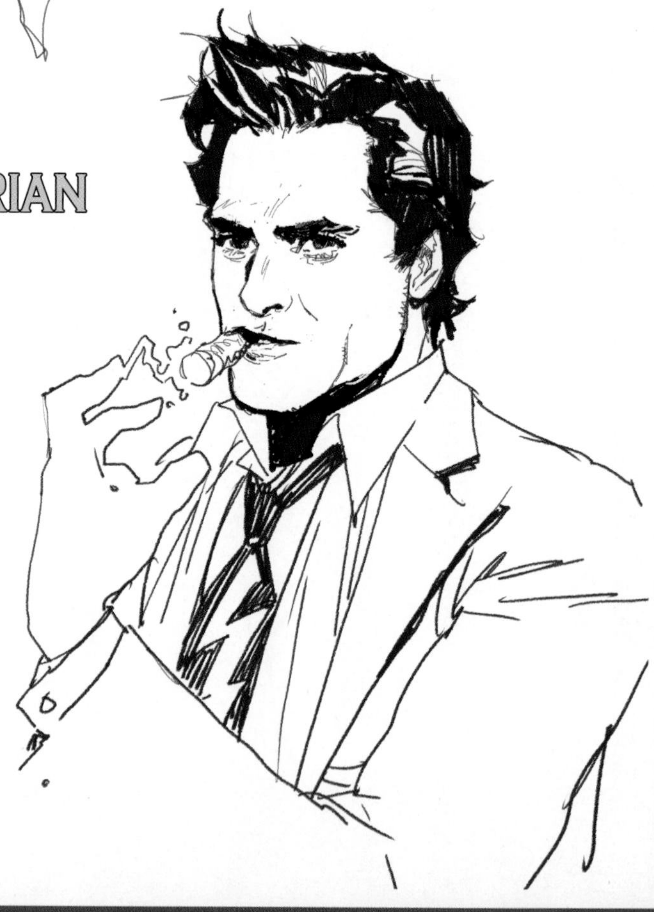

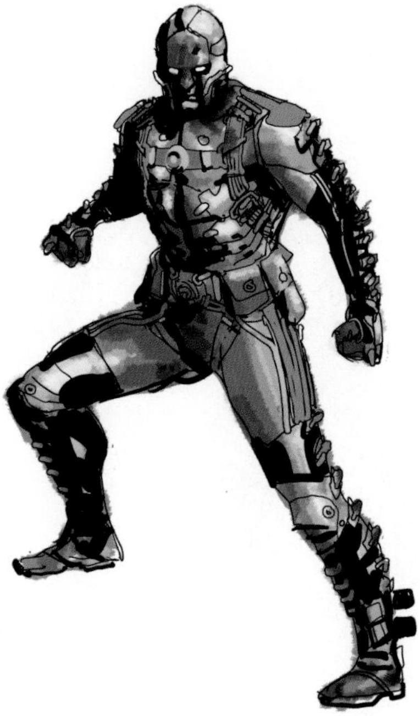

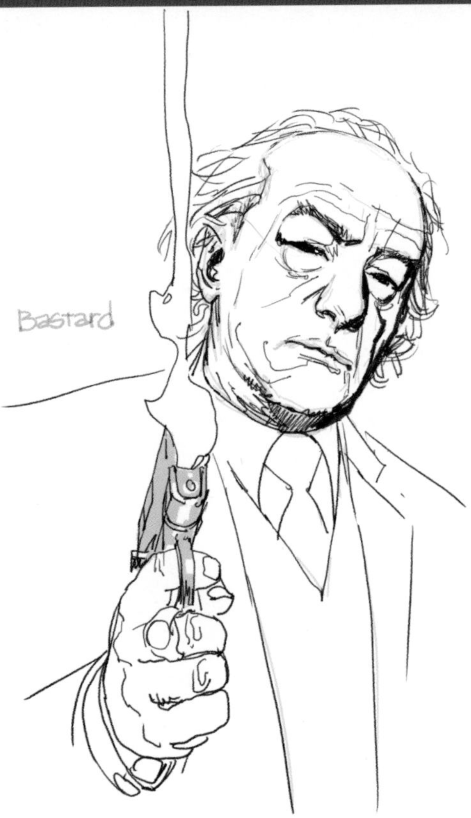
Bastard

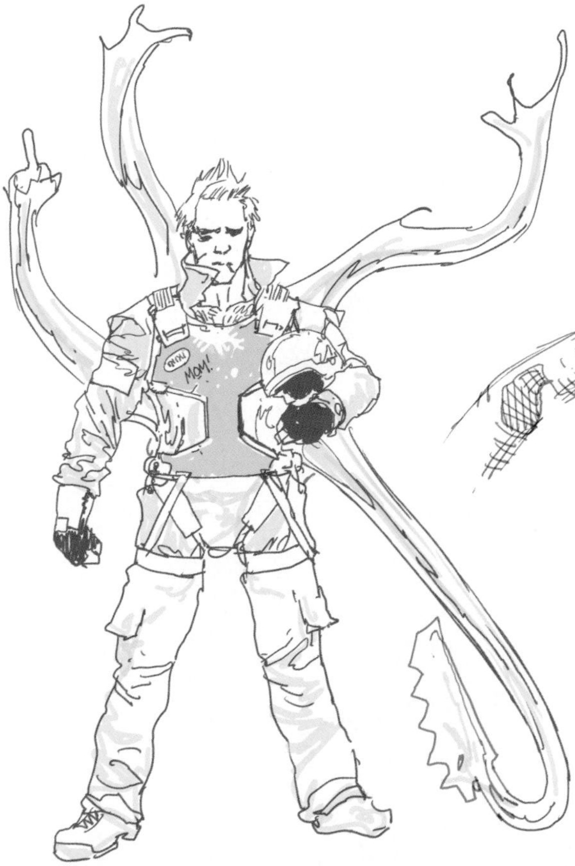
MOM!

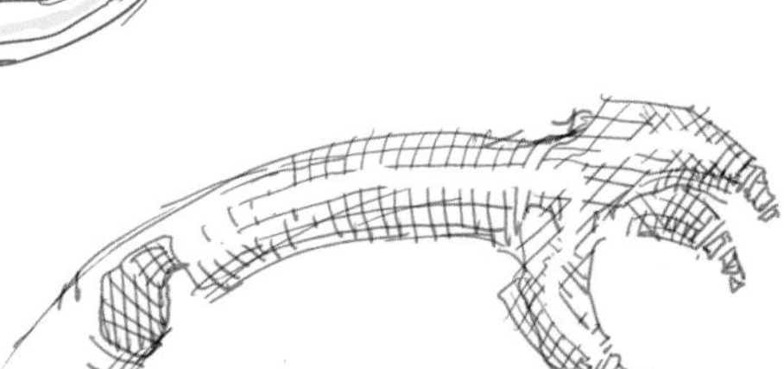

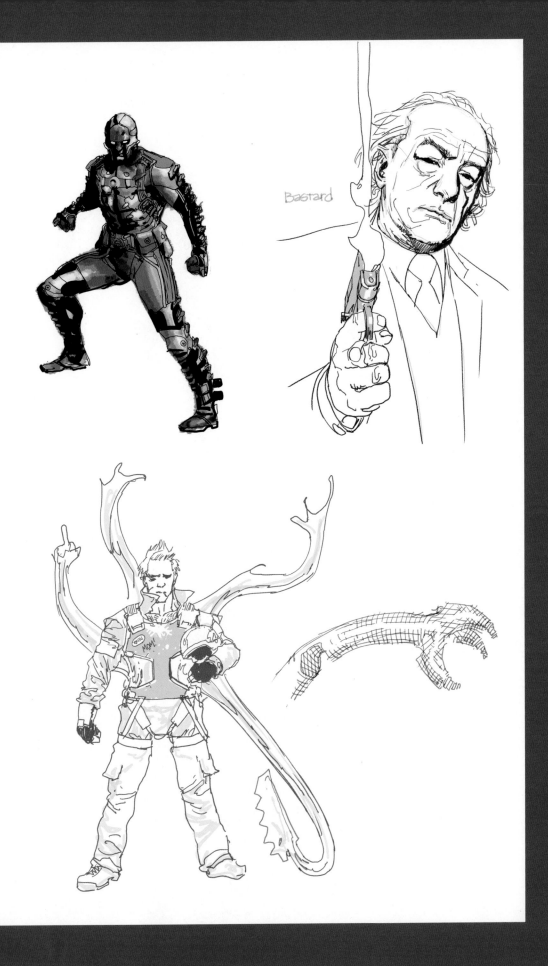

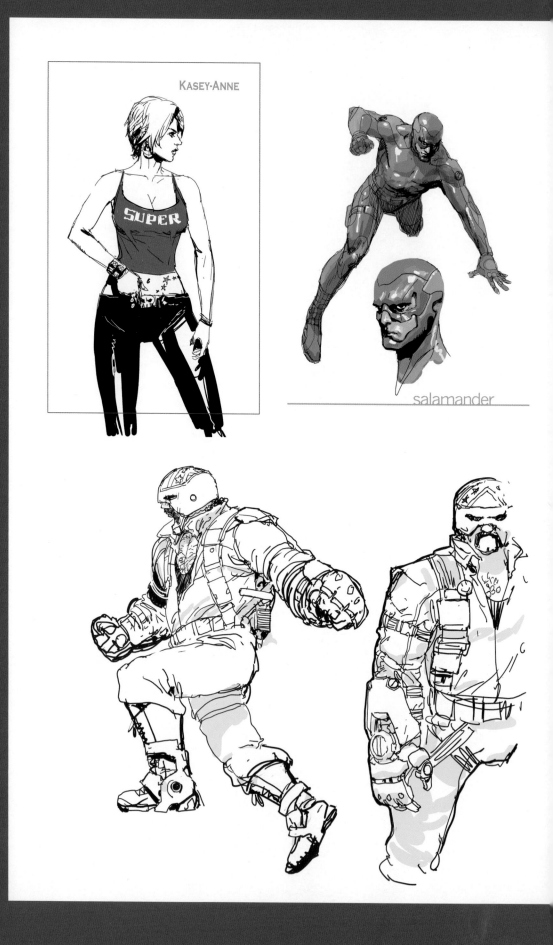

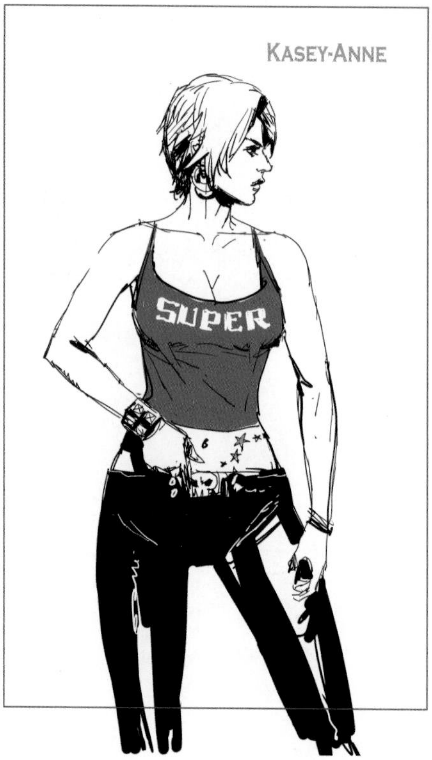
Kasey-Anne
SUPER

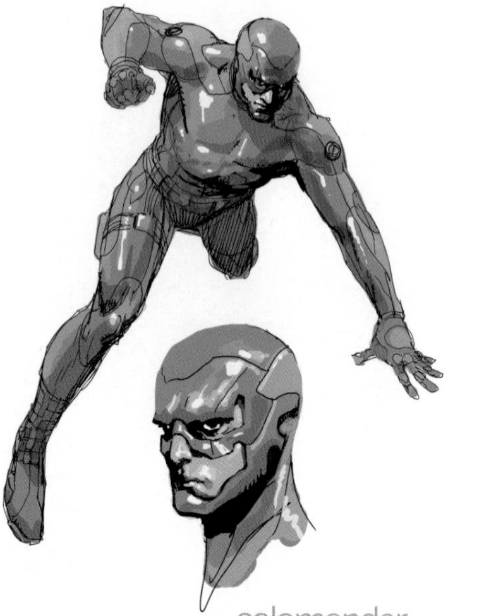

salamander

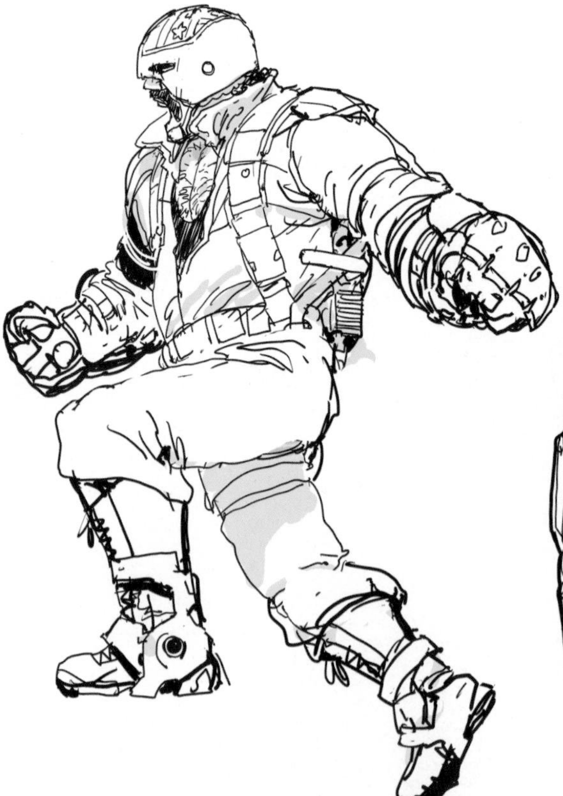

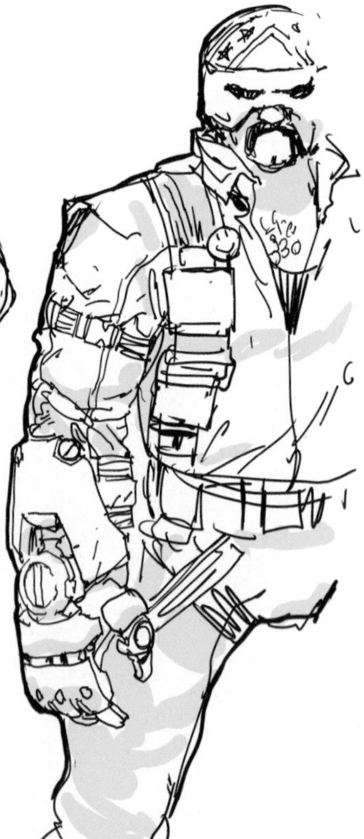

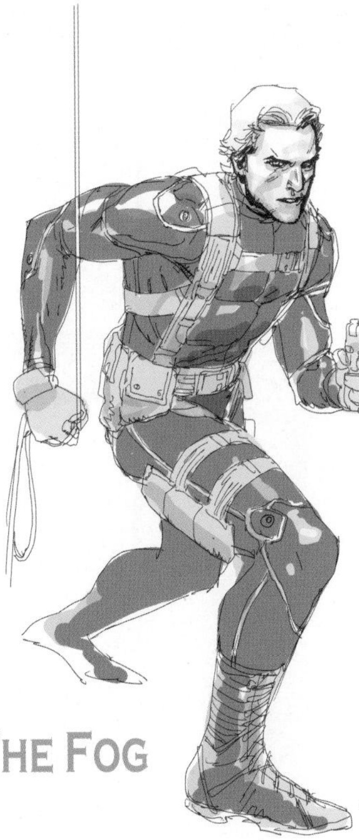

THE FOG

TK McCABE

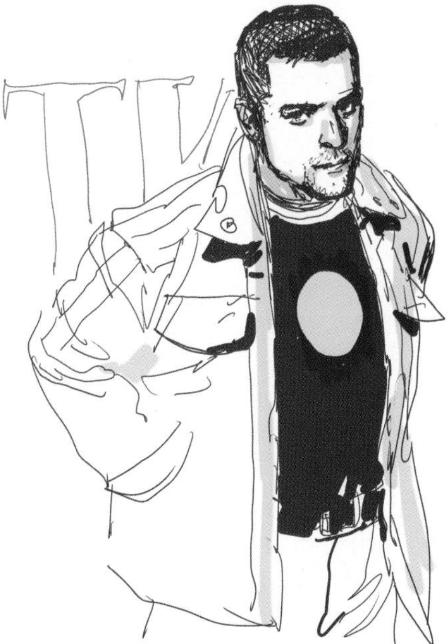

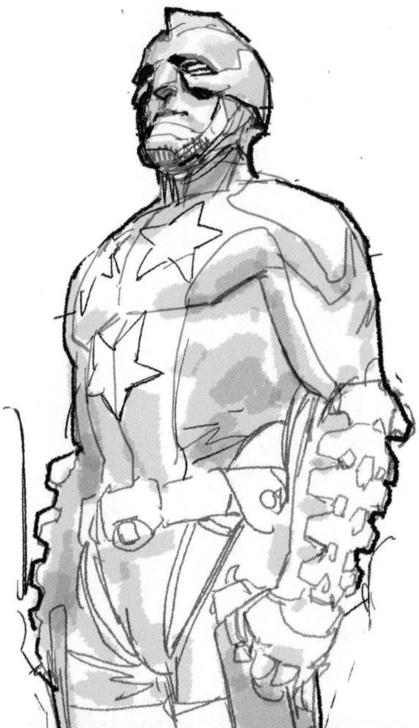

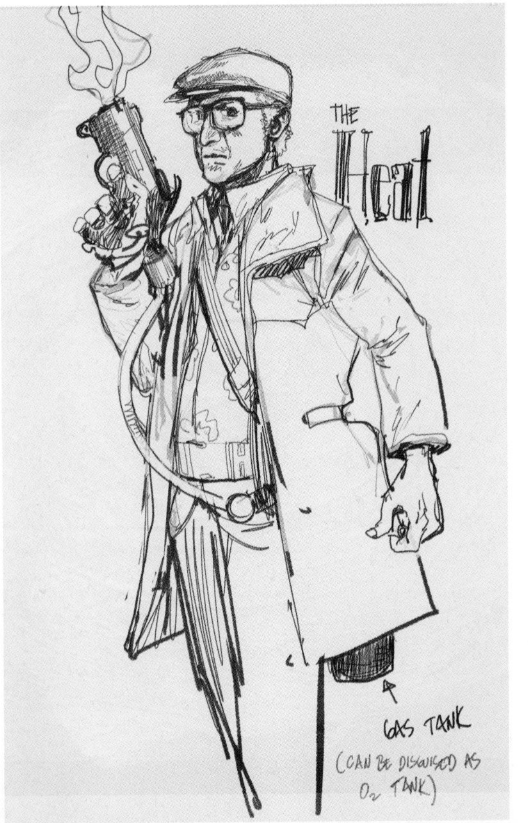
THE Heat
GAS TANK
(CAN BE DISGUISED AS
$O_2$ TANK)

# MOVIE PRODUCTION PLANS

## ART BY LEINIL YU

When Mark Millar sold a SUPERCROOKS movie concept to producers, his next step was to rope in his dear friend Nacho Vigalondo to make it all much better than it was in his head. The film producers suggested that Nacho and Leinil create some concept designs to show the studios. Now, for the first time ever, the team reveals those never-before-seen illustrations — many of which were drawn before the comic book itself.

Nacho's Spanish nationality made him a very logical choice to get involved in SUPERCROOKS, but Mark requested Nacho specifically because he was a fan of Nacho's film Timecrimes (2007), and was delighted to find that Nacho had read a lot of his work as well. They had a great time writing the screenplay together, even though Nacho barely speaks English and Mark can only ask for potato chips in Spanish (this is true).

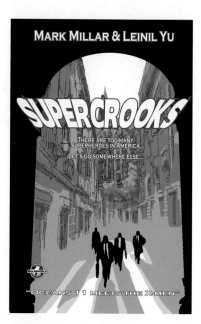

MARK MILLAR & LEINIL YU

SUPERCROOKS

THERE ARE TOO MANY
SUPERHEROES IN AMERICA.
LET'S GO SOMEWHERE ELSE...

"OCEANS 11 MEETS THE X-MEN"

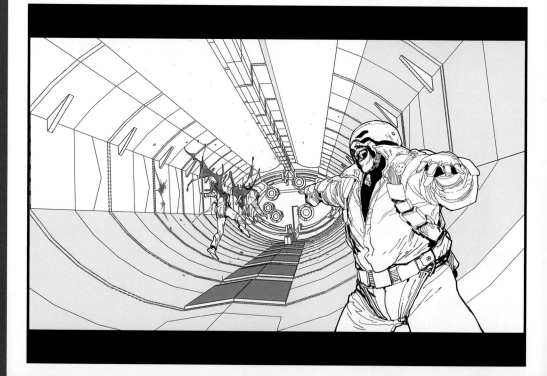

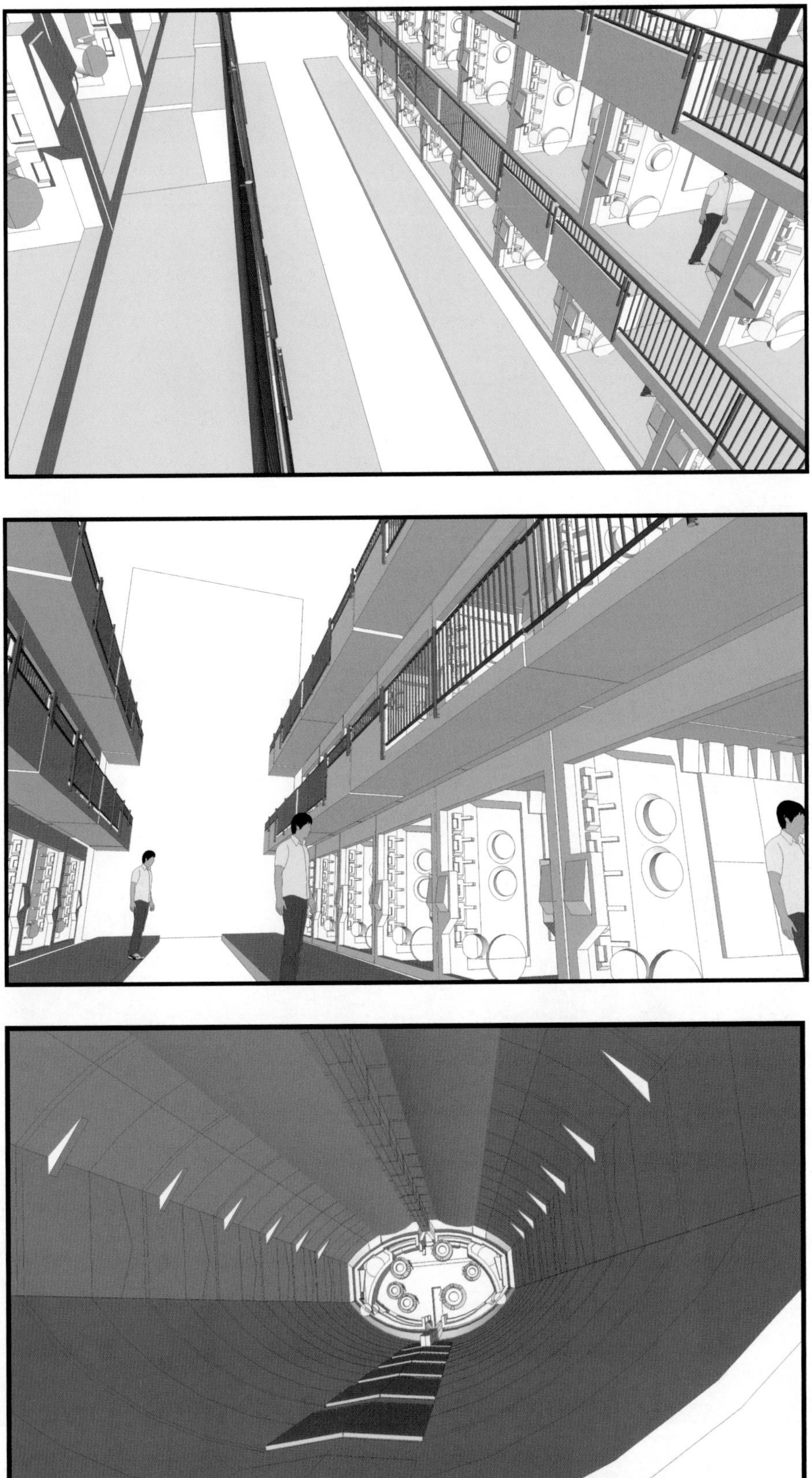

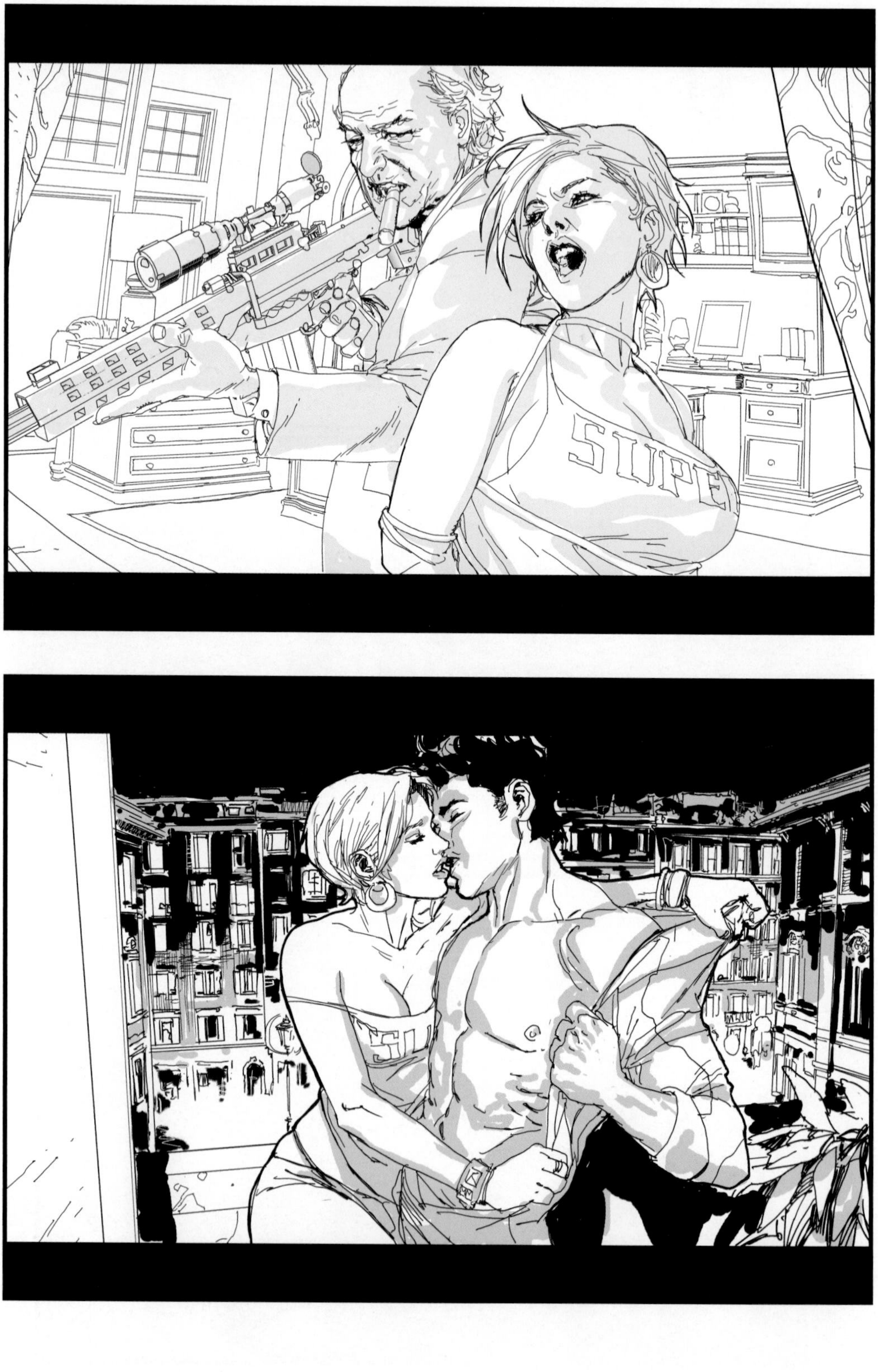

SUPE

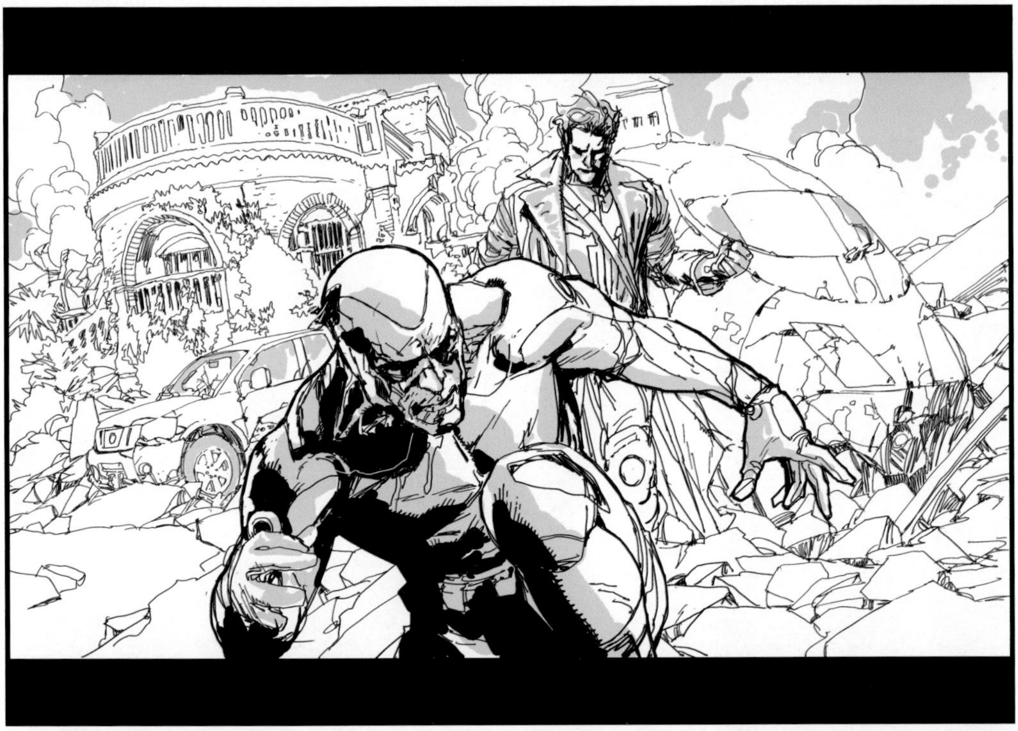

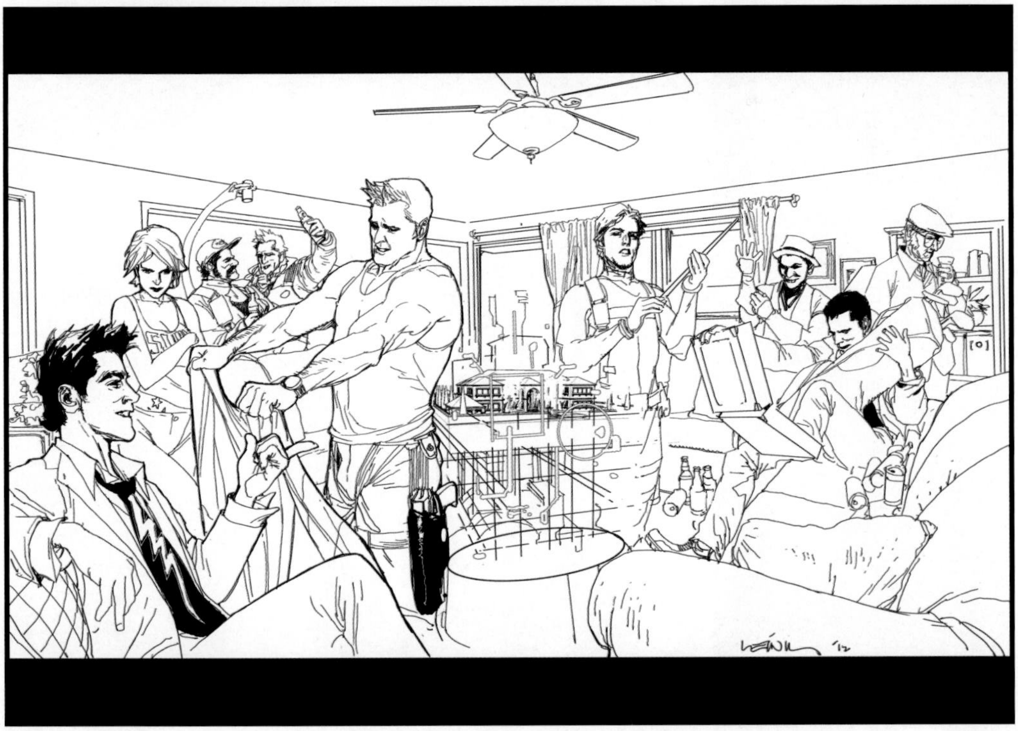

KICK-ASS
NOW A MAJOR MOTION PICTURE!
MARK MILLAR
JOHN ROMITA JR.

THE MILLAR

MARK MILLAR · JOHN ROMITA JR.
HIT-GIRL

KICK-ASS 2
MARK MILLAR
JOHN ROMITA JR.

WANTED
MARK MILLAR • JG JONES • PAUL MOUNTS
NOW A MAJOR MOTION PICTURE FROM
UNIVERSAL PICTURES
WWW.MILLARWORLD.TV

MARK MILLAR & LEINIL YU
SUPERIOR
FROM THE WRITER OF KICK-ASS

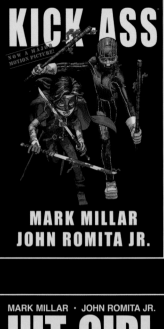

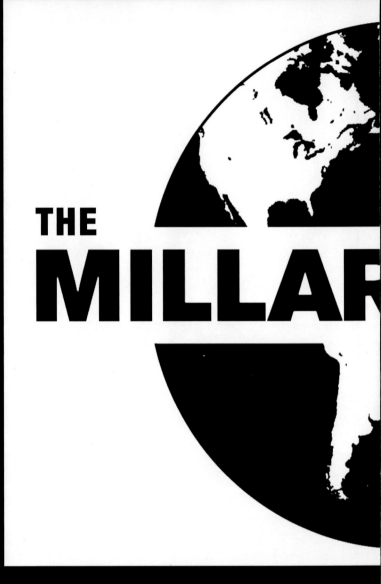

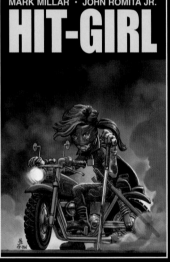

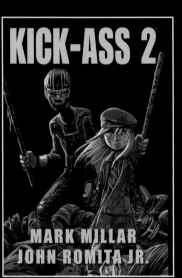

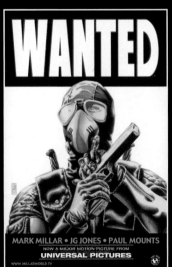

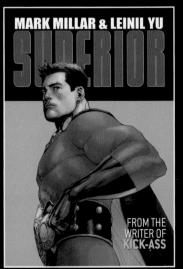

WORLD
COLLECTION

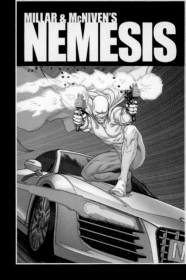

MILLAR & McNIVEN'S
NEMESIS

MILLAR   GIBBONS   VAUGHN
the SECRET
SERVICE

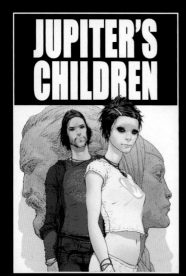

JUPITER'S
CHILDREN

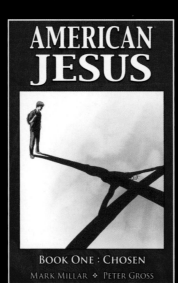

AMERICAN
JESUS

BOOK ONE : CHOSEN

MARK MILLAR ✦ PETER GROSS

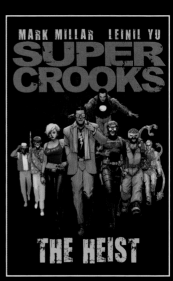

MARK MILLAR   LEINIL YU
SUPER
CROOKS

THE HEIST

# OTHER BOOKS BY MARK MILLAR

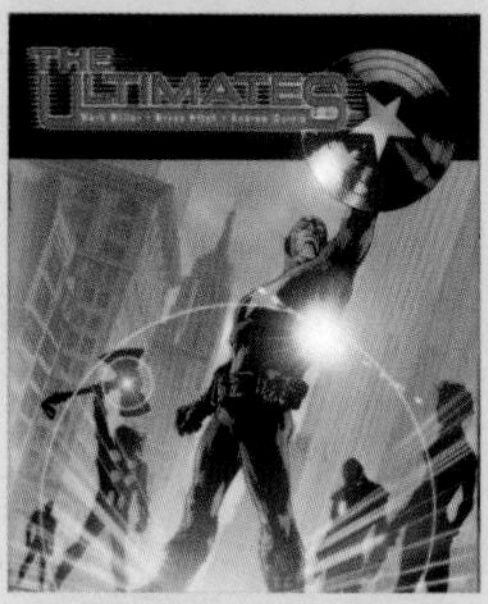
THE ULTIMATES

THE ULTIMATES
Art by Bryan Hitch

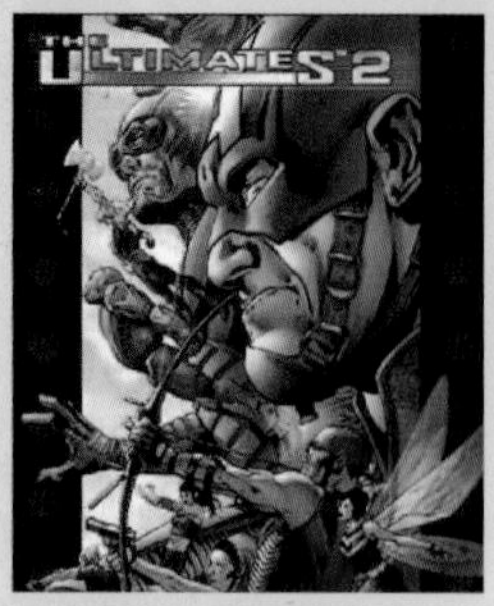
THE ULTIMATES 2

THE ULTIMATES 2
Art by Bryan Hitch

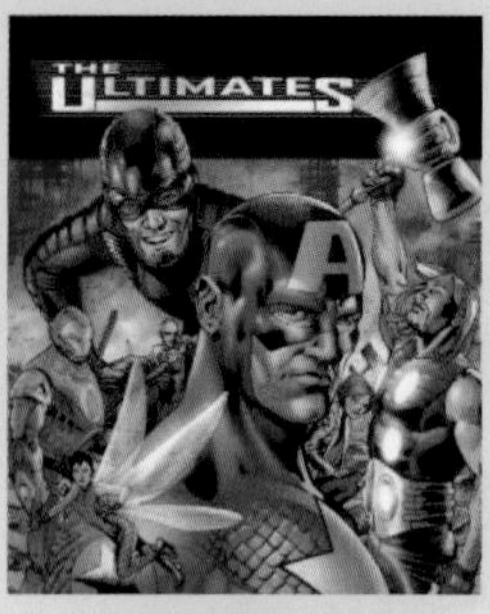
THE ULTIMATES

THE ULTIMATES
OMNIBUS
Art by Bryan Hitch

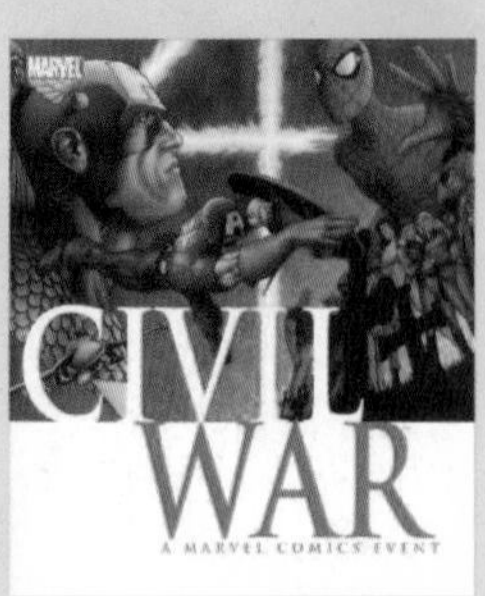
MARVEL
CIVIL WAR
A MARVEL COMICS EVENT

CIVIL WAR
Art by Steve McNiven

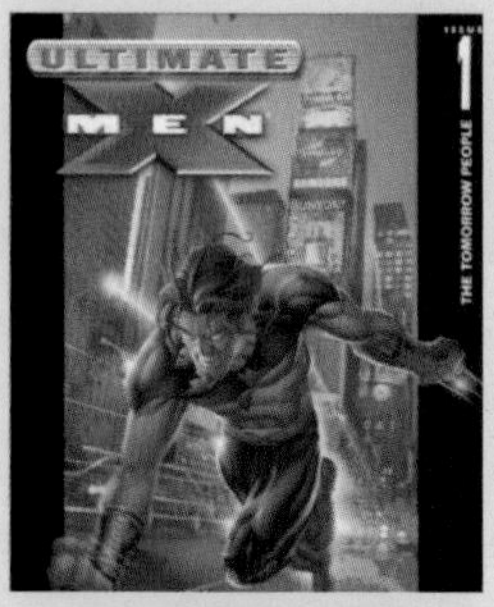
ULTIMATE
X-MEN
1
THE TOMORROW PEOPLE

ULTIMATE X-MEN
Art by Adam Kubert

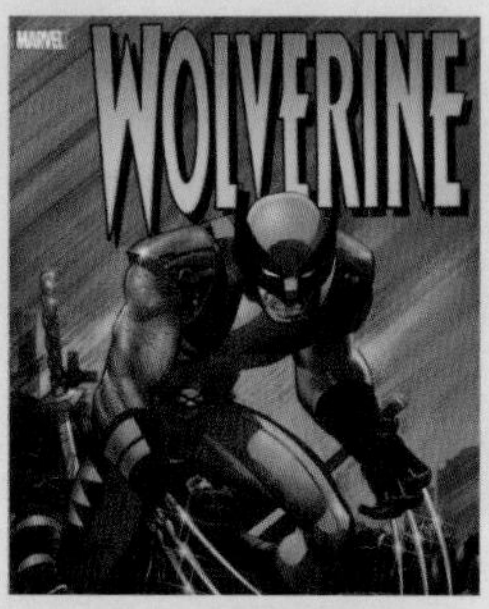
WOLVERINE

WOLVERINE:
ENEMY OF THE STATE
Art by John Romita Jr.

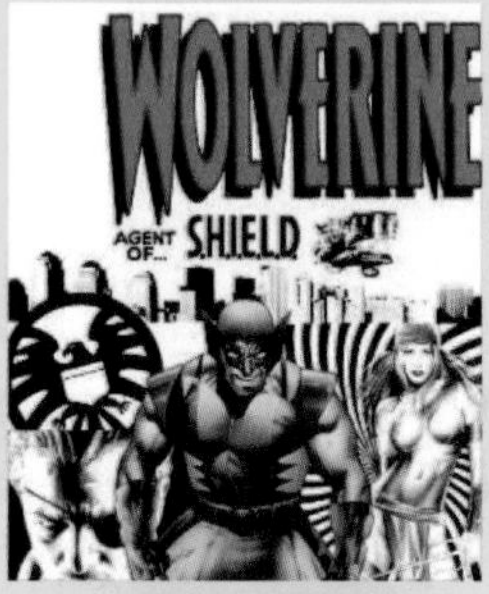
WOLVERINE
AGENT OF... S.H.I.E.L.D.

WOLVERINE:
AGENT OF S.H.I.E.L.D.
Art by John Romita Jr.

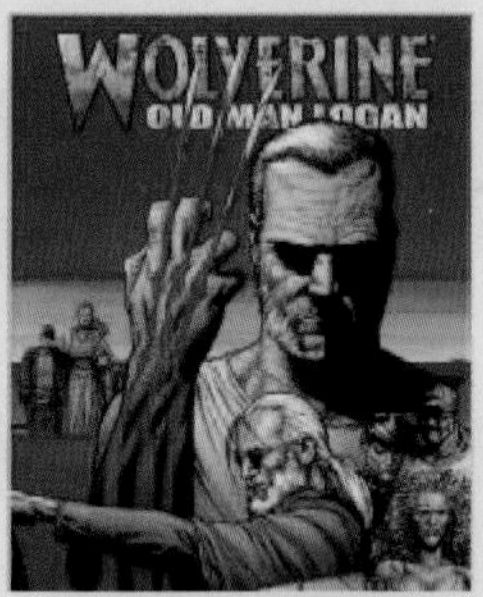
WOLVERINE
OLD MAN LOGAN

WOLVERINE:
OLD MAN LOGAN
Art by Steve McNiven

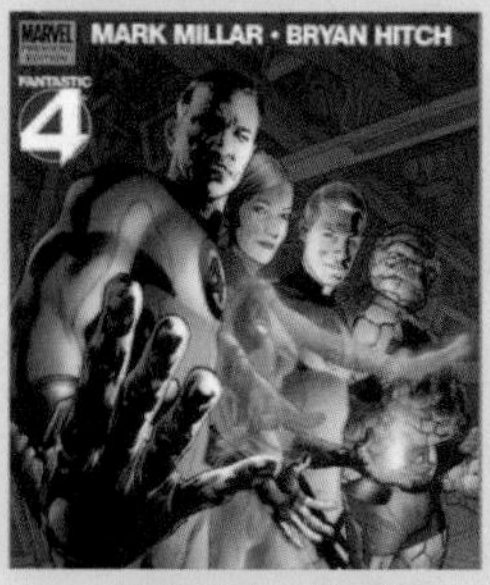
MARK MILLAR • BRYAN HITCH
4

FANTASTIC FOUR:
WORLD'S GREATEST
Art by Bryan Hitch

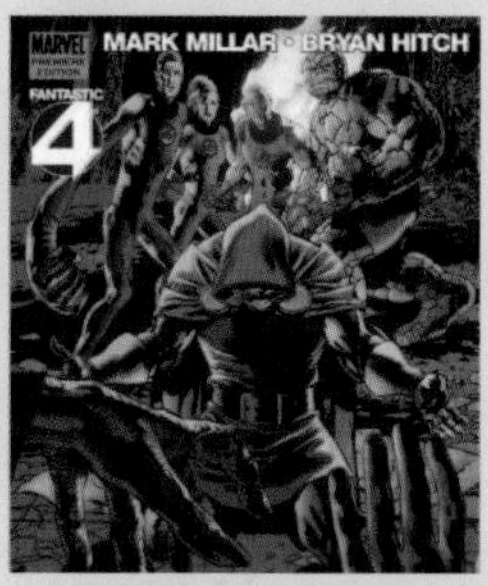
MARK MILLAR • BRYAN HITCH
4

FANTASTIC FOUR
MASTERS OF DOOM
Art by Bryan Hitch

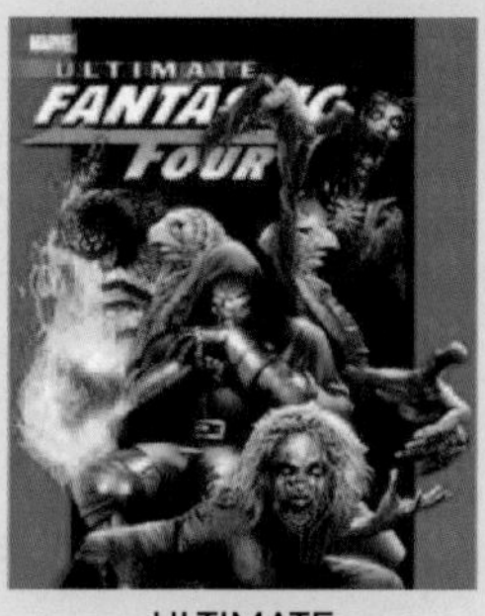
ULTIMATE
FANTASTIC FOUR

ULTIMATE
FANTASTIC FOUR
Art by Greg Land

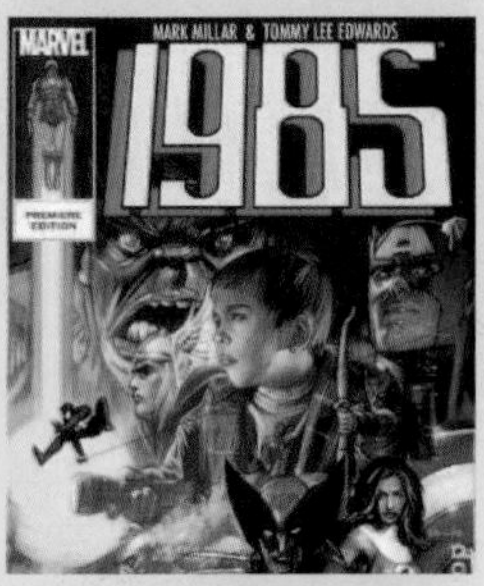
MARVEL
MARK MILLAR & TOMMY LEE EDWARDS
1985

1985
Art by Tommy Lee
Edwards

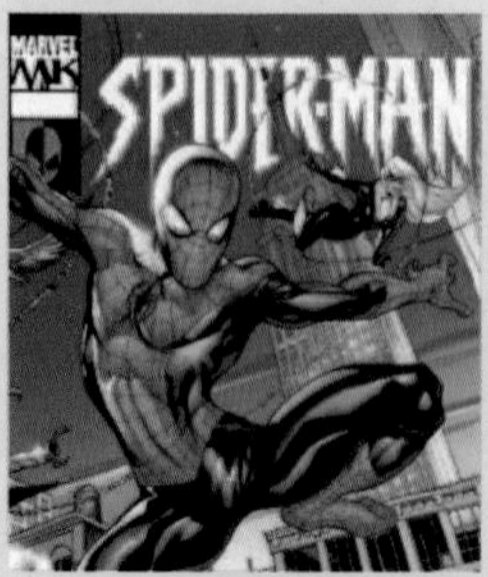
SPIDER-MAN

MARVEL KNIGHTS
SPIDER-MAN
Art by Terry Dodson

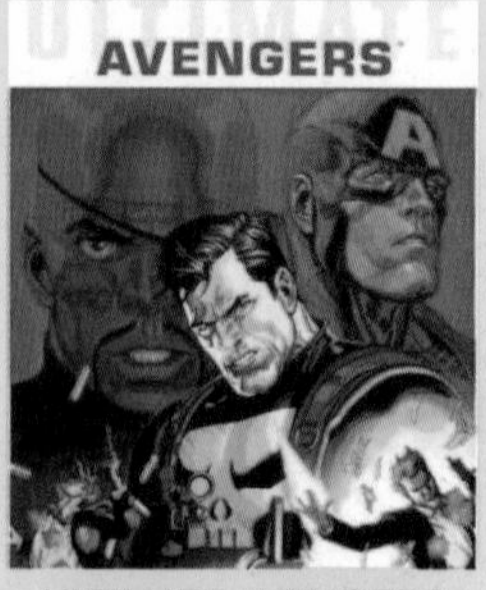
AVENGERS

ULTIMATE AVENGERS
Art by LEINIL YU

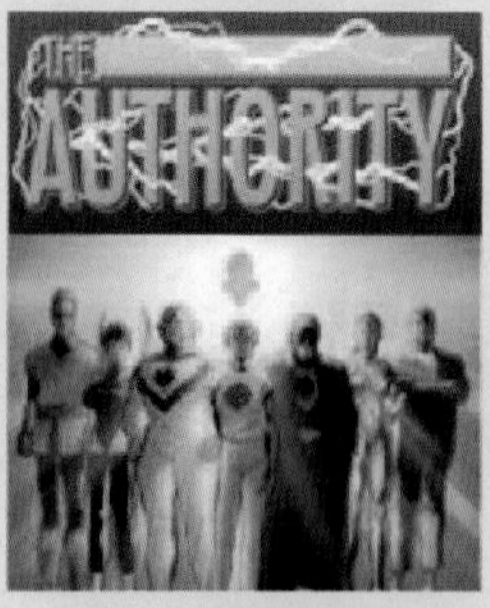
THE AUTHORITY

THE AUTHORITY
Art by Frank Quitely

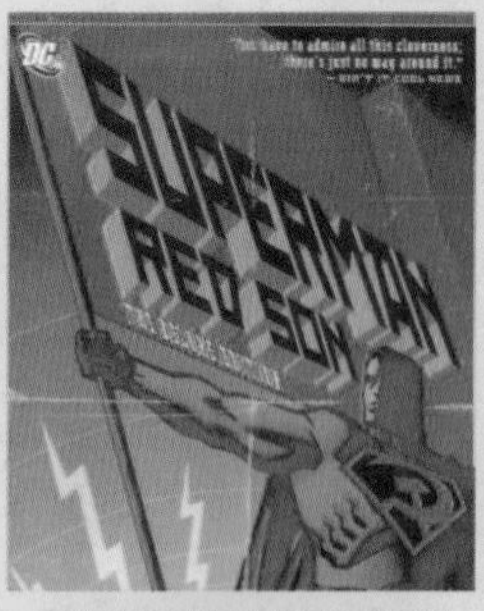
SUPERMAN
RED SON

SUPERMAN: RED SON
Art by Dave Johnson